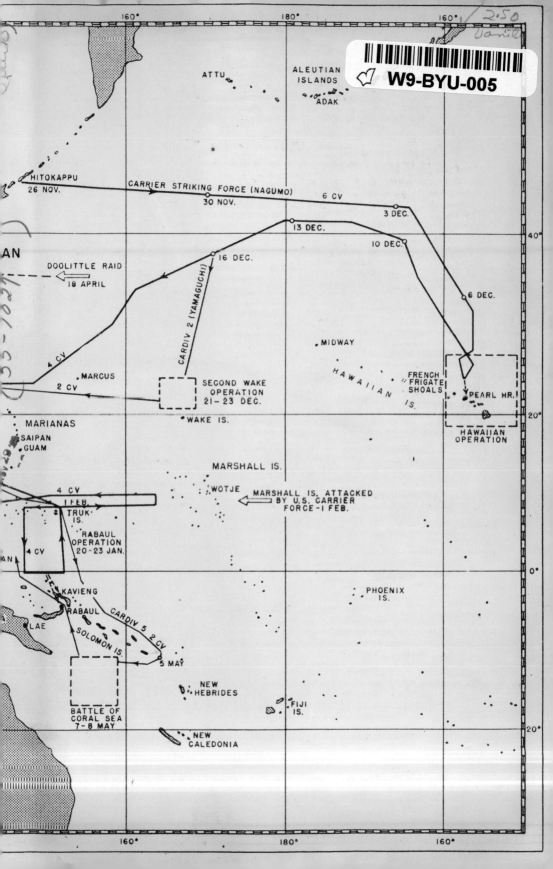

MIDWAY

the battle that doomed Japan

A
NAVAL INSTITUTE
PUBLICATION

Japanese Heavy Cruiser *Mogami* on Fire After Attack by American Planes in the Battle of Midway, 6 June 1942

MIDWAY

the battle that doomed Japan

THE JAPANESE
NAVY'S STORY

By

MITSUO FUCHIDA
Former Captain, Imperial Japanese Navy

and

MASATAKE OKUMIYA
Former Commander, Imperial Japanese Navy

Edited by
CLARKE H. KAWAKAMI
and ROGER PINEAU

With a Foreword by Admiral Raymond A. Spruance, *United States Navy (Ret.)*

A N A V A L I N S T I T U T E P U B L I C A T I O N

To the Memory of
The Brave Men
Who Fell in the
Battle of Midway

Foreword

It is always interesting and instructive after a naval operation or battle to try to get as complete a picture as possible from the enemy's point of view. During the Battle of Midway the "fog of war" was fairly thick, in spite of the excellent intelligence which we had prior to it. For instance, we were not sure of the fate of the HIRYU until a number of days after her sinking, when our Midway search located and rescued a boatload of survivors from her engine rooms. Similarly, the identity and the fate of the MIKUMA were in doubt for sometime. The last we knew of the MIKUMA was when we photographed her late on the afternoon of 6 June, as she lay disabled and dead in the water, with survivors on her bow and stern. The next morning she had disappeared when one of our submarines investigated the area. The fact that Admiral Yamamoto with seven battleships, one carrier, cruisers, and destroyers was operating to the northwestward of Midway was not known to us for several months after the battle.

The present volume is a most valuable historical contribution to our knowledge of Japanese naval planning and operations, from the months leading up to the outbreak of war through the first six months of the war itself.

In reading the account of what happened on 4 June, I am more than ever impressed with the part that good or bad fortune sometimes plays in tactical engagements. The authors give us credit, where no credit is due, for being able to choose the exact time for our attack on the Japanese carriers when they were at the greatest disadvantage—flight decks full of aircraft fueled, armed and ready to go. All that I can claim credit for, myself, is a very keen sense of the urgent need for surprise and a strong desire to hit the enemy carriers with our full strength as early as we could reach them.

Two other points may be of interest in reading the Japanese

account of Midway. One is our retirement to the eastward for some hours during the night of 4-5 June. The situation toward sundown on 4 June was that Admiral Fletcher's afternoon search from YORKTOWN had located and reported HIRYU; then YORKTOWN had been disabled by two torpedo hits from HIRYU's second attack; and finally ENTERPRISE and HORNET's planes had knocked out HIRYU. After ENTERPRISE and HORNET had recovered aircraft, I decided to retire to the eastward so as to avoid the possibility of a night action with superior forces, but to turn back to the westward during the night, so that at daylight we would be in air supporting distance of Midway in case the enemy were to attack there. The Japanese did order a night attack.

The second point concerns what occurred on 6 June, the third and last day of the battle. I had desired to chase and to inflict as much damage as possible on the retreating enemy. We knew, however, that the Japanese had strong air forces on Wake waiting to garrison Midway after its capture. I had decided in advance that I would keep outside of the 700 mile circle from Wake to avoid attack by these forces. When the day's action on 6 June was over—one search mission, three attack missions, and one photographic mission—we were short of fuel and I had a feeling, an intuition perhaps, that we had pushed our luck as far to the westward as was good for us. Accordingly, we turned back to the eastward and headed for the oiler rendezvous which Admiral Nimitz had set up for us. Had we continued on to the westward during the night of 6-7 June, we would probably have run foul of Admiral Yamamoto and his superior Japanese forces the next morning.

Our success at the Battle of Midway was based primarily on the excellent intelligence which enabled Admiral Nimitz to exercise to the full his talent for bold, courageous and wise leadership. He recalled Task Forces 16 and 17 from the South Pacific and, with no time to spare, had them lying in wait to the northeast of Midway. He disposed his available submarines to the northwestward of Midway. He strengthened the defenses of Midway itself with Marines, artillery, and aircraft, and instituted air searches over the critical areas. He sent forces to the Aleutians.

Admiral Fletcher, Commander Task Force 17, was also in over-all command of Task Forces 16 and 17, and played a very important part in the battle. The YORKTOWN's air group did splendid work as a unit until their ship was disabled, and after that the individual aircraft recovered by ENTERPRISE and HORNET continued in the fight for the following two days.

I feel sure that all of us who took part in the Battle of Midway, as well as those who have studied it, will enjoy and profit by reading this Japanese account. The authors are to be congratulated on the research they have done and the book they have written.

RAYMOND A. SPRUANCE
Admiral, United States Navy (Ret.)

April 1955

Introduction

The Battle of Midway was without question a turning point of the Pacific War. That much is clear from the results of this great sea battle. But as to why the operation was planned and how it was fought, there have been few, if any, detailed and accurate accounts on the Japanese side.

The explanation for this lies in the fact that the plans for the operation were studied and drawn up exclusively by Combined Fleet Headquarters and the Naval General Staff in Tokyo. Admiral Yamamoto did not want his fleet commanders, whose energies were fully occupied with the conduct of the first-phase operations in so many far-flung theaters, to be bothered by other matters.

At this time I commanded the Second Fleet and also was alternate Commander in Chief Combined Fleet in case Admiral Yamamoto should be unable to act. Yet even I was not consulted concerning the Midway plans and did not learn of them until after the completion of the southern operations. By the time I returned to Yokosuka on 17 April 1942, the day before the Doolittle air raid, the plans were already fixed and decided, allowing of no modification.

Our forces tried to carry out these plans and suffered defeat —a defeat so decisive and so grave that the details, like the plans, were kept the guarded secret of a limited circle, even within the Japanese Navy. The result is that today few, even among high-ranking former naval officers, are familiar with the details of the operation.

In this book, at last, the full story is told. There is nothing that I can add to it, nor is there anything that I would wish to add.

The author, Captain Mitsuo Fuchida, was an outstanding officer in the Naval Air Force. At the outbreak of war he was senior air wing commander in the Carrier Task Force, which was actually the main striking strength of the Japanese Fleet. In this capacity he led the air assault on Pearl Harbor as well as subsequent air strikes by the same task force. In every operation he performed brilliantly and capably. Captain Fuchida was present at the Midway battle from start to finish on board aircraft carrier AKAGI, flagship of the Nagumo Force. Immediately afterward he was transferred to the Naval War College as an instructor, with the special assignment of studying and making a report on the battle using all available records, official and private. This he did. Later in the war he served as Air Operations Officer in Combined Fleet Headquarters.

Commander Masatake Okumiya, who collaborated with Captain Fuchida in writing the present volume, observed the Midway battle from a different vantage point. He was in light carrier RYUJO, flagship of the Second Task Force, which operated in the Aleutians area as the northern prong of the offensive. Later, as a staff officer of the sole carrier division to survive the Midway debacle, he had access to all the detailed action reports concerning the battle and made a painstaking study of them. Toward the end of the war he was assigned to the Naval General Staff, where he enjoyed ready access to all operational records and reports.

Now that the Japanese Navy has passed out of existence, it is unlikely that any more complete information concerning the Battle of Midway will be forthcoming than has been assembled by the authors of this book. It seems to me in every way desirable that an accurate record of this vital battle should be left to posterity. I feel that the authors have produced such a record—not only factually accurate, but eminently fair and objective.

As the senior commander, still living, who participated in this operation, I dedicate the fine work of these two men to those, on both sides, who perished in the battle. I am pleased that their families, relatives, and friends may now know the facts surrounding their death. For all others I hope that this book will serve as material for criticism and reflection.

近藤信竹

February 1951

Nobutake Kondo
Formerly Admiral, Imperial Japanese Navy

Authors' Preface

For Japan, the Battle of Midway was indeed a tragic defeat. The Japanese Combined Fleet, placing its faith in "quality rather than quantity," had long trained and prepared to defeat a numerically superior enemy. Yet at Midway a stronger Japanese force went down to defeat before a weaker enemy.

Not only were our participating surface forces far superior in number to those of the enemy, but the initiative was in our hands. Nor were we inferior, qualitatively, in the crucial element of air strength, which played the major role throughout the Pacific War. In spite of this we suffered a decisive defeat such as the modern Japanese Navy had never before experienced or even dreamed possible.

With Midway as the turning point, the fortunes of war appeared definitely to shift from our own to the Allied side. The defeat taught us many lessons and impelled our Navy, for the first time since the outbreak of war, to indulge in critical self-examination.

The Japanese public, of course, was not told the truth about the battle. Instead, Imperial General Headquarters announcements tried to make it appear that both sides had suffered equal losses. The United States, however, promptly announced to the whole world the damage inflicted on the Japanese, accurately naming the ships damaged and sunk. Thus it was clear that our efforts to conceal the truth were aimed at maintaining morale at home rather than at keeping valuable knowledge from the enemy.

I myself had a rather painful taste of the extreme measures taken to preserve secrecy. During the battle I had been wounded on board AKAGI and then transferred to hospital ship HIKAWA MARU, which brought me to Yokosuka Naval Base. I was not moved ashore until after dark, when the streets of the base were deserted. Then I was taken to the hospital on a covered stretcher and carried in through the rear entrance. My room was placed in complete isolation. No nurses or corpsmen were allowed entry, and I could not communicate with the outside. In such manner were those wounded at Midway cut off from the rest of the world. It was really confinement in the guise of medical treatment, and I sometimes had the feeling of being a prisoner of war.

Naturally all documentary materials pertaining to the battle were classified "Top Secret." Preparation of after-action reports based on these materials also was drastically restricted, and such reports as were prepared were kept highly secret throughout the war. Following Japan's surrender in 1945, almost all of these papers were burned. It is not surprising, therefore, that even since the return of peace there have been but fragmentary and frequently erroneous accounts of the Japanese side of the Midway battle.

After my discharge from the hospital, I was temporarily assigned to the Yokosuka Naval Air Corps as an instructor, since my leg wound was still not completely mended. As additional duty I was appointed instructor at the Naval War College in Tokyo. A Battle Lessons Research Committee had been established at the War College and I was ordered to serve as secretary of the Sub-committee for Aviation. In this capacity I researched the records of past sea and air actions and compiled studies analyzing the strategic and tactical lessons taught by these actions.

Research on the Battle of Midway was limited to specially authorized persons. Since it was my job to draw up the final draft of the study, I had access to all official materials as well as private records. In addition, dozens of officers who had participated in the battle were called in for interviews. When the study was completed, only six copies were made and distributed. What became of those copies I do not know, but I was fortunate enough, after the war, to discover the original manuscript hidden away in one of my foot lockers.

Even with this valuable document to supplement my own experience, I was still doubtful of my ability to write a comprehensive and accurate history of the Midway battle. It was fortunate, therefore, that I found in Commander Masatake Okumiya, whom I have known for many years, a ready and well-qualified collaborator. A naval aviator like myself, he fully shares my belief in the importance of bringing forth an accurate account of the battle from the Japanese side. He is chiefly responsible for those portions of this book which do not pertain directly to the Nagumo Force.

We have tried to describe the development of the battle as objectively as possible so that this account may be of true historical value. I wish to add that accounts of United States naval actions in this book have been drawn from official publications of the United States.

淵田美津雄

February 1951

Mitsuo Fuchida

The Pacific War saw air power finally come of age. So predominant did the air element become in naval warfare that battles between great surface fleets were decided without their exchanging a single shot. And so decisive was the force of strategic air power, coupled to be sure with the attrition wrought by American submarines, that the Japanese Army and Navy were compelled to surrender before a single enemy soldier had set foot upon our home soil. In this new type of warfare the Battle of Midway was the outstanding defeat suffered by Japan

By June of 1942 I was already experienced in carrier force operations and my assignment placed me in an advantageous position to follow the development of the entire battle. Moreover, in order to obtain additional data, I have toured Japan three times since the end of the war questioning former naval officers who took part in the battle.

As a consequence of my studies, I am firmly convinced that the Pacific War was started by men who did not understand the sea, and fought by men who did not understand the air. Had there been better understanding of the sea and air, Japan would have pondered more carefully the wisdom of going to war. And even if she had then decided that no other course was possible, many of the blunders she made could have been avoided. Because she judged the sea by land standards and applied to air warfare the concepts of sea fighting, Japan's tragic fate was foreordained.

If and when we should again underestimate the importance of air power, the day will surely come when we will have to pay for such negligence—politically, economically, and otherwise.

February 1951

奥 宮 正 武

Masatake Okumiya

Editors' Preface

When Captain Fuchida and Commander Okumiya brought out the original edition of their book on the Battle of Midway in 1951, the Japanese public learned for the first time the story of the disastrous naval defeat which turned the tide of the Pacific War. Now, with the publication of a revised version of their work in English, American readers for the first time will be able to round out their knowledge of this great battle with a full and detailed account from the Japanese side.

A considerable part of the rather meager Japanese documentary material on the battle remaining in existence at the end of the war has long been available to interested American students in translations contained in publications by the United States Strategic Bombing Survey and the Office of Naval Intelligence. The documents by themselves, however, are not enough to provide a coherent, integrated story; and in interpreting them American naval historians are necessarily at a heavy disadvantage. It is only key Japanese participants in the battle, such as the authors of the book, who can fill in the gaps and interpret accurately the fragmentary data given in the documents.

The United States Naval Institute expressed an interest in publishing this work on the basis of a preliminary translation by Commander Masataka Chihaya, on condition that it be put into acceptable form for American readers. This has been a more exacting task than the editors anticipated, as it developed into a thoroughgoing revision of the original and not just the polishing of a translation.

The reason for this is that the original book was written primarily for popular consumption in Japan, where, because of wartime secrecy, little or nothing was known about the Midway battle. The authors' account therefore was sketchy on some points of crucial interest, and they made no attempt to document their story as required by American historical practice. In the United States most of the facts of the battle have long been known, and what was lacking was an authentic and documented account of the Japanese side. This is what the editors, in long-distance collaboration with the authors, have attempted to provide.

To this end, Commander Chihaya's translation has been closely checked against the original text, and statements of fact have been checked against all available documents and records —Japanese as well as American. Footnotes, entirely absent in the original, have been added to supplement the Japanese account and provide documentation and substantiation for statements of fact which challenge hitherto accepted versions. Finally, the book has been reorganized to follow a more nearly chronological order than the original.

The Japanese edition used the time of the homeland (East Longitude date, Zone minus 9 time) throughout, regardless of the locale under consideration, as do all Japanese military documents. An effort has been made to render dates and times more understandable to American readers, primarily by using the local time of the place where action occurs.

In checking the authors' accuracy on American details of the story, extensive use has been made of American publications. Foremost of these is the careful and colorful study in *Coral Sea, Midway and Submarine Actions*, Volume IV of the *History of United States Naval Operations in World War II* by Rear Admiral Samuel E. Morison, USNR (Ret.). Points of conflict with American versions of the battle have been resolved and explained to the best of our ability.

We are grateful to the authors for the latitude they have allowed in our reorganization of the text, which they approved in its final version, and for their patience in answering the many searching questions occasioned by our skepticism about some of their conclusions. We also appreciate the interest that Vice Admiral Ralph A. Ofstie, USN, has shown and the encouragement he has given to this work. Finally, gratitude must be expressed to Lieutenant (jg) Richard S. Pattee, USNR, for his advice on technical problems, and to the aviation historian, Mr. Adrian O. Van Wyen, who read the finished manuscript.

CLARKE H. KAWAKAMI
ROGER PINEAU

Washington, D.C.
30 March 1955

Publisher's Note

Most of the photographs in this book have been obtained from Japanese sources. Because of the destruction of many official Japanese archives, the photographs available are frequently less sharp than comparable American photographs would be. The emphasis in this edition, however, has been on following the original Japanese edition as closely as possible. For this reason only a limited number of American photographs have been used to supplement the Japanese.

The line drawings have been redrawn by Commander W. M. Shannon, (N), U.S. Power Squadrons, from those appearing in the original Japanese edition.

Likewise, the narrative itself, as the Editors have stated in their Preface, is the *Japanese* story. Supplementary documentation in the Footnotes reflects the conclusions of the Editors, Mr. Kawakami and Mr. Pineau, and these conclusions are not to be attributed to the U. S. Naval Institute.

U.S. NAVAL INSTITUTE

May 1955

Contents

List of Photographs

LIST OF LINE DRAWINGS

Battleship *Yamato*, Flagship of Combined Fleet

ADMIRAL YAMAMOTO, COMMANDER IN CHIEF COMBINED FLEET (sixth from left, front row), WITH HIS STAFF ON BOARD *Yamato* EARLY IN 1942

CHAPTER 1 Sortie from Hashirajima

As day broke over the western Inland Sea on 27 May 1942, the sun's rays slanted down on the greatest concentration of Japanese fleet strength since the start of the Pacific War.

The setting was at the island of Hashirajima, which lies to the south of the well-known city of Hiroshima and southeast of the lesser-known coastal town of Iwakuni. The anchorage at Hashirajima is surrounded by hilly little islands, most of which are cultivated from water's edge to summit. Camouflaged anti-aircraft batteries atop almost every hill belied the peaceful appearance of these islands. The anchorage was large enough to accommodate the entire Japanese Navy and was well off the ordinary routes of merchant ships. It was a wartime stand-by anchorage for Combined Fleet, whose headquarters had been functioning in safety from a battleship group stationed there since the start of the war. It had remained there so long, in fact, that naval officers had come to speak of Combined Fleet Head-quarters simply as "Hashirajima."

Within the anchorage Commander in Chief Combined Fleet Admiral Isoroku Yamamoto's 68,000-ton flagship, YAMATO, was moored to a red buoy. Underwater cables to shore permitted instant communication with Tokyo. Gathered around YAMATO were a total of 68 warships, constituting the greater part of the surface strength of the Combined Fleet.

Admiral Yamamoto's Battleship Division 1 consisted of YAMATO, NAGATO, and MUTSU, which with ISE, HYUGA, FUSO, and YAMASHIRO of Battleship Division 2 made the total of seven battleships. Torpedo nets were extended around each of these giants. Pearl Harbor had impressed on us the importance of protecting ships against torpedo attacks, even in home waters. The other ships were disposed around the battleships as further

I

protection against attacks by planes or submarines. There were light cruisers KITAKAMI and OI of Cruiser Division 9, flagship SENDAI and 12 destroyers of Destroyer Squadron 3, eight destroyers of Destroyer Squadron 1, light carrier HOSHO with one destroyer and two torpedo boats, and seaplane carriers[1] CHIYODA and NISSHIN, each of which had six midget submarines on board.

All these ships and units except Battleship Division 1 belonged to the First Fleet commanded by Vice Admiral Shiro Takasu, whose flag flew in ISE. Both the First Fleet and Battleship Division 1 had remained at Hashirajima since the outbreak of war, awaiting an opportunity for decisive surface battle. Aviators of the Carrier Force sarcastically referred to them as the "Hashirajima Fleet."

The 21 ships of our force, commanded by Vice Admiral Chuichi Nagumo, were anchored to the north of the so-called "main strength" just described. To the west of us was a force under Vice Admiral Nobutake Kondo, commander of the Second Fleet. Here were heavy cruisers ATAGO (Kondo's flagship) and CHOKAI of Cruiser Division 4, MYOKO and HAGURO of Cruiser Division 5, fast battleships HIEI and KIRISHIMA of Battleship Division 3, light cruiser YURA and seven destroyers of Destroyer Squadron 4, and light carrier ZUIHO with one destroyer.

This massive gray armada swung silently at anchor, each ship riding low in the water under a full load of fuel and supplies taken on board at Kure in preparation for the sortie. The only traffic in the whole area consisted of chugging yellow Navy tugboats which emitted heavy black smoke from their tall stacks. On board the warships there was little evidence of activity other than the occasional fluttering of signal flags as

---

[1] *Editors' Note:* A ship type not found in the U.S. Navy, these are not to be confused with seaplane tenders, mother-ships which serve as a fueling and minor-repair base for a dozen or so float planes. The four seaplane carriers (CHIYODA, CHITOSE, NISSHIN, and MIZUHO) were ships of over 10,000 tons, capable of making 28 or 29 knots; they carried in deck hangars a normal complement of 24 planes ("Jakes" and "Rufes") which were launched by catapults, of which each ship had four. Later in the war CHIYODA and CHITOSE were converted to aircraft carriers by the addition of flight decks.

messages were exchanged. But despite the general quiet of the anchorage, one could feel the excitement which permeated the entire fleet.

It was Navy Day, the anniversary of Admiral Togo's great victory over the Russian Fleet in the Battle of Tsushima. Japan's achievements during the first six months of war in the Pacific seemed to rival that triumph of 37 years earlier. Spirits were high—and why not? Now we were embarking on another mission which we confidently thought would add new glory to the annals of the Imperial Navy.

At 0800 AKAGI's ensign was raised. Then on her signal mast went up a single flag which gave the tensely awaited order, "Sortie as scheduled!"

Standing at the flight deck control post, I turned to watch the ships of Destroyer Squadron 10. White water splashed from the anchor cables of each destroyer, washing mud from the heavy links as they dragged through the hawseholes. The destroyers soon began to move, and they were followed by Cruiser Division 8, the second section of Battleship Division 3, and Carrier Divisions 1 and 2, in that order. The Nagumo Force was on its way toward the scene of one of the most significant naval actions in history.

As we steamed out of the anchorage the ships of the other forces, which would sortie two days later, gave us a rousing send-off. The crews lined the rails and cheered and waved their caps as we passed. They seemed to envy our good fortune in being the first to leave. We waved back a farewell, and a general gaiety prevailed. Every man was convinced that he was about to participate in yet another brilliant victory.

Two hours later we were halfway across the Iyonada and before long would enter Bungo Strait. Beyond the strait it was expected that we might encounter enemy submarines. Combined reports on their activities were sent out daily from Imperial General Headquarters. Latest reports indicated that a dozen or more of them were operating close to the homeland, reporting on ship movements and seeking to destroy our lines of communication. Occasionally they would send radio reports to Pearl Harbor, and it was at such times that our scattered radio direction finders would endeavor to spot them.

AKAGI, the sleek aircraft carrier flagship of Admiral Nagumo, headed westward through Kudako Strait, cruising easily at 16 knots on her course toward Bungo Channel and the broad Pacific. Through scattered clouds the sun shone brightly upon the calm blue sea. For several days the weather had been cloudy but hot in the western Inland Sea, and it was pleasant now to feel the gentle breeze which swept across AKAGI's flight deck.

The fleet had formed a single column for the passage through the strait. Twenty-one ships in all, they cruised along at intervals of 1,000 yards, resembling for all the world a peacetime naval review. Far out in front was Rear Admiral Susumu Kimura's flagship, light cruiser NAGARA, leading the 12 ships of Destroyer Squadron 10. Next came Rear Admiral Hiroaki Abe's Cruiser Division 8—TONE, the flagship, and CHIKUMA—followed by the second section of Battleship Division 3, made up of fast battleships HARUNA and KIRISHIMA. (The first section of Battleship Division 3, HIEI and KONGO, had been assigned to Admiral Kondo's Aleutians Force for this operation.) Behind KIRISHIMA came large carriers AKAGI and KAGA, comprising Carrier Division 1, under Admiral Nagumo's direct command. Rear Admiral Tamon Yamaguchi's Carrier Division 2—HIRYU and SORYU—brought up the rear, completing the Nagumo Force.

Presently a dozen or so fishing boats waiting for the tide hove into sight to starboard, and their crews waved and cheered as we passed. To port the tiny island of Yurishima appeared to be floating on the surface of the sea, its thick covering of green foliage set off against the dim background of Aoshima. Beyond, the coast of Shikoku lay hidden in mist.

As the fleet steamed on, three seaplanes of the Kure Air

Corps passed overhead, their pontoons looking like oversized shoes. The planes were on their way to neutralize any enemy submarines which might be lying in wait for us outside Bungo Strait.

Yashirojima soon appeared to starboard. Wheatfields, cultivated high up the mountainsides, were lightly tinged with yellow, proclaiming the nearness of summer. Offshore a small tug belched black smoke as she struggled to pull a string of barges. We soon left them far behind as the tiny islands of Ominasejima and Kominasejima came into view, lying peacefully on the sea.

To me this was familiar ground. My career had started at the Japanese Naval Academy at Etajima, which lay but 20 miles to the north. In the score of intervening years I had viewed every corner of the scenic Inland Sea, both from the sea and from the air, and I knew this region like a book. Now, as these familiar places passed by, I was lost in reminiscences which were suddenly interrupted by the loud voice of the chief signalman as he relayed an order through the voice tube.

The flight deck control post, where I sat, was situated on the port side, amidships. Directly forward of it rose the island which housed the bridge and the central battle command station, the ship's nerve center. At this moment all the top-ranking officers of the Striking Force, as well as AKAGI's own skipper and his staff, were assembled on the bridge, for regulations required all hands to be at their stations when passing through a narrow strait.

Scarcely had the chief signalman ceased calling the order when four flags were quickly hoisted on the small signal mast just abaft the flight deck control post. The first flag indicated a maneuvering order. Since we had now passed through the strait, I concluded, without knowing the other three flags, that the order was for all ships to move into normal cruising disposition.

Atop the signal mast fluttered the flag of the Striking Force

Commander. I wondered at the vast importance which Navy men attribute to such symbols. It is the hope and dream of every naval officer some day to fly his own flag. There were almost one hundred such flags in the Japanese Navy at this time, and four of them were flying in this very force.

Suddenly the ship's loudspeakers blared: "Passage through strait completed. Stow gear. Restore normal condition of readiness!" Men in undress whites and green work uniforms began drifting up to the flight deck to enjoy a last glimpse of the receding coastline. Some twenty communications men, their watch just completed, appeared on deck, doffed their shirts and began to exercise.

Commander Minoru Genda, First Air Fleet Operations Officer, came down from the bridge and joined me. A classmate of mine at the Naval Academy, he was also an aviator, and our friendship was of long standing. He sat down beside me on a folding chair, lit a cigarette, and said, "I heard that you were ill back at Kagoshima. Are you all right now?"

"Not so good," I replied. "My stomach still bothers me occasionally."

"What's the trouble?"

"Well, back at the base they sent me to an Army hospital for examination, and the doctors seemed to think it was ulcers. Anyway they told me to quit drinking for a while. Pretty rough!"

"Aha," laughed Genda. "So that's why you were on such good behavior back at the base?"

"That's right," I admitted, "and I'm still not feeling up to par. But my fliers are in good shape. They didn't have much time for training, but they are ready and confident. I suppose you've been busy, too, preparing for the sortie."

"It was terrific! We were supposed to wind up the southern operations and get ready for this one at the same time. We really had no time to study this operation thoroughly. Why, the Chief of Staff was still running around trying to put through promotions for the fliers killed in the Pearl Harbor operation!"

This last remark of Genda's touched on a sore point. Following the Pearl Harbor attack, the nine[2] men who lost their lives there in midget submarines had promptly been promoted two ranks and glorified as national war heroes. The First Air Fleet had endeavored to obtain similar promotions for the 55 airmen lost in the attack, but the authorities had disapproved them on the ground that there were too many.

"The fliers are really disgusted with that situation," I told Genda. "Why, now the authorities are even giving the small subs credit for sinking battleship ARIZONA! And that's obviously ridiculous, because there was an oiler moored outboard of ARIZONA, so a submarine torpedo couldn't possibly have scored on her. Furthermore, the big explosion in ARIZONA came immediately after KAGA's second squadron of high-level bombers got two direct hits.

"We don't mean to discredit the midget submarines and their crews. They certainly did their part. But the morale of the air units has to be considered too. After all, they are the backbone of the Fleet. And their morale would be much higher right now if the airmen's promotions had been granted before this sortie. SORYU's air officer, Commander Kusumoto, has been saying that the top echelons in Tokyo seem to be deliberately trying to discourage us."

"I know," nodded Genda. "The Naval General Staff isn't acting energetically enough, and Combined Fleet Headquarters also seems to have lost some of its prewar enthusiasm. Our own Chief of Staff seems to be the only one really sticking up for us;

[2] *Editors' Note:* There were five midget submarines in the attack, each with a two-man crew. One submariner, Ensign Kazuo Sakamaki, survived his boat (hence missed promotion and deification), was taken prisoner, and repatriated at war's end. He later wrote *I Attacked Pearl Harbor*, which describes his brief wartime submarine experience and his life as a prisoner of war in the United States.

and, instead of that, he ought to have been devoting himself exclusively to studying this operation."

"Well, at least we're sortieing according to plan," I remarked.

"Sure," Genda laughed somewhat sarcastically, "the sortie is going as scheduled. We just swallowed the Combined Fleet plan down whole and rushed out. The trouble is that there are several things in it that just don't add up. But then, I think the Nagumo Force can handle this operation all by itself. The other forces can operate as they please."

"Yes, I guess you're right," I agreed. "But one thing that worries me is the way information about the sortie has leaked out. Everybody seems to know of it. One officer I know was getting a shave the other day and was surprised to hear his barber remark, 'You're going out on a big one this time, aren't you?' "

"Barbers always have quick ears," said Genda. "With so many ships docking at Kure for repairs, loading supplies and so forth, nobody in town could have helped knowing we were preparing to sortie. Also, some of our forces were rather obviously being fitted out for cold weather. With summer practically here, any fool could guess that northern operations were in prospect."

I remarked on the difference in security measures between this and the Pearl Harbor operation, in which strictest precautions had been taken.

"It just couldn't be helped," replied Genda. "Our entire Fleet had to prepare for sortie on such short notice. It would have been better if the Fleet could have made an intermediate move—say, to the Marshalls—and waited for a while until attention was diverted from them. That way, we might have kept the enemy guessing longer as to where and when we intended to strike."

I asked Genda why Combined Fleet hadn't taken this factor

into consideration in planning the operation.

"They still think that the initiative is entirely in our hands," he explained. "Their plans are made far in advance, based entirely on their own thinking. The result is that they will never budge from them an inch."

Our attention now shifted to the planes overhead. Bungo Strait was defended by the Saeki Defense Force and the planes of the Kure Naval Air Corps. To ensure the safe passage of our powerful task force, their entire strength had been assigned to sweep the channel and hunt out enemy submarines. But there were no alerts from either ships or planes.

By noon we had passed through the eastern channel of Bungo Strait into the deep blue waters of the Pacific, and the destroyers had spread out for a swift antisubmarine sweep before assuming their positions in a ring formation.

At the center of the formation four carriers steamed in two columns, AKAGI and KAGA on the right, HIRYU and SORYU on the left. Surrounding them were two circles of screening ships. The inner circle consisted of heavy cruisers TONE and CHIKUMA, disposed diagonally forward of the carriers, and battleships HARUNA and KIRISHIMA diagonally to the rear. Light cruiser NAGARA and 12 destroyers formed the outer circle, with NAGARA out in front as the lead ship.

The atmosphere was tense in every ship. Antisubmarine stations were fully manned, and all hands were alert and ready for action. There was not even time for sentimental looks backward at the receding coast of the homeland.

Our ships sped to the southeast, making better than 20 knots to escape possible pursuit by enemy submarines. Evening twilight soon spread over the ocean and we were cloaked in the security of darkness. No submarines had been sighted, nor was there any indication that one had observed our sortie and reported it back to base. We had passed safely through the danger area and were speeding toward our destination—Midway!

CHAPTER 2 Evolution of Japanese Naval Strategy

1. PREWAR DEVELOPMENT

To comprehend fully what lay behind the fateful sortie of the Japanese Combined Fleet in late May 1942, it is necessary to hark back to the strategic concepts which dominated prewar Japanese naval thinking and to trace their evolution through the initial phase of our operations in the Pacific War.

For many years prior to Pearl Harbor, it had been common knowledge among the rank and file of Japanese citizens that the Imperial Navy was building up its strength and formulating its strategy with the United States Navy as the hypothetical antagonist, while at the same time the Imperial Army based its preparedness and planning on the hypothesis of a contest with the Russian Army.

This dual-standard policy, however, had not always existed. Up to the close of World War I, there had been a unified one-power standard for both the fighting services. China was the hypothetical enemy until near the turn of the century; then Tzarist Russia filled this role for roughly two decades, until World War I and its aftermath radically altered the international picture.

Having fought on the side of the victorious Allies, Japan emerged from World War I a first-class world power and thus became the rival of her erstwhile companion in arms, the United States, for primacy in the Pacific. At the same time the Communist Revolution in Russia reduced the threat of Russian imperialism in Asia and relegated the new Soviet state to a place of secondary importance in Japanese military planning.

Accordingly, the new Imperial Defense Policy adopted in

1918 designated the United States as potential enemy No. 1, and the U.S.S.R. as potential enemy No. 2, for purposes of future preparedness. From that time onward, the Navy program was geared to this policy. However, it was not long before the Army, seeing in the rise of Soviet power an obstacle to its own ideas of continental expansion, again began looking upon Russia as the primary potential enemy. So began the dual-standard preparedness policy which prevailed until the eve of the Pacific War.

By the time I entered the Naval Academy in 1921, the Navy was already indoctrinating its future officers with the idea that "the potential enemy is America." We were instructed that the Navy stood for southward advance, which meant clashing with the United States, as opposed to the Army's policy of northward expansion involving friction with Russia.

Thus developed the Navy's practice of sending its most promising officers to serve as Naval Attachés in Washington, just as the Army commonly assigned honor graduates of the Army General Staff College to duty in Moscow. Admirals Osami Nagano and Isoroku Yamamoto, who as Chief of Naval General Staff and Commander in Chief, Combined Fleet, respectively, were the two central figures in the Japanese Navy at the start of the Pacific War, both had behind them tours of duty in the United States capital. Many others had the same experience.

Consequently, I believe it can be said that nearly all the high-ranking officers who occupied leading positions in the Japanese Navy for nearly two decades before Pearl Harbor were amply equipped to make an accurate evaluation of the fleet capabilities of the United States. Based on such evaluation, they formulated the defensive concept of fleet strategy which came to be the virtual tradition of the Imperial Navy. So firmly, indeed, was this concept established and maintained that it almost petrified the strategic thinking of the naval service.

The defensive principle manifested itself most concretely in the special characteristics of Japanese warship construction. In the event of war, the Navy's strategists figured, the superior American Fleet would most probably carry the offensive into the Western Pacific, and it would be the role of the Imperial Navy to intercept and attack it in waters close to the Japanese homeland. Japanese ships, therefore, should be so designed as to assure every possible advantage in this type of operation.

For this purpose, it was decided to sacrifice to the limit living accommodations for the crews, defensive armament, and radius of action, in order to achieve maximum offensive power and speed. The goal was to produce ships which would be individually superior to those of the enemy, even by a single gun or torpedo tube, or by a single knot of speed.

Hull design also reflected the defensive concept. With light cruiser YUBARI as the forerunner, the Navy began building ships whose freeboard was of almost uniform height from bow to stern, giving the deck line a peculiar, flat appearance. The reason was that ships of this design were considered best suited to operate in the rough seas surrounding the Japanese homeland.

In such manner the leaders of the Navy sought to offset Japan's inability to compete in a quantitative naval armaments race with the United States by emphasizing efforts to achieve qualitative superiority of ships for the specific type of operations envisaged. At the same time they developed special tactical systems for waging decisive fleet action in the course of interception operations, stressing employment of the "balanced fleet" principle, with battleships as the backbone.

By means of hard and unremitting training, these tactical concepts were thoroughly and uniformly inculcated throughout the fleet, and a high level of proficiency in their application was developed. Tireless effort finally produced a naval establishment whose confidence in its own fighting ability was expressed in the motto, "We rely not upon the enemy's not attacking us, but upon our readiness to meet him when he comes."

Japan's naval preparedness, however, remained restricted within the bounds of the defensive concept. It was designed only to insure safety against attack and to preserve peace. Naturally such a thought as sending the Fleet out to attack distant Hawaii never entered the minds of the Navy's leaders. Nor was it ever considered that Japan could afford involvement in an international conflict which might result in her small Navy's being pitted singlehanded against those of more than one enemy power.

Toward the end of 1936 I was ordered to the Naval War College as a student. It was a critical time, for shortly thereafter Japan was to become free of the yoke of the naval arms limitation treaties. For some time past there had been alarming outcries at home that 1936 would be a year of crisis, and that it might well witness the outbreak of war between Japan and the United States.

Naval rivalry was, indeed, a sore spot in Japanese-American relations. At the Washington Conference of 1921 Japan had strongly pressed for a fleet ratio of 7 to 10 vis-à-vis the United States, basing her stand on the principle that the relative strengths of the two navies should be such that each could defend itself successfully against the other, but neither could attack or menace the other. This was the so-called principle of "non-menace and non-aggression."

Naval experts at the time generally agreed that in fleet warfare an invading force needed to be 50 per cent stronger than the defending. Under the 7 to 10 ratio demanded by Japan, the United States Fleet would have had only a 43 per cent margin of superiority—in other words, not quite enough to wage an aggresive campaign.

The Conference, however, finally adopted a 3 to 5 ratio applicable to capital ships—capital ships meaning battleships, since in those days aircraft carriers were practically non-existent.

This ratio gave the American Fleet a 67 per cent margin of superiority in the key battleship category and therefore, in the eyes of the Japanese Navy, made it an aggressive menace to Japan. The Navy's efforts to develop superior ship types for defensive operations, referred to earlier, were largely spurred by this threat.

In 1930 the London Naval Conference was convoked for the purpose of extending the limitation of naval armaments to categories other than capital ships. At this conference Japan again insisted upon a ratio of 7 to 10 in global tonnage of non-capital ships for the same reasons as she had advanced earlier, but again her demands were rejected.

Confronted by the unbending attitude of the other powers, Japan decided to regain her freedom by refusing to renew the naval limitation treaties upon their scheduled expiration at the end of 1936. In accordance with treaty stipulations, notice of this intention was given by the Japanese Government in December 1934, two years ahead of the expiration date.

Earlier in the same year the United States had enacted the Vinson naval expansion program, which it contended was necessary in view of changed conditions in Europe and Asia. This program aimed at building up American fleet strength to the full limits allowed by the Washington and London Naval Treaties by 1939. Prior thereto, the United States had not built up to treaty levels, whereas the Japanese Fleet was already at full authorized strength. Consequently, until the Vinson program, Japan had actually enjoyed some sense of security in spite of the treaty ratio. However, if the Vinson program were carried to completion, the United States Fleet would achieve, actually as well as on paper, the 67 per cent margin of superiority which Japanese naval strategists feared would enable it to carry out successful offensive operations against Japan.

As soon as the naval limitation treaties lapsed, Japan promptly acted to counter the Vinson program. In 1937 she adopted what was known as the "*Marusan* Program," the third naval expansion undertaken by Japan since the conclusion of the Washington Treaty. Under this program greater stress than ever was placed upon building special, superior-type ships and armament designed to offset numerical inferiority. YAMATO and MUSASHI, the world's largest and most heavily armed battleships, were conceived as part of this effort.

At the Naval War College the problems of naval armament and possible war with the United States naturally came up for frequent discussion among the students. I particularly recall one of these debates, in which the majority of those present agreed that eventual war with America was inevitable. As usual, I seized the opportunity to voice my own pet—and somewhat iconoclastic—opinions.

"If it is accepted that war is inevitable," I asserted, "our present naval preparedness policies are, in my opinion, entirely inadequate, and as long as we adhere to them we shall never be in a position to win. The trouble is that we are trying to prepare ourselves to fight—and fight successfully—at an unforseeable time, whenever an enemy challenge may force us to do so. But for us to maintain constantly the armaments level necessary to assure victory regardless of when the war may come is, I believe, utterly impossible.

"Consequently, if we are really convinced that war must come, we should ourselves determine in advance when to fight, and we should formulate a systematic, long-range plan of preparedness based on that decision. We should stick to the plan at the sacrifice of everything else, above all avoiding involvement in war prior to the time we have fixed. Then, when the time comes and we have attained the level of preparedness necessary to assure victory, we should deliberately provoke hostilities."

My thesis did not fail to evoke sharp opposition I was accused of advocating a heretical perversion of the preparedness principle.

"Armaments," argued my opponents, "are intended to preserve peace, not to prepare for war. Their true objective is to avoid the necessity of fighting."

This, of course, was the accepted version of the preparedness theory. But there was an inconsistency in my colleague's reasoning which I hastened to point out.

"How can you hold to this contention," I asked, "and at the same time accept the premise that war with the United States is inevitable? Your premise itself is heretical. Japan and the United States were not particularly ordained by fate to be irreconcilable enemies.

"As a matter of fact," I went on, "I am not opposed to the accepted concept of preparedness. What I take exception to is the manner in which we are presently carrying out our naval preparations. First of all, I think that it is meaningless to build up our armament with a view to counterbalancing that of another power. Let us assume that we were successful in expanding our armament to a point where we could fight the American Fleet, our presumed antagonist, on even terms. Still we would not have any real security, for under present conditions any war that breaks out is likely to develop into a world conflict. We may go ahead and build super-battleships like YAMATO and MUSASHI, but even they cannot give us the ability, singlehanded, to come out on top in any international conflict. Therefore, I believe that Japan must also adopt a more flexible and conciliatory attitude in her foreign policy.

"In the second place, I consider our present naval armament policies wrong because they have not kept pace with the radical change in methods of warfare. We must abandon the idea that all we need to do is to outbuild our rivals in warships. In the future, aircraft will be the decisive factor. Conventional naval armament based on surface strength has become largely ornamental. Moreover, air warfare will be total warfare, requiring the complete mobilization of all national resources and activities.

Courtesy Shizuo Fukui

BATTLESHIP *Nagato*

Courtesy Shizuo Fukui

BATTLESHIP *Fuso*

Courtesy Shizuo Fukui

BATTLESHIP *Haruna*

Light Cruiser *Nagara*, Flagship of the Screening Force

I fear, however, that our present level of national development is not far enough advanced to enable us to achieve security through building up our own air power. We must first have a more farsighted policy of internal development."

My colleagues listened to these remarks with pained expressions, as if to say, "There he goes, spouting off again about his all-powerful air force!" And so the discussion broke off.

Whatever were the shortcomings of the fleet preparedness program, the Army, ever since the Manchurian Incident of 1931, had successfully exploited our naval armaments as a springboard and flank protection for its continental expansion moves. In 1937 these maneuvers culminated in the so-called North China Incident, which soon developed into a full-scale Sino-Japanese war. The theater of hostilities gradually spread southward, finally leading, in September 1940, to the forcible stationing of Japanese troops in northern Indochina. In the same month Japan entered into a military alliance with Germany and Italy, and her relations with the United States thereafter deteriorated swiftly toward a rupture.

By the fall of 1941 the Navy's leaders found themselves confronted by the difficult necessity of choosing between war and peace. I honestly believe that the majority of them were disposed toward peace.

Pacifist sentiment was particularly strong among the elder admirals, who cautioned against blind belief in Japanese invincibility, pointing out that the wars of 1895 and 1904, instead of being the "overwhelming Japanese triumphs" described by propagandist historians, had actually been barely won through political as well as military effort. As shown in the Tokyo war crimes trials after Japan's surrender, Admirals Keisuke Okada and Mitsumasa Yonai, both on the retired list in 1941, and Admiral Soemu Toyoda, still in active service, were representative spokesmen of the antiwar viewpoint.

Even Admiral Isoroku Yamamoto, then Commander in Chief

of the Combined Fleet and the man to whom, above all others, the Navy looked for leadership, is known to have opposed Japan's plunging into war. On the basis of his estimate of Japan's naval strength and national resources, he gave a clear-cut warning that the Fleet could not be counted upon to fight successfully for longer than a year.

This hesitancy on the part of the Navy's leaders was taken as cowardice and indecision by the Army, whose primary concern had been Russia more than the United States and Britain, and by a certain section of the public, who blindly believed in Japan's invincibility. Also, within the Navy itself there was a pro-war faction which argued that Japan must take up arms or suffer slow but certain strangulation in the tightening strictures of Anglo-Dutch-American economic reprisals.

Ever since Japan, dazzled by German victories in Europe, had concluded the military alliance with the Axis, the United States, Great Britain, and the Netherlands had applied increasing economic pressure against her. When Japanese troops moved into southern Indochina in July 1941, the three powers struck back with their most damaging blow to date—a concerted embargo on oil exports to Japan.

The cutting off of oil supplies hit the Navy at its most vulnerable spot. Its reserve of 6,450,000 tons diminished daily, and, even with the strictest economy, would be exhausted in three or four years at the most. Since without oil the Japanese fighting services would become powerless, Japan would be reduced to a situation in which she would have to bow to any and all demands by the Anglo-American camp.

It had been hoped, when Japanese-American negotiations were begun in the spring of 1941, that a peaceful solution might be found. But as the talks dragged on with no apparent hope of achieving a mutually acceptable agreement, the war faction pointed to the disastrous effects of the oil embargo and declared that Japan must either take up arms before it was too late or else reconcile herself to eventual complete capitulation.

Generally speaking, however, the overwhelming majority of naval officers stood aloof from the long and bitter controversy over the issue of war or peace. Leaving this fateful question to be decided on the highest level of the national political leadership, they went on pouring all their energies into augmenting the combat efficiency and readiness of the Fleet.

Meanwhile, since the beginning of 1941, Navy planners had been giving careful thought to a revamping of fleet strategy. It was readily apparent that the traditional concept of purely defensive operations in waters close to the Japanese homeland would not be adequate for the type of war in which Japan now seemed increasingly likely to become involved.

2. STRATEGY OF INITIAL OPERATIONS

Whereas, in the past, Japanese naval strategists had thought almost exclusively in terms of an isolated contest against a single enemy, the United States, they now had to remold their plans to fit Japanese participation in a multilateral world war. As an Axis ally, Japan had to count on waging simultaneous hostilities against the combined Pacific forces of the world's two strongest naval powers, Britain and the United States, not to mention Holland as well. With China, of course, Japan had already been at war since 1937.

Such a large-scale conflict obviously would be a long drawn-out struggle, in which possession of ample supplies of strategic natural resources would be a vital determinant of ultimate victory. Above all, Japan would have to gain quick access to oil, the most vital sinew of modern warfare. Oil, therefore, was the paramount factor in shaping Japanese strategy for the initial phase of hostilities, just as it was to become later the final precipitant of Japan's decision to fight.

To secure a source of oil supply, it was essential that Japan seize the rich petroleum-producing areas of Southeast Asia as soon as possible after the outbreak of war. The prompt acquisition of these areas was, accordingly, the common central objective of the Navy's war planners, but a clear-cut divergence of opinion arose between the two principal strategy-formulating organs—the Naval General Staff and Combined Fleet—as to how this could best be accomplished.

The basic war plan elaborated by the Naval General Staff under Admiral Osami Nagano was the more orthodox and, superficially at least, the more cautious. Adhering firmly to the principle of maximum concentration of force, it called, in brief, for employing the bulk of the Navy's surface and air strength, including the Carrier Force, in a bold and direct thrust southward to capture the oil areas at the outset of hostilities. The General Staff strategists thus hoped to accomplish the seizure before the main body of the U. S. Pacific Fleet, based far away at Pearl Harbor, could interfere. And if it later came out to attack, the Japanese Fleet would intercept and destroy it in the western Pacific according to the tenets of the old defensive doctrine.

While the Naval General Staff was planning along these lines, however, certain key officers in Combined Fleet were independently probing the feasibility of a much more daring and aggressive strategic plan. It is generally accepted that the basic concept of this plan originated in the mind of Admiral Isoroku Yamamoto, Commander in Chief Combined Fleet, early in 1941.

As supreme commander at sea, Admiral Yamamoto was concerned above all with the potential threat posed by the strong American naval forces concentrated in the Hawaiian Islands. If, as envisaged by the Naval General Staff, the greater part of Japan's naval strength were committed to the invasion of the southern area without immobilizing these forces at least temporarily, Admiral Yamamoto saw serious danger that the

United States might attack in the western Pacific before the Japanese fleet could redispose itself to counter such an attack. He felt, therefore, that it was absolutely essential to eliminate this danger by striking a crippling offensive blow at the U. S. Pacific Fleet simultaneously with the launching of the southern operations. Here was the genesis of the surprise assault on Pearl Harbor.

Admiral Yamamoto confidently outlined his bold concept to Rear Admiral Takijiro Onishi, then Chief of Staff of the Eleventh Air Fleet, and instructed him to study its practicability. Onishi, who later was to become the organizer of the first Kamikaze air units, was one of the Navy's foremost career aviators and was highly respected throughout the Naval Air Corps as a man of intelligence and foresight. He proceeded to give careful thought to Yamamoto's idea.

It was clear from the beginning, however, that the only effective means of attacking the Pacific Fleet within its Hawaiian base lay in the employment of the Japanese Carrier Force, the First Air Fleet, which then contained four large carriers, two small carriers, and a destroyer screen. Onishi's own organization, the Eleventh Air Fleet, consisted chiefly of shore-based attack planes, and was obviously incapable of delivering an attack on Hawaii from bases in the Marshalls, 2,000 miles away. It could be used effectively only against the Philippines and Malaya.

To assist him in his study, therefore, Onishi turned to Commander Minoru Genda, a brilliant staff officer of the First Air Fleet, who shared Onishi's belief in the key role of naval air power. Though short in stature, Genda was endowed with a strong fighting spirit which was reflected in his hawk-like countenance. He had begun his naval career as a fighter pilot, and his skill and daring in that capacity had won for him and his unit the nickname of "the Genda Circus."

Genda, however, was more than a skillful flier; he was also

an outstanding air tactician. As Operations Officer of the 2nd Combined Air Group dispatched to the Shanghai area in 1937, he had been instrumental in introducing new and vastly improved methods for mass, long-range operations by fighter aircraft. Later, after graduating with honors from the Naval War College, he had served two years in London as Assistant Naval Attaché for Air, an experience which further broadened his outlook.

Genda's most noteworthy contributions in the realm of air tactics were the mass employment of fighters to gain control of the air where friendly bombers were to operate, and the concerted use of several carrier task groups in a single tactical theater. These new methods, applied so effectively in the opening phase of the Pacific War, were to become widely known in American aviation circles under the name of "Genda-ism."

In compliance with Admiral Onishi's request, Genda made an exhaustive study of whether Admiral Yamamoto's Hawaiian attack concept could be put into practical execution, finally drawing up his ideas in a full report. The report stated as its conclusion that the proposed attack could be successfully carried out provided that the following essential conditions were met:

(1) That all six of the Fleet's large carriers[1] be assigned to the operation;

(2) That special care be taken to select only the most competent commanders and the best-trained flying personnel; and

(3) That complete secrecy be maintained so as to ensure the advantage of surprise.

Commander Genda's report convinced Admiral Yamamoto that the idea of a carrier-borne air assault on Pearl Harbor was sound, and Combined Fleet pushed ahead with further concrete planning. However, when the tentative scheme was finally broached to the Naval General Staff, which had already con-

---

[1] The number of large fleet carriers was augmented from four to six by the commissioning of ZUIKAKU and SHOKAKU in August 1941.

cluded that the main strength of the Fleet should be employed in the invasion of the southern area, it naturally encountered strong opposition.

In support of its stand the Naval General Staff argued that the diversion of a considerable portion of fleet strength, including virtually all available carriers, to the Pearl Harbor attack might seriously compromise the success of the southern operations. This argument, indeed, was not lacking in cogency, for few even in aviation circles then thought that shore-based air alone would suffice to cover and support the southern invasions. At the same time, there was no inclination to underestimate the strength of the American, British, and Dutch naval forces in Far Eastern waters.

The Naval General Staff critics further assailed Yamamoto's plan for the Pearl Harbor attack as being too much of a gamble because its success depended entirely upon taking the American Fleet by surprise within its base. If, for any reason, this could not be accomplished, the attack would fail—possibly with disastrous consequences.

Nor were such doubts limited to the Naval General Staff. Vice Admiral Chuichi Nagumo, whose First Air Fleet would have to play the central role in the Hawaiian assault, himself opposed the plan at first. Nagumo concurred in the General Staff contention that maximum strength should be thrown into the conquest of the oil regions to the south, as this was of primary strategic importance. He also underlined further the riskiness of the Yamamoto plan, pointing to the high vulnerability of carriers to air attack. Even a large carrier, he warned, could be quickly and effectively disabled by a few bomb hits.

But Admiral Nagumo's views were not shared by all his subordinate commanders in the First Air Fleet. Rear Admiral Tamon Yamaguchi, Commander Carrier Division 2, enthusiastically supported the Yamamoto plan. The U.S. Pacific Fleet, he argued, was the mainstay of Allied strength in the entire Pacific area, and its destruction should therefore be the first and foremost objective of Japanese strategy. Were the American Fleet left free and undamaged, Japan would become unable to exploit any success in the south. Conversely, if it were destroyed at Pearl Harbor at the start of hostilities, the conquest and exploitation of the rich oil areas would become easy tasks.

Admiral Yamamoto himself was firm and unbending in his insistence on the Pearl Harbor attack plan. Opposed as he unquestionably was to Japan's going to war, once that decision was taken he would be responsible for the successful prosecution of the war at sea. The U.S. Pacific Fleet stood out as his strongest antagonist, and therefore its destruction had to be his first and paramount mission. Thanks to the remarkable advance in naval air force capabilities, it was now possible to attack that Fleet at Hawaii without waiting for it to come out to the western Pacific. Despite the risk, Yamamoto could see no reason for hesitating to take the gamble.

The Naval General Staff did not yield easily, however. Admiral Yamamoto, it is understood, finally threatened to resign as Commander in Chief Combined Fleet unless his plan was adopted, and he also declared himself ready to take personal command of the Carrier Striking Force in the attack if Admiral Nagumo remained halfhearted. Confronted by this ultimatum, Admiral Nagano, Chief of Naval General Staff, had no choice. Records now available show that Nagano at last gave his consent at a meeting with Yamamoto in Tokyo on 3 November 1941, only 35 days before the Pearl Harbor attack was actually delivered.

Japan's fleet strategy for the opening phase of the Pacific War was now fixed. The defensive concepts of prewar days were dead and buried. The new watchword was "Attack!"

On the political front, meanwhile, developments were rapidly pointing toward war. On 5 November, the Government and High Command jointly decided that Japan would take up arms if diplomatic negotiations failed to achieve a settlement by the end of November. On that same day Admiral Yamamoto ordered Combined Fleet to make final preparations for war, and issued an outline of the initial operations, including the attack on Pearl Harbor. On 7 November a further Combined Fleet order tentatively fixed 8 December as the date for the start of hostilities.

3. THE PEARL HARBOR ATTACK

By 22 November the Pearl Harbor Task Force of 31 ships, under command of Vice Admiral Nagumo, had assembled in utmost secrecy at Tankan Bay, in the Kurile Islands. The assemblage consisted of a Striking Force of six fleet carriers (Carrier Divisions 1, 2, and 5); a Screening Force of two fast battleships (Battleship Division 3), two heavy cruisers (Cruiser Division 8), and one light cruiser and nine destroyers (Destroyer Squadron 1); an Advance Patrol Unit of three submarines; and a fleet train of eight tankers.

At 0600 on 26 November this Force sortied and headed via a devious route for a prearranged stand-by point at latitude 42° N, longitude 170° W. At this point it was to receive final orders depending upon the ultimate decision taken on the question of whether or not to go to war.

On 1 December this decision was made, and it was for war. A Combined Fleet order dispatched the following day to Nagumo's eastward moving Task Force definitely set 8 December[2] as the date for attacking Pearl Harbor.

On 3 December (4 December in Japan) the Task Force altered course southeastward, and at 1130 on the 6th it turned

Editor's Note: In Japan, which is 7 December at Pearl Harbor. At this point the narrative is shifted to local (Hawaiian) time, Zone plus 9½, and West Longitude date.

due south to close the island of Oahu, increasing speed to 24 knots.

In the very early morning of the 7th, with only a few hours to go before the target would be within plane striking distance, the Task Force received disturbing information from Tokyo. An Imperial General Headquarters intelligence report, received at 0050, indicated that no carriers were at Pearl Harbor.[3] These were to have been the top-priority targets of our attack and we had counted on their being in port. All of the American carriers, as well as all heavy cruisers, had apparently put to sea. But the report indicated that a full count of battleships remained in the harbor.

Despite this late-hour upset, Vice Admiral Nagumo and his staff decided that there was now no other course left but to carry out the attack as planned. The U.S. battleships, though secondary to the carriers, were still considered an important target, and there was also a faint possibility that some of the American carriers might have returned to Pearl Harbor by the time our planes struck. So the Task Force sped on toward its goal, every ship now tense and ready for battle.

In the predawn darkness of 7 December, Nagumo's carriers reached a point 200 miles north of Pearl Harbor. The zero hour had arrived! The carriers swung into the wind, and at 0600 the first wave of the 353-plane Attack Force, of which I was in over-all command, took off from the flight decks and headed for the target.

The first wave was composed of 183 planes: level bombers, dive bombers, torpedo planes, and fighters. I flew in the lead plane, followed closely by 49 Type-97 level bombers under

[3] *Editors' Note:* The Japanese believed that four American carriers—YORKTOWN, HORNET, LEXINGTON, and ENTERPRISE—were based at Hawaii at this time. Actually, only LEXINGTON and ENTERPRISE were based there, YORKTOWN and HORNET being in the Atlantic. The Japanese were correctly informed that SARATOGA was on the U.S. West Coast and would shortly rejoin the Pacific Fleet.

my direct command, each carrying one 800-kilogram armor-piercing bomb.

To starboard and slightly below flew Lieutenant Commander Shigeharu Murata of AKAGI and his 40 planes from the four carriers, each carrying one torpedo slung to its fuselage. Above me and to port was a formation of 51 Type-99 carrier dive bombers led by Lieutenant Commander Kakuichi Takahashi from SHOKAKU. Each of these planes carried one ordinary 250-kilogram bomb. A three-group fighter escort of 43 Zeros, commanded by Lieutenant Commander Shigeru Itaya from AKAGI, ranged overhead, on the prowl for possible enemy opposition.

The weather was far from ideal. A 20-knot northeast wind was raising heavy seas. Flying at 3,000 meters, we were above a dense cloud layer which extended down to within 1,500 meters of the water. The brilliant morning sun had just burst into sight, setting the eastern horizon aglow.

One hour and forty minutes after leaving the carriers I knew that we should be nearing our goal. Small openings in the thick cloud cover afforded occasional glimpses of the ocean, as I strained my eyes for the first sight of land. Suddenly a long white line of breaking surf appeared directly beneath my plane. It was the northern shore of Oahu.

Veering right toward the west coast of the island, we could see that the sky over Pearl Harbor was clear. Presently the harbor itself became visible across the central Oahu plain, a film of morning mist hovering over it. I peered intently through my binoculars at the ships riding peacefully at anchor. One by one I counted them. Yes, the battleships were there all right, eight of them! But our last lingering hope of finding any carriers present was now gone. Not one was to be seen.

It was 0749 when I ordered my radioman to send the command, "Attack!" He immediately began tapping out the pre-arranged code signal: "*TO, TO, TO . . .*"

Leading the whole group, Lieutenant Commander Murata's torpedo bombers headed downward to launch their torpedoes, while Lieutenant Commander Itaya's fighters raced forward to sweep enemy fighters from the air. Takahashi's dive-bomber group had climbed for altitude and was out of sight. My bombers, meanwhile, made a circuit toward Barbers Point to keep pace with the attack schedule. No enemy fighters were in the air, nor were there any gun flashes from the ground.

The effectiveness of our attack was now certain, and a message, "Surprise attack successful!" was accordingly sent to AKAGI at 0753. The message was received by the carrier and duly relayed to the homeland, but, as I was astounded to learn later, the message from my plane was also heard directly by NAGATO in Hiroshima Bay and by the General Staff in Tokyo.

The attack was opened with the first bomb falling on Wheeler Field, followed shortly by dive-bombing attacks upon Hickam Field and the bases at Ford Island. Fearful that smoke from these attacks might obscure his targets, Lieutenant Commander Murata cut short his group's approach toward the battleships anchored east of Ford Island and released torpedoes. A series of white waterspouts soon rose in the harbor.

Lieutenant Commander Itaya's fighters, meanwhile, had full command of the air over Pearl Harbor. About four enemy fighters which took off were promptly shot down. By 0800 there were no enemy planes in the air, and our fighters began strafing the airfields.

My level-bombing group had entered on its bombing run toward the battleships moored to the east of Ford Island. On reaching an altitude of 3,000 meters, I had the sighting bomber take position in front of my plane.

As we closed in, enemy antiaircraft fire began to concentrate on us. Dark gray puffs burst all around. Most of them came from ships' batteries, but land batteries were also active. Suddenly my plane bounced as if struck by a club. When I looked back to see what had happened, the radioman said: "The fuselage is holed and the rudder wire damaged." We were fortunate that the plane was still under control, for it was imperative to fly a steady course as we approached the target. Now it was nearly time for "Ready to release," and I concentrated my attention on the lead plane to note the instant his bomb was dropped. Suddenly a cloud came between the bomb sight and the target, and just as I was thinking that we had already overshot, the lead plane banked slightly and turned right toward Honolulu. We had missed the release point because of the cloud and would have to try again.

While my group circled for another attempt, others made their runs, some trying as many as three before succeeding. We were about to begin our second bombing run when there was a colossal explosion in battleship row. A huge column of dark red smoke rose to 1,000 meters. It must have been the explosion of a ship's powder magazine.[4] The shock wave was felt even in my plane, several miles away from the harbor.

We began our run and met with fierce antiaircraft concentrations. This time the lead bomber was successful, and the other planes of the group followed suit promptly upon seeing the leader's bombs fall. I immediately lay flat on the cockpit floor and slid open a peephole cover in order to observe the fall of the bombs. I watched four bombs plummet toward the earth. The target—two battleships moored side by side—lay ahead. The bombs became smaller and smaller and finally disappeared. I held my breath until two tiny puffs of smoke flashed suddenly on the ship to the left, and I shouted, "Two hits!"

When an armor-piercing bomb with a time fuse hits the target, the result is almost unnoticeable from a great altitude.

[4] *Editors' Note:* It was battleship ARIZONA, whose boilers and forward magazines exploded as a result of several direct hits by heavy bombs, rendering her a total loss.

On the other hand, those which miss are quite obvious because they leave concentric waves to ripple out from the point of contact, and I saw two of these below. I presumed that it was battleship MARYLAND we had hit.[5]

As the bombers completed their runs they headed north to return to the carriers. Pearl Harbor and the air bases had been pretty well wrecked by the fierce strafings and bombings. The imposing naval array of an hour before was gone. Antiaircraft fire had become greatly intensified, but in my continued observations I saw no enemy fighter planes. Our command of the air was unchallenged.

Suddenly, at 0854, I overhead Lieutenant Commander Shigekazu Shimazaki, flight commander of ZUIKAKU and commander of the second wave, ordering his 170 planes to the attack. The second wave had taken off from the carriers at 0715, one hour and fifteen minutes after the first, and was now over the target. My plane did not withdraw with the first attack wave, but continued to fly over the island so that I could observe results achieved by both assaults. Furthermore, it was planned that my plane would remain until the last to serve as guide back to the carriers for any straggling fighters, since these carried no homing devices.

The 54 level bombers of the second wave, under Lieutenant Commander Shimazaki, were Type-97s ("Kates"), armed with two 250-kilogram or one 250-kilogram and six 60-kilogram bombs. Their targets were the air bases. The dive bomber group, led by Lieutenant Commander Takashige Egusa, SORYU's flight commander, consisted of 80 Type-90 bombers ("Vals"), armed with 250-kilogram bombs, and its original assignment had been to attack the enemy carriers. Since there were no carriers present, these planes were to select targets from among the ships which remained unscathed or only

---

[5] *Editors' Note:* Battleship MARYLAND was hit by two bombs which did little damage; she was repaired and ready for active service by February 1942.

slightly damaged by the first-wave attack. Fighter cover for the second wave was provided by 36 Zeros commanded by Lieutenant Saburo Shindo of AKAGI.

On the heels of the attack order, Lieutenant Shindo's fighter group swooped down to strafe Pearl Harbor and the airfields. Egusa's dive bombers then came in over the east coast mountains and dove to the attack, following the lead of the commander's plane, which was easily distinguishable because of its red-painted tail. Billowing smoke from burning ships and harbor installations greatly hampered the attack, but the dive bombers flew in doggedly to accomplish their mission.

Most of Shimazaki's level bombers, which followed the dive bombers in, concentrated on Hickam Field; the rest attacked Ford Island and Kaneohe Air Base. They flew at no more than 2,000 meters in order to bomb from beneath the clouds. In spite of this, no planes were lost to antiaircraft fire, although nearly half of them were holed.

By 1300 all surviving aircraft of both attack waves had returned to the carriers. Of the total of 353 planes, only 9 fighters, 15 dive bombers, and 5 torpedo planes, along with their crews aggregating 55 officers and men, were missing. Against these almost negligible losses, 8 battleships—virtually the entire battleship strength of the U.S. Pacific Fleet—were believed to have been sunk or severely damaged.[6] Besides, enemy air strength based on Oahu appeared to have been decisively smashed, with the result that not a single plane attacked the Japanese force.

[6] *Editors' Note:* Of the vessels in Pearl Harbor on the morning of 7 December, the following were either sunk or damaged: Battleships—ARIZONA, CALIFORNIA, WEST VIRGINIA sunk; OKLAHOMA capsized; NEVADA heavily damaged; MARYLAND, PENNSYLVANIA, TENNESSEE damaged. Light cruisers—HELENA, RALEIGH heavily damaged; HONOLULU damaged. Destroyers—CASSIN, DOWNES burned and heavily damaged; SHAW heavily damaged. Repair ship VESTAL badly damaged; minelayer OGLALA sunk, seaplane tender CURTISS damaged, miscellaneous auxiliary UTAH capsized. (Data from Report of the Joint Committee on the Investigation of the Pearl Harbor Attack, *Investigation of the Pearl Harbor Attack*, p. 64).

Undeniably this added up to a remarkable success—one which even the old believers in battleship primacy would hail as a complete triumph. Even so, the fliers returning from the initial attack were all in favor of continuing the offensive to inflict still further damage on the enemy. Our striking power remained virtually intact. Control of the air was completely ours. Nothing seemed to stand in the way.

This certainly was the unanimous sentiment of the flying officers on board flagship AKAGI as we gathered at the flight deck command post after landing to analyze attack results and plan for possible further action. But though everyone favored pressing the attack, our keenest desire was not so much to inflict additional damage on the targets already hit as it was to find and destroy the enemy carriers which had so fortuitously eluded us.

A hasty plan for accomplishing this came into my mind. It was our guess that the missing carriers and heavy cruisers must be somewhere to the south of Oahu, engaged in training exercises. A further air strike, I thought, might help draw them in; and then if the task force, instead of retiring by the same route that it had come, skirted around to the south of the islands and headed toward the Marshalls, carrying out air searches as it went, there might be a reasonable chance of locating the American carriers.

This spur-of-the-moment idea received an enthusiastic reception from my fellow officers, but it had to be dismissed because of one insuperable obstacle. Our tanker train was already heading for a prearranged stand-by point on the northern withdrawal route, and if it were now redirected southward, it could not possibly catch up with the task force in time to provide the much-needed fuel.

So the last hope of hitting the enemy carriers was reluctantly abandoned. As the next best thing, when I reported to Admiral Nagumo the results of the initial strike, I strongly

ATTACK ON WHEELER FIELD, OAHU, 7 DECEMBER 1941

PEARL HARBOR ATTACK, 7 DECEMBER 1941

DECK OF JAPANESE AIRCRAFT CARRIER

PRE-TAKEOFF BRIEFING FOR PILOTS OF
RECONNAISSANCE SEAPLANES

recommended a further attack on Oahu. His decision, however —which I believe was influenced to a considerable degree by his Chief of Staff, Rear Admiral Ryunosuke Kusaka—was to terminate the attack and withdraw. At 1330, upon a flag signal from AKAGI, the Task Force set a north-northwest course and retired as swiftly and silently as it had come.

With the exception of a specially organized force composed of Carrier Division 2 (SORYU, HIRYU), Cruiser Division 8 (TONE, CHIKUMA), and two destroyers, which was detached on 16 December[7] by Combined Fleet order to support the invasion of Wake Island, the Task Force headed back for the Inland Sea and Hashirajima anchorage, where it arrived on 23 December.

The reasons for Admiral Nagumo's decision to retire without further exploiting his success have puzzled naval experts and historians, particularly abroad. I know of only one document which gives the Admiral's own estimate of the situation at the time he made this decision. Therein he says:

1. The first attack had inflicted practically all the damage that we had anticipated, and a further attack could not have been expected to augment this damage to any great extent.

2. Even in the first attack, the enemy's antiaircraft fire reaction had been so prompt as virtually to nullify the advantage of surprise. In a further attack, it had to be expected that our losses would increase out of all proportion to the results achievable.

3. Radio intercepts indicated that the enemy still had at least 50 large-type aircraft in operational condition, and at the same time the whereabouts and activities of his carriers, heavy cruisers, and submarines were unknown.

4. To remain within attack range of enemy land-based planes was distinctly to our disadvantage, especially in view of the limited range (250 miles) of our own air searches and the undependability of our submarine patrol then operating in the Hawaiian area.

Related to, but certainly less logical than the queries con-

[7] *Editors' Note.* Tokyo date and time are resumed at this point.

cerning Admiral Nagumo's decision to retire is the speculation so frequently indulged in since the war as to why Japan did not seize Hawaii outright instead of merely delivering a hit-and-run attack on Pearl Harbor. In the first place, this speculation arises only because the Pearl Harbor attack turned out to be such an unexpectedly great success. At the time the attack was decided upon, we were by no means so confident of success; indeed we felt very much as if we were about to pull the eagle's tail feathers. Naturally nothing so ambitious as the conquest of Hawaii had even entered our calculations.

Furthermore, as explained earlier, the primary objective of our initial war strategy was to secure oil resources. The Pearl Harbor attack itself was conceived purely as a supporting operation toward that objective. As our military resources were limited and oil was our immediate goal, there was no reason at this stage to contemplate the seizure of Hawaiian territory.

All in all, the Pearl Harbor operation did achieve its basic strategic objective of preventing the U.S. Pacific Fleet from interfering with Japanese operations in the south. But the failure to inflict any damage on the enemy carriers still weighed heavily on the minds of Admiral Nagumo's air staff and flying officers as the task force cruised back toward home waters. We immediately began laying plans for subsequent operations to achieve what we had been unable to accomplish at Pearl Harbor.

On the one hand, we labored to perfect a new tactical doctrine for a sea engagement against the enemy carrier force. The essence of this doctrine was the amalgamation of the air units on board all six of our carriers into a single powerful attack group of fighters, bombers, and torpedo planes, which would strike the enemy all at once in overwhelming strength. We were fully confident that these new tactics would assure us of victory.

On the other hand, Commander Genda, as Operations Officer on Nagumo's staff, gave exhaustive thought to the broader strategic and tactical problems. His conclusion also was that our next operation must be an all-out effort to destroy the enemy carriers. And as a means of luring the enemy out from his base so that we might engage him in battle, he thought that invasion operations should be undertaken against Midway Island and also against Kingman's Reef, 960 miles south-southwest of Pearl Harbor. Thus it was Genda who first thought up the basic idea that six months later culminated in the Midway operation.

Genda's scheme, of course, met with our wholehearted approval. To us it was the logical way to exploit and complete our initial successes, and we felt that the time to strike was now. So anxious were we to get started that suggestions were even made that the whole task force put in to Truk to support the Wake invasion and then stand by for operations against the enemy carriers.

Upon our return to the homeland, however, we found Japanese naval leaders complacently elated over the destruction of so many battleships at Pearl Harbor and not at all receptive toward plans for prompt follow-up action against the enemy carriers. To my knowledge, the only important naval officer who criticized the failure to inflict any damage on the enemy carriers was Rear Admiral Keizo Ueno, then commander of the Yokosuka Naval Air Corps.

4. NAGUMO FORCE IN SOUTHERN OPERATIONS

By the time the main body of the victorious Pearl Harbor Attack Force got back to home waters, the key Japanese operations in the southern area were well under way. Army forces were already pushing down the Malay Peninsula toward Singapore. Thailand had been occupied. Conquest of the vital Borneo oilfields had begun with the capture of Miri on 16 December. At sea, shore-based naval aircraft had scored a signal success only two days after the start of hostilities by sinking battleships PRINCE OF WALES and REPULSE, mainstays of the British Far Eastern Fleet, in the waters east of Malaya.

Elsewhere, too, the war was going well for Japan. Conquest of the Philippines, essential to protect the southward line of advance, was proceeding satisfactorily, with enemy air opposition smashed and the first of the two main landings on Luzon already accomplished at Lingayen Gulf. The oceanic perimeter to the east had been strengthened by the seizure of Guam in the Marianas, of Makin and Tarawa in the Gilberts, and of Wake, which finally fell under reinforced Japanese assault on 23 December, the same day that the Nagumo Force dropped anchor at Hashirajima.

Returning amid nationwide rejoicing over Japan's successes everywhere, Admiral Nagumo found that plans had already been made for the next employment of his force. Both the Naval General Staff and Combined Fleet were fully satisfied with the results achieved at Pearl Harbor and saw no need for further neutralizing action against the U.S. Pacific Fleet. They had therefore decided to transfer the Nagumo Force forthwith to the southern theater of operations, where its first mission was to support the impending invasions of Rabaul and Kavieng, in the Bismarck Archipelago.

Accordingly the Nagumo Force, less the units which had been detached to support the Wake invasion, sortied from the Inland Sea on 5 January 1942 and, after calling briefly at Truk, continued south to launch preinvasion air strikes. On 20 January attack groups took off from the four carriers northeast of New Ireland and struck Rabaul. The following day Kavieng was hit, simultaneously with neutralization strikes by aircraft from ZUIKAKU and SHOKAKU on airfields at Lae and Salamaua, on the eastern New Guinea coast.

Nowhere, however, was any appreciable enemy air strength discovered. Leading a powerful force of 90 bombers and fighters in the Rabaul attack, I saw just two enemy planes. They were attempting to take off from one of the two airfields and were promptly disposed of by our fighters. The second airfield was empty. Dive bombers dispatched a lone cargo ship caught in the harbor, and my level bomber group, for lack of any more worthwhile target, finally let loose its full load of 800-kilogram bombs on a coastal gun emplacement commanding the harbor entrance.

A further strike on Rabaul was carried out on the 22nd, but it was superfluous. The next day our landing forces occupied Rabaul and Kavieng without a struggle. All in all, the employment of the Nagumo Force in this operation struck me as wasteful and extravagant. If ever a sledge hammer had been used to crack an egg, this was the time.

The Nagumo Force put back to Truk and prepared to set out for the Celebes, where it was to support southwest area operations. A sudden development intervened, however. Early in the morning of 1 February, the very day we were scheduled to sortie, a report came in that enemy carrier-borne aircraft were attacking the Marshalls. Our departure for the Celebes was immediately called off, and instead we headed eastward at top speed to catch the enemy task force.

This impulsive action really made little sense. It would take us two full days to cover the 1,200-mile distance from Truk to the Marshalls, and in that interval the enemy was sure to retire to safety. Nevertheless, I inwardly rejoiced. Futile as it seemed, I thought our mad dash might be just the gesture that was needed to persuade Combined Fleet to re-direct the Nagumo Force eastward against its logical and potentially most dangerous opponent, the U.S. carrier force.

Throughout 1 February reports kept coming in from the Marshalls detailing the enemy raid, but by that night it was evident that the enemy carriers had already vanished from the area. Still the Nagumo Force kept speeding eastward during 2 February, and it was only after picking up an American news broadcast announcing the execution of "successful raids on the Marshall and Gilbert Islands" that it finally turned back, knowing for certain that the enemy was beyond its grasp.

Combined Fleet's reaction, also, proved highly disappointing. It viewed the Marshalls attack merely as an enemy attempt to divert strength from our southern operations. It was quick to criticize the local island defense command for having been taken by surprise, but it failed on its own part to produce any positive and effective plan for dealing with the enemy carrier force. Instead, it took a feeble and purely negative countermeasure which struck me as worse than no action at all.

This countermeasure was an order directing the detachment of Carrier Division 5 (ZUIKAKU, SHOKAKU) from the Nagumo Force to carry out defensive air patrols east of the homeland. It sprang from Combined Fleet apprehension that the enemy, having directed a successful carrier strike against the Marshalls, might be emboldened to attempt similar strikes against objectives closer to Japan—conceivably even the Imperial capital itself! The detachment of the two fleet carriers for patrol duty was designed only to guard against this worst eventuality. Unfortunately, its effect was to dissipate the strength of the one Japanese force which, with all six of its carriers operating together, could have confidently taken the offensive against any enemy in the Pacific, including the undamaged American carrier force.

For the main part of the Nagumo Force, however, Combined Fleet had other ideas. The Hashirajima headquarters continued to focus its attention exclusively on the southern area, where it was now most concerned over probable Allied use of northwest Australia as a base from which to impede Japanese seizure of the Dutch East Indies. Proposals for mounting an amphibious invasion of Port Darwin met a flat rebuff by the Naval General Staff and the Army, so Combined Fleet decided upon the next best alternative, a carrier air strike to completely wreck base installations in the area. An order was issued assigning this mission to the Nagumo Force, less Carrier Division 5.

Admiral Nagumo received word of his new assignment as he headed back from the futile sortie toward the Marshalls. Since Rear Admiral Yamaguchi's splinter force, which had been operating separately since 16 December,[8] was to rejoin the main body for the Darwin strike, Admiral Nagumo set his course for Palau and ordered Yamaguchi to rendezvous with him there. En route to Palau, Carrier Division 5 broke away from the main body and headed for the homeland.

After completing battle preparations, the Nagumo Force— now consisting of carriers AKAGI, KAGA, SORYU and HIRYU, battleships HIEI and KIRISHIMA, heavy cruisers TONE and CHIKUMA, light cruiser ABUKUMA, and nine destroyers— sortied from Palau on 15 February and headed for the Banda Sea. Early in the morning of the 19th, it reached a position about 220 miles north-northwest of Port Darwin and launched a strike of 188 planes under my command.

As at Rabaul, the job to be done seemed hardly worthy of the Nagumo Force. The harbor, it is true, was crowded with all kinds of ships, but a single pier and a few waterfront buildings appeared to be the only port installations. The airfield on the outskirts of the town, though fairly large, had no more than two or three small hangars, and in all there were only

[8] *Editors' Note:* After completing its mission in support of the Wake invasion, the Yamaguchi Force (Carrier Division 2, Cruiser Division 8 and two destroyers) had returned to the homeland, where it received orders to proceed south and support amphibious operations in the Banda Sea area. The force carried out pre-invasion air strikes on Ambon on 24-25 January, and on 4 February SORYU and HIRYU aircraft, operating from a shore base at Kendari, took part in a highly effective attack on an Allied surface force of four cruisers and seven destroyers south of Kangean Island.

twenty-odd planes of various types scattered about the field. No planes were in the air. A few attempted to take off as we came over but were quickly shot down, and the rest were destroyed where they stood.

While the fighter group went after the enemy planes, I detailed the dive bombers to attack ships in the harbor and led the main strength of my level bombers in an attack on the harbor installations and a nearby cluster of oil tanks. The rest of the level bombers went to destroy the airfield hangars. Antiaircraft fire was intense but largely ineffectual, and we quickly accomplished our objectives. The final tally was 11 ships, including some destroyers, sunk, over 20 enemy planes destroyed, and all base installations effectively smashed.

The Nagumo Force withdrew to Staring Bay,[9] on the southeast coast of the Celebes, but did not stay there long. The invasion of Java, culmination of the southern operations, was to begin on 1 March. To support it, the Nagumo Force, together with Vice Admiral Nobutake Kondo's Southern Force Main Body of four battleships, was to skirt around to the south of Java and cut off any possible enemy reinforcement or escape. The combined force sortied from Staring Bay on 25 February and headed into the Indian Ocean through Ombai Strait. On 3 March, a 180-plane strike was launched from our carriers against the south Javanese port of Tjilatjap, netting a bag of about 20 ships sunk. In addition, up to 5 March, 3 enemy destroyers and 14 transports were sunk trying to escape southward, and 3 other transports were captured. The landing operations meanwhile went off on schedule, and on 9 March Java surrendered. The Nagumo Force returned to Staring Bay to await orders.

By the latter part of March Sumatra was also in Japanese hands, as were the Andaman Islands in the Bay of Bengal. In Burma, Japanese forces had taken Rangoon and were pushing

[9] *Editors' Note:* Also known as Teluk Bay, it is in latitude 04°05′ S, longitude 122°44′ E.

HMS *Cornwall* SINKING, 5 APRIL 1942

BRITISH CARRIER HMS *Hermes* SUNK OFF THE
EAST COAST OF CEYLON, 9 APRIL 1942

on to the north. To secure these newly won areas and make it possible to supply the Burma forces directly by sea, Combined Fleet decided that it was necessary to strike a blow at British surface and air strength in the Indian Ocean. Enemy forces there were estimated at 2 carriers, 2 battleships, 3 heavy cruisers, 4 to 7 light cruisers, and a number of destroyers,[10] plus a shore-based air strength of about 300 planes.

Admiral Kondo, as Commander in Chief of Japanese Naval forces in Southeast Asia, assigned the mission to the Nagumo Force. Carrier Division 5, detached in February, was now restored to Admiral Nagumo's command for the operation, and the task force was further reinforced by two of Admiral Kondo's battleships. Sortieing from Staring Bay on 26 March, the Force headed into the Indian Ocean and opened its offensive with a surprise air strike at Colombo, Ceylon, on 5 April. All the carriers that had hit Pearl Harbor were participating except KAGA, which had gone to the homeland for repairs.

The first attack wave took off from the carriers at thirty minutes before dawn, about 200 miles south of Ceylon. This force, under my command, consisted of 36 fighters, 54 dive bombers, and 90 level bombers. We were expecting trouble this time, since an enemy flying boat had spotted us the preceding day and, though shot down by our combat air patrol, had undoubtedly reported the presence of our Force.

As we closed the target, flying through dense but occasionally broken clouds, I suddenly spotted a formation of 12 enemy Swordfish-type torpedo planes. They were flying at a much lower altitude, without any fighter escort, and obviously had not noticed us. I quickly signalled Lieutenant Commander Itaya, the fighter group commander, who was flying to port, to close me. When he had done so, I pointed down toward the

---

[10] *Editors' Note:* This Japanese estimate was not very accurate. Actually the British Far Eastern Fleet at this time contained 3 carriers, 5 battleships, 8 cruisers, 13 destroyers, and 7 submarines. Two of the cruisers and two of the submarines were Dutch.

enemy formation and motioned for him to attack. After a few moments, Itaya nodded and veered off to lead his fighters against the still unsuspecting enemy. The lumbering Swordfish, caught from above, were shot down to the last plane in one swift attack.

Since the luckless enemy planes must have been on their way to attack our carriers, I was sure now that enemy fighters were out to intercept us. To avoid them, I led the whole attack force around to the north of Colombo, and then we dashed in toward the objective. Still wet from a recent rain squall, the city lay glistening in the sun. No airborne fighters were visible as we came over, and the big airfield southeast of the city was also empty of planes, so it was apparent that the enemy interceptors had gone south to meet us.

While Commander Itaya's fighters and a few of my level bombers headed to attack the airfield, the other level bombers and the dive bomber group struck at shipping in the harbor. No warships were present, but considerable damage was inflicted on cargo vessels, with which the harbor was jammed. As the last bombers made their attack runs, I prepared to radio back to flagship AKAGI that our mission was accomplished and that a second-wave attack would be unnecessary.

Just then a terse message was overheard from one of the Nagumo Force float planes, which had taken off simultaneously with the air attack force to search over a broad sector of the western Indian Ocean: "Two enemy heavy cruisers sighted heading south."

It appeared that the enemy had sent out his surface units to attack the Nagumo Force, and the consequences might be serious if the air attack force did not get back to the carriers quickly. I immediately ordered all units to reassemble, and we were just about to head for home when some 20 Hurricane fighters appeared from the south. Itaya's Zeros again peeled off and engaged them, while the rest of our force streaked for the carriers. It was hard to leave the fighters to find their way back alone, but it had to be done. Most of them did return safely, but several never made it.

Back on AKAGI, I was relieved to learn from Commander Genda that the two enemy cruisers had been running away, not attacking, and that no other enemy forces had been spotted. The second-wave dive bomber group of 80 planes, led by Lieutenant Commander Egusa, was already on its way to attack them. A few minutes later Egusa radioed, "Enemy sighted." Twenty minutes thereafter the attack was over, and both enemy cruisers—identified as DORSETSHIRE and CORNWALL—had been sent to the bottom. The dive bombers scored hits with close to 90 per cent of their bombs—an enviable rate of accuracy, even considering the windless conditions. But rather than feeling exultation over the proficiency of Egusa's bombardiers, I could only feel pity for these surface ships assailed from the air at odds of forty to one.

The Nagumo Force now retired southward beyond range of Ceylon-based air patrols, but a few days later it again headed north to attack the important British base of Trincomalee, on the east coast of Ceylon. The air task organization was the same as for the Colombo strike. The first attack wave, which I again led, took off in the predawn darkness of 9 April. The weather was fine.

Enemy radar must have detected our approach, for Hurricane fighters came out to intercept before we reached the target. Our fighter group took care of them in short order, however, and we pressed on to launch the attack. As we came in over the base, enemy antiaircraft batteries immediately put up a heavy barrage.

Despite this opposition the attack was highly effective. Our dive bombers found numerous carrier-type aircraft lined up on the apron of the field and quickly set them ablaze. My level bombers, carrying 800-kilogram bombs, concentrated on the airfield installations and naval base facilities. One of the targets, a munitions depot, went up in a spectacular display of fireworks.

Lying in the anchorage were two light cruisers, a number of destroyers, and about ten cargo ships. I detailed some bombers to attack the cruisers, but decided that it would be best to leave the main job of destroying the enemy ships to the dive bomber group of the second attack wave. I radioed back to AKAGI to this effect, and our first wave then headed back to the carriers.

On the way back there was a repetition of what had occurred on the Colombo strike. One of our search planes was suddenly overheard reporting that it had sighted two enemy ships heading south—only, this time, one was a destroyer, the other an aircraft carrier! We opened our throttles and sped for home, not without some apprehension.

Luckily the enemy ships had been spotted before our second wave had taken off for Trincomalee, and by the time we landed on the carriers, Egusa again was leading his dive bombers to attack the enemy. Above, our full combat air patrol was on the alert. Below, on the carriers, there was a steady hum of activity as the planes back from Trincomalee were refueled and rearmed to attack in case Egusa's dive bombers failed to eliminate the enemy carrier. My level bombers were being armed this time with torpedoes.

Suddenly AKAGI's loudspeakers blared, "AA action!" Almost simultaneously there was the stunning noise of bomb explosions, and six white columns of water rose off the ship's bow, four to starboard and two to port. Looking up, I saw a formation of six Wellington[11] bombers passing over at 4,000 meters. They had somehow caught our combat air patrol flatfooted, though not for long. The fighters quickly pursued them and eventually shot down every one in a running battle.

Shortly thereafter Egusa's dive bombers reached the enemy

[11] *Editor's Note:* Actually the bombers were Blenheims, and there were nine; five were shot down, the others were damaged.

carrier, which had been identified as HMS HERMES. In a swift 15-minute attack they sank this carrier and her lone destroyer escort, as well as a large merchant ship which was spotted farther to the north. No fighters were protecting HERMES, nor were there any aircraft on her deck. Just before the attack, she had been overheard calling repeatedly to Trincomalee asking if fighters had been dispatched. From this it seemed evident that it was her planes we had destroyed on the Trincomalee airfield a few hours earlier. Needless to say, they never rejoined her; nor were there further air attacks on the Nagumo Force from any quarter.

With the sinking of HERMES, Admiral Nagumo decided to write *finis* to the Indian Ocean operation. After recovering Egusa's planes, the Force headed eastward for the Strait of Malacca. The "first-phase operations" were now completed, and Combined Fleet shortly ordered our return to the homeland. On the way, Rear Admiral Hara's Carrier Division 5 (ZUIKAKU, SHOKAKU) was again detached and ordered to Truk, whence it was to sortie in early May to support the planned invasion of Port Moresby, on the southeast coast of New Guinea.

As we left the tropic seas behind, I had time to think back on the operations of the past four hectic months. In that brief span, the Nagumo Force had covered almost 50,000 miles of ocean, ranging all the way from Hawaii nearly to the shores of India. We had acquitted ourselves well in every operation. Morale, along with combat efficiency, had risen steadily.

Still, I was convinced now more than ever that the Nagumo Force had been improperly and wastefully employed ever since its return from the attack on Pearl Harbor. Where in the southern area had there been an enemy powerful enough to require the use of our superior striking power? Surely the southern operations could have been carried out quite adequately by the naval forces already assigned, without commitment of the

Nagumo Force in an unneeded and unworthy supporting role.

Indeed, it looked to me as if, after Pearl Harbor, the naval high command must have thought that there was nothing important for the Nagumo Force to do, and so, rather than let it remain idle, had assigned it to secondary missions in the southern area. But was it true that no vital task remained? Were not the Naval General Staff and Combined Fleet forgetting that our main adversary at sea was the United States Fleet? And were they not at the same time deliberately closing their eyes to the very lesson that our success at Pearl Harbor had taught— namely, that it was no longer the battleship, but the aircraft carrier, which was the decisive element of fleet strength? The enemy's battleships had been effectively smashed, but his carriers, with the heavy cruisers to screen them, remained unscathed. Therefore, before sending the Nagumo Force to the south where it was not really needed, should not Combined Fleet have kept it operating to the east with the paramount mission of destroying the American carrier force?

This trend of thought called to my mind the seven big battleships, which had lain idle in the Inland Sea ever since the outbreak of war—the "Hashirajima Fleet." If the Nagumo Force had been wasted, what about these doughty battlewagons, the supposed heart and core of the Japanese Fleet's combat strength?

Evidently the idea was to save them for the great decisive battle which our fleet strategists had long planned to fight in a war against the United States—a contest in which the battleships of the two fleets would slug it out with their big guns in approved World War I style. At Pearl Harbor, however, Japanese carrier air power had smashed the enemy's battleships, and with them the myth of battleship supremacy. Thus, on two counts at once, the retention of the "Hashirajima Fleet" under wraps at its Inland Sea anchorage as a decisive battle force became meaningless. Yet there it was kept, contributing

no more to the prosecution of the war than the enemy battleships left in wreckage at Pearl Harbor!

One cannot help wondering what might have been the course
of the war had our top naval command been more prompt to
revise its outmoded thinking in the light of new experience.
Suppose it had fully absorbed the lesson of Pearl Harbor and
had recognized without delay that the Nagumo Force with its
six carriers, not the seven battleships at Hashirajima, constituted the main combat strength of the Japanese Fleet. Suppose,
having recognized this, that it had fused the Nagumo Force
and the seven idle battleships into a single powerful carrier task
force, with the battleships in a supporting role, and had assigned
to it the sole mission of operating eastward to complete the destruction of the United States Fleet.

It is undoubtedly too much to say that, had this been done,
the ultimate outcome of the war at sea would have been different. At the very least, however, it seems reasonable to
believe that the American carrier force, which had survived
Pearl Harbor, could speedily have been crushed, and that the
Japanese Fleet would not nearly so soon have lost its advantage
to an enemy who was quicker to learn from defeat than our
naval leaders were to learn from victory.

CHAPTER 3

Debate on Future
Strategy

1. EASTWARD VS. WESTWARD ADVANCE

At the start of the Pacific War, Japan's strategy-makers had
been so engrossed in the immediate problem of acquiring oil
resources that they had formulated no concrete strategic program for the ensuing course of hostilities after these resources
had been won. Also, they had been keenly conscious of the
many risks involved in the initial operations—the Pearl Harbor
attack not the least of such risks—and had by no means been
certain of the outcome. They therefore had decided to wait
and see how the operations progressed before attempting to
formulate subsequent war strategy.

By early January of 1942, Japanese successes on all fronts
had assured the planners that the first-phase operations would
be completed without a hitch, and accordingly they began
weighing the problem of future strategy. Many vital questions
posed themselves. With her initial strategic objectives attained,
should Japan go on the defensive to hold what she had won,
or should she remain boldly on the offensive in an effort to
break the fighting determination of the Allies? If the latter,
should she first strike westward against Britain or eastward
against the United States, and specifically what offensive action would be most effective?

In theory, the formulation of Army and Navy strategic
policies was the function, respectively, of the Army and Naval
General Staffs operating as sections of Imperial General Headquarters. The Chief of Naval General Staff was automatically

Chief of the Navy Section of Imperial General Headquarters and, in the latter capacity, issued orders and directives to Commander in Chief Combined Fleet embodying top-level strategic and operational decisions. Actually, however, Combined Fleet, rather than the Naval General Staff, often played the dominant role in shaping fleet strategy.

Time had been when Commander in Chief Combined Fleet was a naval commander in the true Nelsonian tradition, who led the fleet in battle and issued orders from the bridge of his flagship amidst a hail of enemy fire. But, owing to the expansion of the naval establishment and the vast enlargement of operational theaters, it had become difficult for the Commander in Chief to exercise over-all tactical command if he went to sea with the combat forces. So Combined Fleet became primarily a shore-based headquarters which, in addition to planning and directing tactical operations, exerted a potent and frequently decisive influence on the formulation of basic fleet strategy.

Combined Fleet's ability to impress its views on the highest organ of naval command had been demonstrated at the start of the war by Admiral Yamamoto's successful insistence upon the Pearl Harbor attack over strong Naval General Staff opposition. Needless to say, the striking victories won by the Fleet in the first month of hostilities served only to reinforce this influence. Combined Fleet staff officers were filled with elated self-confidence, while the Naval General Staff felt constrained to talk softly in its dealings with the Fleet Headquarters.

It was not surprising, therefore, that the initiative in formulating naval strategy for the second phase of the war was taken by Combined Fleet rather than by the Naval General Staff. Rear Admiral Matome Ugaki, Combined Fleet Chief of Staff, began studying the problem toward the middle of January on board flagship NAGATO anchored in Hiroshima Bay. According to his diary, he spent four days in quiet and exhaustive deliberation. The first-phase offensive operations, he estimated, would be largely accomplished by the middle of March, which meant that a decision on subsequent strategy should be reached by the end of February at the latest.

Ugaki concluded first of all that the Japanese armed forces, instead of reverting to a defensive strategy which would yield the initiative to the enemy, must remain vigorously on the offensive. As to the direction of the next offensive move, he considered three major alternatives: toward Australia, toward India, or toward Hawaii. His final conclusion was in favor of a move against Hawaii, to be initiated with preliminary operations in June for the seizure of Midway, Johnston and Palmyra Islands. As soon as adequate air strength had been moved up to these advance bases, amphibious operations would be launched against Hawaii itself, with the main strength of Combined Fleet advancing to Hawaiian waters to support the invasion and, if possible, challenge the U.S. Fleet in decisive battle. The reasons which impelled Ugaki to favor this plan, according to his diary, were as follows:

1. Seizure of Hawaii and destruction of American fleet strength constituted the most damaging blows which could be inflicted upon the United States.

2. Despite the apparent risks involved in the invasion attempt and in fighting a decisive fleet engagement in waters close to Hawaii, the chances of success appeared preponderant since the Japanese Fleet had a three-to-one advantage in aircraft carriers in addition to overwhelming superiority in battleships.

3. Time would work against Japan because of the vastly superior national resources of the United States. Consequently, unless Japan quickly resumed the offensive—the sooner, the better—she eventually would become incapable of doing anything more than sitting down and waiting for the American forces to counterattack. Furthermore, although Japan had steeled herself to endure a prolonged struggle, it would be obviously to her advantage to shorten it if at all possible, and the only hope of so doing lay in offensive action.

4. In the event Germany succeeded in conquering England,

it appeared possible that the British European Fleet might reinforce American naval strength in the Pacific, thus doubling the
pressure upon the Japanese Navy. The surest way to avert this
threat would be to destroy the American Fleet before such an
eventuality arose. Then the British Fleet could be dealt with
separately thereafter, and the destruction of the two Allied Navies
would offer the best possible hope of speedily ending the war.

Admiral Ugaki promptly instructed subordinate staff officers
to make a detailed study of the practicability of his plan. The
conclusion reached, however, proved negative on three principal grounds. First, the Japanese forces could no longer expect
to achieve surprise as in the Pearl Harbor attack. Second, it
would be beyond the capability of the Japanese air strength
which could be brought to bear, both carrier and shore-based,
to gain control of the skies over so large an area as the Hawaiian
Islands, where the enemy air forces would be widely dispersed.
Third, in a contest between ships and shore batteries, the odds
would be against the former.

In view of these unfavorable findings, Admiral Ugaki reluctantly set aside his plan and directed the Combined Fleet
staff to begin studying an alternative scheme of offensive operations to the west, advanced by the Senior Fleet Operations Officer, Captain Kameto Kuroshima. Ugaki, who did not fully
concur in Kuroshima's ideas, instructed that the study be carried
out subject to the following conditions:

1. Although there appeared to be no imminent danger of
Soviet-Japanese hostilities, sufficient precautions should be taken
to meet such an eventuality.

2. Similarly, adequate measures should be provided to suppress
hit-and-run attacks by U.S. carrier task forces from the east.

3. Launching of any operations to the west should await re-
fitting of the naval forces following completion of the first-phase
operations and also should be timed to synchronize with German
offensives in the Near and Middle East.

4. The objectives of the western operations would have to be
clearly defined from the start. They would be (a) destruction of

the British Fleet, (b) capture of strategic points and elimination of enemy bases, and (c) establishment of contact between the Japanese and European Axis forces.

Thus, Combined Fleet began its study of the Kuroshima plan with the idea that the proposed westward operations would be part of a closely-coordinated Axis offensive from two directions. However, this concept suffered an early setback when the headquarters received a copy of the new tripartite Axis military agreement concluded on 19 January. The agreement, though it made passing reference to Germany's advance eastward and Japan's advance westward, said nothing at all with regard to a future joint offensive effort. Ugaki was keenly disappointed and concluded that, rather than attempt to coordinate her action with that of the European Axis, Japan could best promote over-all Axis success by fixing her own strategy independently.

Hence, the idea of a joint offensive was abandoned, and Combined Fleet continued its study of the western operations as a purely Japanese project. The primary tactical objectives were to be destruction of the British Fleet, capture of Ceylon, and acquisition of air control over the Indian Ocean. The broader strategic aims were to safeguard the Dutch East Indies and Malaya against a threat from the west and to facilitate an early juncture with German forces in the Near East.

By late February the study had been completed and a tentative plan worked out. The plan was then put to the test in a war game staged on board super-battleship YAMATO, which had just been designated flagship of Combined Fleet. The game continued over a four-day period with representatives of the Naval General Staff attending. As a result, the Naval General Staff formulated an official Navy plan for the western operations, and this was laid before a joint conference of the Army and Navy Sections of Imperial General Headquarters in the middle of March.

The Navy plan, which envisaged amphibious operations against Ceylon, of course required the participation of Army forces. The Army, however, voiced strong opposition on the ground that it had to be on guard against the Soviet Union and therefore could not afford to extend itself any further in Southeast Asia. From the Navy viewpoint, this argument appeared somewhat specious in view of the Army's current operations in Burma; but specious or not, the Army's refusal to cooperate meant that the proposed offensive in the Indian Ocean could not be carried out.

Combined Fleet nevertheless remained convinced that it must take the offensive somewhere as soon as possible. The headquarters therefore resumed its planning studies looking toward offensive operations to the east, this time lowering its sights somewhat from the earlier Ugaki plan to invade Hawaii and envisaging operations which could be carried out by Naval forces alone or with minimum Army participation. A factor of key importance at this stage was the increasingly alarming activity of enemy carrier task forces which, since the beginning of February, had successively attacked the Marshalls, Rabaul, Wake, Marcus Island and eastern New Guinea. To curb this activity, the Combined Fleet planners concluded that it was advisable to seize Midway Island, only 1,130 miles from Hawaii, as an advance base for air patrols. At the same time they calculated that a move against Midway would draw out the enemy Fleet so that it could be destroyed in decisive battle.

The preparatory studies conducted by Admiral Ugaki and the staff of Combined Fleet had now progressed as far as they could without a decision by the Commander in Chief. Admiral Yamamoto had not intervened in the planning activities of his subordinates and had taken no part in the protracted debate on eastward vs. westward advance. Now, however, the decision was up to him, and he quickly and strongly came out in favor of the proposed eastward offensive. Accordingly, on 29 and 30

March, a preliminary plan was drawn up at Combined Fleet Headquarters for the Midway operation.

All that was now needed to put the plan into final form was the sanction of the Naval General Staff. The latter had been briefly informed, around the middle of March, that Combined Fleet was studying plans for an attack on Midway, but no further discussions had taken place. Consequently, on 2 April, Commander Yasuji Watanabe, Operations Officer on Admiral Yamamoto's staff, was sent to Tokyo to present officially the preliminary Combined Fleet plan. He quickly discovered that the plan would not have easy sailing.

2. THE AUSTRALIA-FIRST SCHOOL

While Combined Fleet had displayed greater energy and initiative in planning second-phase naval strategy, the Naval General Staff had not exactly been idle. Its main attention, however, had been focussed on an area different from either of the two major alternatives considered by Combined Fleet. This was the so-called southeast area, centering on the Australian subcontinent.

Neither Admiral Nagano, Chief of Naval General Staff, nor his Deputy Chief, Vice Admiral Seiichi Ito, was the kind of officer who actively directed the planning of his subordinates. They allowed the staff to take the initiative and expressed themselves only when a plan had been drafted and submitted for their approval. Naval General Staff thinking, therefore, was largely the thinking of the Plans Division of its First (Operations) Section. Rear Admiral Shigeru Fukudome headed the First Section, and under him the Plans Division was led by Captain Sadatoshi Tomioka. It was Tomioka who sparked the Australia-first school of strategy.

The key importance of Australia in the minds of the Tomioka group stemmed from their estimate that the subcontinent, because of its size and strategic location on the Japanese defensive perimeter, would almost certainly become the springboard for an eventual Allied counteroffensive. This counteroffensive, they reasoned, would be spearheaded by air power in order to take full advantage of American industrial capacity to produce planes by mass-production methods, and the effective utilization of this massive air strength would require the use of land bases in Australia. Consequently, there would be a weak spot in Japan's defensive armor unless Australia were either placed under Japanese control or effectively cut off from the United States.

Following the easy conquest of the Bismarcks in January, the most aggressive proponents of the Australia-first concept started advocating outright occupation of key areas in Australia. This extreme initial proposal, however, was speedily rejected by the Army, which flatly stated that it could not scrape together the more than ten combat divisions that would be required for such an operation, not to mention the impossibility of amassing enough ships to transport such a force and keep it supplied.

The reasons for the rejection were persuasive enough, but Navy circles suspected that they were a camouflage for the Army's real intentions. The Army High Command, it was surmised, was confidently counting upon the success of the major offensive which Germany planned to launch in the Caucasus in the spring. Such success, of course, would radically alter the European war situation in Germany's favor, and it was suspected that the Army desired to hold back a large part of its forces with a view to committing them on the continent against Russia when this favorable situation developed.

In any event, it was abundantly clear that the Army did not want to commit substantial forces to the southeast area and would have no part of an attempt to invade Australia. The Naval General Staff strategists therefore began concentrating their efforts on less ambitious plans to isolate Australia and cut off the flow of American war matériel by gradually extending

Japanese control over eastern New Guinea, the Solomons, and the New Caledonia-Fiji Islands area.

By early April, when Combined Fleet presented its Midway attack plan, a beginning had already been made toward carrying out the Naval General Staff program. Lae and Salamaua, in eastern New Guinea, had been occupied as the first step, and the Army had agreed to the use of its South Seas Detachment, currently at Rabaul, in the second move—the simultaneous invasion of Port Moresby, on the southeast New Guinea coast, and of Tulagi, in the Solomons. The Port Moresby-Tulagi operations were waiting only upon the dispatch of one of Admiral Nagumo's carrier divisions to reinforce the naval covering forces. Meanwhile, the Naval General Staff was already trying to talk the Army into participating in further invasion operations against New Caledonia, the Fiji Islands and Samoa as soon as Port Moresby and Tulagi had been taken.

In view of these circumstances, the Combined Fleet plan for Midway could hardly have come at a more inauspicious moment. The plan specifically provided that the move against Midway, to be accompanied by a diversionary invasion of the western Aleutians, be carried out in the early part of June, and that the New Caledonia-Fiji-Samoa operations proposed by the Naval General Staff be deferred until after the completion of the Midway-Aleutians venture. Thus, the stage was set for another crucial test of strength between Combined Fleet and the Naval General Staff to see which would have the more powerful voice in determining fleet strategy.

3. MIDWAY DEBATE

Discussions concerning the Midway plan promptly got under way on 2 April with a lengthy exchange of views between Commander Watanabe, representing Combined Fleet, and Commander Tatsukichi Miyo, First Section Air Officer, representing the Naval General Staff. Commander Miyo pleaded vigorously, and on occasion almost tearfully, against the plan, voicing a long series of objections ranging from the difficulty of amassing the vast amount of materiel required to the unfavorable tactical aspects of the operation itself and the questionable strategic value of Midway even if it were successfully occupied.

As far as materiel requirements were concerned, Commander Miyo argued that prior execution of the New Caledonia-Fiji-Samoa operations, as planned by the Naval General Staff, would be more feasible since, in fact, some preparations had already been started. He emphasized particularly that it would be next to impossible, owing to the short supply of aircraft and air materiel in general, to re-equip the depleted air groups of Admiral Nagumo's carriers in time to meet the Combined Fleet attack deadline.

The problem of aircraft supply was one that directly concerned Miyo, since it was his responsibility to see that naval air units engaged in combat operations were furnished with necessary plane replacements. The situation was, indeed, becoming increasingly serious. Every air unit was supposed to be equipped with reserve aircraft amounting to one-third of its regular operational complement. Actually, the vast majority of units not only had no reserve planes whatever but were below normal operating strength. Miyo had just been obliged to shunt aside an urgent request from the shore-based Eleventh Air Fleet for enough planes to bring its units up to operational level, proffering the excuse that even carrier Ryujo had not yet been equipped with Zero fighters to replace her outmoded Type-96 planes.

Miyo went on to say that, even if the supply problem could somehow be solved, the Naval General Staff still viewed the Midway venture as unwise from both the tactical and the strategic standpoint. He outlined the principal objections as follows:

1. Because of Midway's proximity to the United States' main Pacific base at Hawaii, the enemy could effectively use, in addition to his carrier forces, both submarines and, more important, large land-based aircraft from Hawaii to support the defense of the island. Also, it had to be assumed that the enemy, as a result of the Pearl Harbor experience, was now fully on guard and keeping a close watch on Japanese fleet movements, so that surprise was not likely to be achieved.

2. The Japanese forces, on the other hand, would have to operate without land-based air support even for scouting and reconnaissance purposes. This would mean a reduction of the effective striking power of the carrier-borne air forces, since part of their strength would have to be diverted to scouting duty to supplement the float reconnaissance planes of the battleships and cruisers.

3. Although not excluding the possibility that an invasion of Midway might bring about a decisive fleet engagement as hoped by Combined Fleet, the Naval General Staff considered it questionable that the enemy would gamble his meager remaining fleet strength for the sake of defending Midway. He might very well choose to conserve his surface strength and, if the island were taken, launch operations later to recapture or neutralize it, taking advantage of its remoteness from Japan and corollary proximity to Hawaii.

4. This last possibility pointed to the very serious problem of whether Japan, if she successfully occupied Midway, would be capable of keeping it supplied and of defending it against enemy counterattack. In addition to being remote from the Japanese homeland, Midway was so small in size that aircraft based there could not be dispersed to minimize losses that might be inflicted by surprise attack from the air or sea. Continuous day and night air patrols on a very large scale would have to be carried out to forestall such attacks, and this would require a huge number of planes as well as a vast quantity of gasoline. The resultant supply and shipping problem might prove beyond Japan's capabilities over any extended period of time.

5. The Naval General Staff further regarded as dubious Combined Fleet's estimate that Midway would be strategically valuable to Japan as an advance base for air patrols to facilitate the discovery of enemy carrier task forces advancing toward the Japanese homeland. In the first place, Midway-based patrols could only

cover an area between 600 and 700 miles in radius from the island with the existing range of Japanese patrol aircraft. Further, the interference of occasional bad weather as well as enemy action to obstruct the use of the airfields would have to be taken into account.

6. Finally, Combined Fleet's view that the seizure of Midway, by threatening Hawaii, would effectively undermine America's will to fight and thus pave the way for a negotiated peace was considered far too optimistic. In the opinion of the Naval General Staff, operations against Hawaii would still be extremely hazardous even if Midway were in Japanese possession, and occupation of the island obviously would pose no threat whatever to the continental United States. Its effect on American morale would therefore be negligible.

Having set forth the Naval General Staff's arguments against the Midway operation, Commander Miyo proceeded to defend its alternative plan for a move against New Caledonia, Fiji and Samoa. He emphasized that, although these islands were situated farther from Japan than Midway, they were almost equally distant from the United States' main Hawaii base, so that one advantage the American forces would have in defending Midway would be nullified. Also, the size of the islands as compared with Midway would make them of much greater military value.

As for drawing out the American Fleet so that it could be engaged in decisive battle, Commander Miyo argued that operations against New Caledonia, Fiji and Samoa would be more likely to achieve this objective than an assault on Midway because Australia would feel itself seriously threatened and would undoubtedly appeal for American naval assistance. The United States would be strongly impelled to act even without such an appeal since severance of the American supply route to Australia would effectively block the eventual use of Australia as an Allied counteroffensive base.

Finally, the Naval General Staff believed that the successful seizure of New Caledonia, Fiji and Samoa would so seriously lower Australian and, indirectly, Allied morale that it would contribute more toward shortening the war than any other move which Japan could make.

While advancing all these arguments, Commander Miyo nevertheless refrained from voicing a flat rejection of the Combined Fleet plan. Instead, on 3 April, the Naval General Staff re-examined the situation in regard to materiel and supplies and concluded that about 70 per cent of Combined Fleet's estimated requirements for the Midway operation could be met. Conferences were resumed on 4 April between Commander Watanabe and members of the Naval General Staff but failed to bring about any concession by either side.

On 5 April the talks continued, this time with Vice Admiral Ito and Rear Admiral Fukudome attending for the Naval General Staff. In the middle of the conference, Commander Watanabe telephoned directly to Combined Fleet headquarters on board flagship Yamato and reported the Naval General Staff's views, requesting instructions as to what stand he should take. After returning to his seat, he stated Admiral Yamamoto's position in the following uncompromising terms:

"In the last analysis, the success or failure of our entire strategy in the Pacific will be determined by whether or not we succeed in destroying the United States Fleet, more particularly its carrier task forces. The Naval General Staff advocates severing the supply line between the United States and Australia. It would seek to do this by placing certain areas under Japanese control, but the most direct and effective way to achieve this objective is to destroy the enemy's carrier forces, without which the supply line could not in any case be maintained. We believe that by launching the proposed operations against Midway, we can succeed in drawing out the enemy's carrier strength and destroying it in decisive battle. If, on the other hand, the enemy should avoid our challenge, we shall still realize an important gain by advancing our defensive perimeter to Midway and the western Aleutians without obstruction."

The statement made it quite evident that Admiral Yamamoto had no intention of giving in to the objections of the Naval General Staff. Since there appeared to be no other way out of the deadlock, Rear Admiral Fukudome turned to Vice Admiral Ito and reluctantly proposed that the Naval General Staff agree to the attack on Midway. Ito quietly nodded his assent.

An accord was thus hammered out on the basic policy of executing the Midway operation, but Combined Fleet and the Naval General Staff continued to disagree on the time of execution. The Naval General Staff strongly urged that D-day, which Combined Fleet proposed to fix early in June, be postponed about three weeks in order to allow more time for preparations. Combined Fleet, however, stood pat on its original proposal, arguing that it was essential to launch the attack when the moon would be full, and that a delay of an entire month might seriously reduce the chances of success. On 13 April Commander Akira Sasaki, Fleet Aviation Officer, was sent to Tokyo to underline these points to the Naval General Staff.

In contrast to the strong opposition which it had evoked from the Naval General Staff, the Combined Fleet plan won the concurrence of the Army General Staff without difficulty. The Army's ready agreement to cooperate, however, was not due to any particular change of heart toward Navy policies, but rather to the fact that the Midway-Aleutians operations were to be predominantly naval in character and the Army would have to furnish only a small number of troops to reinforce the Navy's special landing forces.

Among the lower-echelon fleet commands, reactions to the Midway plan varied. Vice Admiral Moshiro Hosogaya's Fifth Fleet, assigned to guarding the northeastern approaches to the homeland, had long been eager to see a major operation launched on the eastern sea front and naturally welcomed the

Combined Fleet plan. On the other hand, Vice Admiral Nishizo Tsukahaia's Eleventh Air Fleet operating in Southeast Asia was somewhat disappointed. It had expected, on the basis of the atmosphere prevailing at Combined Fleet Headquarters in early March, that the next big operation would take place in the Indian Ocean and had already moved its headquarters to Bangkok as a preparatory step. Its shore-based planes would be unable to play any part in the assault on Midway.

The only forthright opposition within Combined Fleet came from Vice Admiral Shigeyoshi Inouye's Fourth Fleet, responsible for operations in a broad sector of the southwest Pacific. At an early stage of the planning for the Midway operation, Combined Fleet Headquarters had dispatched its Logistics Officer to Truk to confer with Vice Admiral Inouye and his staff concerning the problem of transporting supplies to Midway after its occupation, a mission which was to be assigned to Fourth Fleet. Apparently, however, Inouye felt that, considering Japan's limited resources, the seizure of Midway would dangerously over-extend the area which would have to be defended. He bluntly stated that he had no confidence in Fourth Fleet's ability to fulfill the mission of supplying the island, whereupon the Combined Fleet representative is said to have angrily left the room declaring that, since Fourth Fleet could not be relied upon, the mission would be transferred to the shore-based air forces.

Two fleet commanders who were to play leading roles in the Midway operation—Vice Admiral Kondo of Second Fleet and Vice Admiral Nagumo of First Air Fleet—were not consulted at all during the elaboration of the Combined Fleet plan. Both of these fleets were actively engaged in the southern operations until mid-April, and Admiral Yamamoto did not wish to divert their attention from the tasks at hand by asking them to participate in the Midway planning. As a result of the lack of consultation, however, the question arises whether

Combined Fleet was able to frame its plan on the basis of an accurate knowledge of the condition of these two key forces.

The middle of April found Combined Fleet and the Naval General Staff still haggling over various details of the Midway plan, and it was evident that the latter, in spite of having consented in principle, remained highly skeptical about the whole operation. On 18 April, however, a development intervened which quickly put an end to further debate.

CHAPTER 4

Doolittle Ends Debate

1. CONCERN OVER ENEMY AIR THREAT

Despite Japan's glowing successes on every front in the first four months of the Pacific War, April of 1942 found her Army and especially her Navy leaders unable to free their minds of one ever-present and highly disturbing worry. This was the possibility of a sneak enemy air attack on Tokyo, the capital of the Empire.

The severe damage done to the United States Fleet at Pearl Harbor and the seizure of American bases in the western Pacific eliminated, for some time at least, any fear of sustained, large-scale enemy air action against the homeland, either carrier or shore-based. Still, the enemy's carriers and heavy cruisers, which had escaped injury, remained capable of at least sporadic, small scale attacks of a hit-and-run variety. These, it was feared, might be undertaken as moves in the war of nerves or as a shot in the arm to revive flagging American morale at home. For such "guerrilla" raids, Tokyo seemed a likely target.

Obviously, the physical damage that might be inflicted on the capital by raids of this kind was hardly enough to warrant the exaggerated concern felt by Army and Navy leaders. Their sharp sensitivity to the enemy air threat was largely a spontaneous and unreasoned expression of the almost religious devotion to the Emperor which has long characterized the Japanese national psychology. The fighting services, especially, were imbued with the idea that their foremost duty was to protect the Emperor from danger. Naturally, they felt that it would be a grave dereliction of this duty if the Emperor's safety were jeopardized by even a single enemy raid on Tokyo.

Under the terms of an Army-Navy agreement covering defense of the homeland, primary responsibility for defense against air attack rested with the Army. Nevertheless, a large share of responsibility still rested on the shoulders of the Navy since any air attack at this stage would have to be sea-borne, and it was the Navy's job to intercept and destroy enemy carrier striking forces at sea before they could penetrate within striking distance.

Admiral Yamamoto, as supreme commander of the Fleet, was particularly conscious of this naval responsibility. He himself, by the surprise carrier strike on Pearl Harbor, had set an example which the enemy might follow. Also, he knew from first-hand observation the bold aggressiveness of the American national character and suspected that the United States Fleet would attempt at the earliest opportunity to strike back at the Japanese homeland with a carrier task force.

In Admiral Yamamoto's mind the idea that Tokyo, the seat of the Emperor, must be kept absolutely safe from air attack amounted almost to an obsession. His constant concern on this point was shown by the fact that later, when he was directing operations in the distant southwest Pacific area, he never failed, before giving his attention to any thing else, to ask for the latest Tokyo weather report. If the reports were bad, he felt relieved because they gave added assurance that the capital was safe.

Yamamoto's anxiety was deepened by the recollection of an incident that had occurred during the Russo-Japanese War, when he was a young officer. At that time a Russian naval force had suddenly appeared outside of Tokyo Bay, creating such panic in the capital that many of the inhabitants had fled to the mountains for refuge. Angry mobs had also stoned the home of Vice Admiral Kamimura, whose Second Fleet was responsible for dealing with the enemy force. If Tokyo were now to undergo an air raid, Yamamoto feared that this characteristic instability of the Japanese temperament would manifest itself again and that chaos and confusion would result.

To guard against the penetration of an enemy carrier force within air striking range of the homeland, Admiral Yamamoto, at the start of the war, had established a picket-boat line six to seven hundred miles east of the Japanese coast and extending over a front of about one thousand miles from north to south. The picket line was supplemented by daily long-range air patrols by naval aircraft.

The series of daring enemy carrier strikes which began with the Marshalls raid at the beginning of February 1942 sharply increased Admiral Yamamoto's fear of an eventual attack on the homeland. Immediately after the Marshalls raid, he ordered two of Admiral Nagumo's carriers, ZUIKAKU and SHOKAKU, back from the southwest Pacific to reinforce temporarily the system of defensive air patrols east of the home islands. In the middle of March, the shore-based 21st Air Flotilla was recalled from the Southeast Asia front and stationed in the Tokyo area for both daily patrol duty and defense of the capital against enemy carrier-borne air attack. On 1 April, the 26th Air Flotilla was newly activated and took over this mission from the 21st.

Already on 3 March, an enemy task force commanded by Vice Admiral Halsey and composed of the carrier ENTERPRISE, two cruisers and seven destroyers had struck at Marcus Island, just 1,000 miles from Tokyo and well inside the outer ring of Japanese defenses. It seemed that the time was fast approaching when the precautions taken to guard the homeland against air attack might be put to the test.

2. THE DOOLITTLE RAID

On the morning of 18 April, No. 23 NITTO MARU, a former fishing boat now in naval service under Fifth Fleet, was on her post in the picket patrol line at a point some 720 miles east of Tokyo. Suddenly her crew was electrified by the sight of an enemy naval force steaming westward toward the homeland. Hurriedly studying the silhouettes of the enemy ships through their glasses, the excited officers of the picket boat thought they saw three aircraft carriers in the formation, and at 0630 they flashed a radio message to Combined Fleet Headquarters reporting the sighting.

Unusually brisk enemy radio activity during the preceding several days had already given a hint that something was afoot, and Combined Fleet had ordered a precautionary concentration of naval air strength in the Kanto district around the capital. Upon receipt of NITTO MARU's warning, the headquarters acted swiftly to meet the enemy threat, ordering application of "Tactical Method No. 3 against the United States Fleet."

Vice Admiral Kondo, whose Second Fleet had just returned home from the southern operations, had entered Yokosuka the preceding day in his flagship ATAGO. He was now ordered to put back to sea immediately in command of all available surface units in the Yokosuka area and attack the enemy. Vice Admiral Shiro Takasu's First Fleet, which included four battleships, meanwhile made a hasty sortie from Hiroshima Bay to operate in support of Kondo's force.

At this moment Vice Admiral Nagumo's Carrier Force, en route back to Japan from the Indian Ocean, was passing through Bashi Strait at the southern end of Formosa. An atmosphere of happy excitement prevailed on board flagship AKAGI as all hands thought of their imminent homecoming. Seated in the flight personnel stand-by room, I was lost in similar thoughts when an orderly rushed in to say that Commander Genda wanted me in the operations room immediately. I headed for it on the double, wondering what could be up.

"Well, they've come at last!" said Genda as he handed me a copy of the NITTO MARU's sighting report. He added that Combined Fleet had ordered Tactical Method No. 3, which provided that the Nagumo Force should participate in operations against the enemy force. Admiral Nagumo and other members of the staff were already bent over the chart table plotting a course toward the estimated battle area.

Our distance from the enemy seemed to allow little chance of our being able to join in the anticipated battle. Nevertheless, in compliance with the Combined Fleet order, the Force promptly headed toward the enemy at top speed. All aircraft were brought up from their hangars and lined up on the flight deck ready for action.

Meanwhile, back in the homeland, Rear Admiral Seigo Yamagata's 26th Air Flotilla had already launched planes against the enemy. Thirty-two medium bombers, escorted by 12 Zero fighters, took off from Kisarazu Air Base, near Tokyo, and flew eastward over the Pacific to the limit of their range, but failed to make contact. It looked as if the enemy task force, realizing that it had been discovered, had already given up the attack and begun to retire.

Then, at 1300, AKAGI received a report that Tokyo had been bombed. This was followed in close succession by reports of attacks on Yokohama, Kawasaki, and Yokosuka, and a short time later by another series of reports telling of attacks farther south, on Nagoya, Yokkaichi, Wakayama, and Kobe. Such widespread enemy action came as a distinct shock, and we in the Nagumo Force did not know what to make of it. It appeared that Combined Fleet Headquarters was equally baffled and quite unable to form any estimate of the enemy's intentions.

The situation became clearer, however, as further details were reported. The attacking force had evidently been spread very thin since altogether there were fewer than 20 planes reported. Furthermore, these were not carrier-type aircraft at all, but North American B-25 land bombers, which had a much greater operational range! Still, their range was not enough to make it plausible that they had flown from any shore base, which left only the hypothesis that they had taken off from the carriers sighted by Nitto Maru more than 700 miles offshore. With characteristic Yankee boldness and ingenuity, the enemy had evidently devised a means of launching heavy land-type aircraft from carriers and had employed this new stratagem to penetrate the Japanese defenses.

There were also strong indications that the attack had been planned as a one-way operation. Two of the enemy planes were reported to have retired southward from Kitan Strait, the southern entrance of Osaka Bay, and five more had been sighted off the southern tip of Kyushu flying in a southwesterly direction. The suspicion occurred to us that the enemy plan might have called for the planes to crash-land at sea somewhere off Shikoku, where submarines would be waiting to pick up the crews. A similar surmise was that a Russian steamer, which had been sighted by a Japanese patrol plane 200 miles south of Cape Ashizuri, on the southwestern tip of Shikoku, had been requested to perform this rescue mission. Finally, around midnight on the 18th, the mystery of the enemy's tactics was at last unravelled. A radio message from a Japanese Army unit in China reported that some of the enemy planes had crash-landed in the vicinity of Nanchang.

In the raids themselves, the attacking planes had managed to get in over their targets unopposed despite the forewarning provided by the detection of the enemy carriers. They had accomplished this feat by flying in at a dangerously low altitude so that Japanese Army and Navy interceptors, which were on guard far overhead, completely missed them. More than the admirable skill and daring of the fliers, however, the unforeseen use of the B-25s appeared chiefly responsible for the enemy's success. Taking it for granted that shorter-range carrier planes would be used, the air defense command undoubtedly estimated that there would be no attack before dawn on the 19th, when the enemy carriers would have approached within carrier-plane range. Consequently, it seemed probable that full defensive precautions had not yet been put into effect when the raiders struck.

Thanks to the capture of some of the fliers whose planes had run out of fuel before reaching friendly bases in China, Japanese intelligence soon learned that the raid had, indeed, been mounted from an enemy task group. It contained only two carriers—HORNET and ENTERPRISE—instead of three as reported by NITTO MARU, and the raiders, commanded by Lieutenant Colonel James Doolittle, had all taken off from HORNET. However, not until after the war did we learn from the American side the full story of the raid.

According to this post-war account, the enemy's original plan called for the B-25s to take off in the afternoon of 18 April, about 500 miles off the Japanese coast, so as to reach the targets at night. Colonel Doolittle himself was to fly in ahead of his raiders and make it easier for them to find their way by dropping incendiaries on the capital. As a result of the premature detection of the task group, however, this plan had to be abandoned in favor of a daylight attack, and the launching was carried out at a considerably greater distance than had been intended. To this extent, at least, the picket line interfered with the enemy plans.

A communique issued by Imperial General Headquarters regarding the raid announced that only slight damage had been done and that most of the attacking planes had been shot down or damaged. Later, when it was learned who had commanded the enemy air group, Headquarters spokesmen sarcastically pooh-poohed the attack as not even a "do-little" but rather a "do-nothing" raid.

In point of physical damage inflicted, it was true enough that the raid did not accomplish a great deal. But the same could not be said of its impact on the minds of Japan's naval leaders and its consequent influence on the course of the war at sea. From this standpoint, neither "do-nothing" nor "do-little" were accurate descriptions. On the contrary, it must be regarded as a "do-much" raid.

3. *MIDWAY OPERATION DECIDED*

The greatest importance of the Doolittle raid lay in its immediate effect on the controversy still going on over the Combined Fleet plan for an assault on Midway. Although the Naval General Staff on 5 April had reluctantly agreed to the operation in principle, the time of execution and other vital points were still in dispute when Colonel Doolittle's raiders successfully unloaded their bombs on Tokyo and other Japanese cities.

So far as Combined Fleet was concerned, the raid steeled its determination to press for early execution of the operation as originally proposed. The defeat of all his precautions against an enemy carrier-borne attack on the homeland cut Admiral Yamamoto's pride to the quick, and he resolved that it must not be allowed to happen again at any cost. There must be no delay, he decided, in taking the offensive to destroy the American carrier forces and to push the defensive patrol line eastward to Midway and the western Aleutians.

Nor were the implications of the Tokyo bombing lost on the Naval General Staff. Even the most vociferous opponents of the Midway plan were now hard put to deny that the threat from the east, if not greater than the potential threat from Australia, was at least more pressing and immediate. Moreover, the failure to keep the capital itself safe from attack reflected as much on the Naval General Staff as on Combined Fleet. The result was that all remaining opposition to the early June Midway attack deadline and other moot points of the Combined Fleet proposal promptly vanished, and Fleet Headquarters was enabled to proceed with the elaboration of the final plan of operations.

By the end of April this plan was completed and approved

by Admiral Yamamoto. It was then formally submitted to Chief of Naval General Staff Admiral Nagano, who also gave it his prompt approval. Accordingly, on 5 May, Admiral Nagano, acting in the name of the Emperor, issued Imperial General Headquarters Navy Order No. 18, which briefly directed Commander in Chief Combined Fleet to "carry out the occupation of Midway Island and key points in the western Aleutians in co-operation with the Army."

Simultaneously with the issuance of this basic directive, the Army and Navy Sections of Imperial General Headquarters concluded a joint "central agreement" regulating the terms of co-operation between the two services for the Midway invasion. Under the agreement, the Army promised to furnish a detachment of one infantry regiment, reinforced, to participate in the landing operations, these troops to be withdrawn after completion of the occupation, leaving subsequent defense of the island to naval forces. Saipan was tentatively fixed as the staging point for the amphibious forces, which were to assemble there on or about 25 May. The agreement set no specific invasion date but stated that the operations would begin sometime "in the first twenty days of June" simultaneously with operations against the western Aleutians.

The Midway operation was now definitely decided. Combined Fleet had gained its way, thanks to the unwitting assistance of Colonel Doolittle and his fliers. There still remained the formidable task of organizing and preparing the fleet forces, within barely a few weeks' time, to undertake the most gigantic operation in the 70-year history of the modern Japanese Navy.

Photo courtesy of Admiral Kondo

VICE ADMIRAL NOBUTAKE KONDO

CARRIER *Hiryu*

JAPANESE AIRCRAFT CARRIER *Soryu*

ADMIRAL ISOROKU YAMAMOTO

CHAPTER 5 Midway Operation Plan

1. YAMAMOTO—THE GUIDING SPIRIT

The final Combined Fleet plan for the Midway operation, officially designated "Operation MI" by Imperial General Headquarters, was the composite product of many minds. The basic outline was largely the work of the Senior Operations Officer, Captain Kuroshima. A theoretician given to spending long hours in meditation in his darkened cabin, he was the author of a manual laying down Combined Fleet tactical doctrine for fleet-versus-fleet decisive battle with battleships in the key role. Other members of the staff elaborated detailed parts of the plan, each within his special sphere of competence. Over-all supervision of the drafting activities was performed by the aggressive and resourceful Chief of Staff, Rear Admiral Ugaki, a consistent proponent of offensive fleet action against Hawaii.

But, above all, the Midway plan reflected the ideas and personality of the Navy's dominant figure and Combined Fleet's Commander in Chief, Admiral Isoroku Yamamoto. The task of assessing this forceful leader must necessarily be left to others more competent and better informed than myself. I only wish to put down here some random impressions and thoughts about the man as I, one of thousands of officers who served under his command, saw him.

If, at the start of the Pacific War, a poll had been taken among Japanese naval officers to determine their choice of the man to lead them as Commander in Chief Combined Fleet, there is little doubt that Admiral Yamamoto would have been

73

selected by an overwhelming majority. I am confident, too, that his supporters would have included every flying officer in the Navy. After the war, in fact, American historical investigators put such a hypothetical question to a number of ex-officers of the Japanese Naval Air Corps, including myself. Our unanimous reply was, "Admiral Yamamoto."

The tremendous following which Yamamoto enjoyed among the Navy's fliers stemmed from the fact that he was one of the foremost promoters of naval aviation. Though not a career aviation officer himself, he was appointed Executive Officer of the Kasumigaura Naval Air Training Corps when still a Captain, and he thereafter held a succession of important air posts. The Naval Air Corps was then in its infancy and sorely needed a strong leader and champion. Yamamoto stepped into this role with enthusiasm, bringing to the task his extraordinarily keen foresight and warm-hearted human understanding.

In these early days a flying career was not particularly attractive in view of the frequency of fatal accidents. Indeed, many of the Navy's high-ranking officers would not even set foot in an airplane if they thought that it was going to leave the ground. As recently as the late thirties, Admiral Zengo Yoshida, a classmate of Yamamoto's and then Commander in Chief Combined Fleet, adamantly refused to board a plane which his staff had made ready to fly him on an official trip.

Other high-ranking officers paid lip service to the importance of naval aviation and urged young men starting their careers in the Navy to go into that branch, but their enthusiasm ended abruptly when it came to having their own sons become flying officers or even to having their daughters marry fliers. Admiral Yamamoto was no such part-way enthusiast. His belief in aviation was sincere, and he demonstrated it by encouraging a number of his younger relatives to join the Naval Air Corps.

Yamamoto's fondness for fliers did not extend to sharing one of their common failings, a weakness for alcohol. He was a teetotaler. He did, however, like games of chance and was known to be a highly competent and daring player of bridge and poker. He would have been a gifted gambler, for he had the gambler's all-or-nothing spirit. If it were true, as many said, that the Pearl Harbor attack represented an all-or-nothing strategy, it was in keeping with Yamamoto's character, and perhaps the gambler-like boldness which inspired it was one of the chief reasons for its success.

Beside his capacity to take bold, imaginative decisions, another thing that earned Yamamoto the respect and admiration of the Navy's younger officers was the fact that he exercised strong, unequivocal leadership. In this respect he was an exception rather than the rule among the Navy's admirals. Perhaps influenced by British naval traditions, the Japanese Navy from its early days had laid great stress on instilling gentlemanly qualities in its officers. Unfortunately, however, a tendency arose to equate a lack of assertiveness and an easygoing affability with gentlemanliness, with the result that there were many bright and likable flag officers, but few real leaders and fighting commanders.

The lack of real leadership manifested itself on many occasions. For example, when a fleet command or naval district held maneuvers or battle exercises, the officers usually assembled afterward for a critique. The fleet or naval district commander presided at such conferences, but it was seldom that he actively guided the discussions or offered any incisive comments. The officers consequently had little idea whether they were on the right track or not.

Admiral Yamamoto was quite different. In the study conferences following Combined Fleet maneuvers, he took a leading part in the discussions. If some movement had been carried out improperly, he pointed it out and explained how he wanted it done in the future. He did not employ his staff officers as a brain trust but rather as aides for executing his own policies and decisions. His clear-cut guidance left no doubt as to what these policies were, so that when his subordinates were obliged to make independent decisions, they knew exactly what course of action would correspond to the thinking of their Commander in Chief.

It was these strong qualities of leadership which caused the Navy as a whole to look upon Yamamoto as the man best fitted to be its supreme commander. For in war, the fate of the nation may be staked upon the outcome of a single battle, and in turn victory or defeat in battle hinges largely on the character and ability of a single individual, the Commander in Chief. This is necessarily so because only by concentrating the power of decision can unified action be assured, and without unified action victory is impossible. It is so also because moves in battle cannot be debated around the conference table and decided by majority rule; they must be decided swiftly by the commander on the basis of his own judgment and with full realization that each move, once made, is irrevocable. To make such decisions requires extraordinary courage and self-confidence. Yamamoto had both.

Yet, with all the qualities which seemed to make him an incomparable supreme commander, the test of war showed that Admiral Yamamoto also had his failings. These, it seems to me, were clearly evidenced by his hasty and uncompromising insistence upon the Midway operation in the face of all the cogent arguments against it. It is difficult to avoid the conclusion that his judgment in this instance was warped by his obsession about keeping Tokyo immune from air attack and by his sense of injured pride caused by the Doolittle raid. Had these feelings not unduly swayed him, he surely would have shown greater flexibility in his thinking about future strategy.

Undoubtedly, too, the haste with which Yamamoto plunged into the Midway venture was inspired by his conviction that the balance of military strength between Japan and the United States would shift in the latter's favor within two years at the most from the start of hostilities. Because of this pressing time factor, he felt that Japan's only hope lay in seeking a quick decision which might induce the enemy to come to terms. The move on Midway, he hoped, would force such a decision. He confided to Rear Admiral Yamaguchi and other trusted subordinates that, if he succeeded in destroying the United States Pacific Fleet in the Midway operation, he intended to press the nation's political leaders to initiate overtures for peace.

Yamamoto was unquestionably correct in his judgment that it was essential to engage the enemy fleet in decisive battle at the earliest possible opportunity. Indeed, if any criticism is to be made on this score, it must be directed at his failure to act earlier toward this objective by keeping the powerful Japanese Carrier Striking Force operating to the east after the initial assault on Pearl Harbor. At all events, the destruction of the United States Pacific Fleet was certainly a top-priority task in the spring of 1942. What is open to serious question, however, is whether the occupation of Midway was either the only or the most feasible way to accomplish this goal.

From the tactical standpoint, the Midway plan evidenced an adherence to the outmoded doctrine of the battleship advocates, which was difficult to reconcile with Yamamoto's supposed understanding of the role of air power. It seems strange, to say the least, that the man who conceived the carrier strike on Pearl Harbor was not quicker to institute sweeping changes in fleet organization and tactics so as to make air power the central core of the combat forces. Perhaps Yamamoto himself was afflicted with the characteristic Japanese tendency to cling to the past. Or perhaps he found traditional concepts so firmly entrenched that he was powerless to effect any radical overnight change.

It is often said that warfare is a succession of errors on both sides and that victory goes to the side which makes the fewer. Admiral Yamamoto and his subordinates certainly made their share of mistakes, including some for which it is hard to find any logical explanation. But rather than place blame, it is more important for us to ponder the lessons of such mistakes and of the defeat that followed.

2. OUTLINE OF OPERATIONS

The plan drawn up by Combined Fleet Headquarters for the Midway operation had, as pointed out earlier, two central objectives. The first and more limited objective was the seizure of Midway itself as an advance air base to facilitate the early detection of enemy forces operating westward from the Hawaiian Islands. The second, much broader objective was to draw out the United States Pacific Fleet's remaining strength so that it could be engaged and destroyed in decisive battle.

While the Doolittle raid naturally lent added weight to the first of these objectives, it was nevertheless the annihilation of the enemy fleet which was the dominant goal of the Midway operation. Admiral Yamamoto and his staff were convinced that the move against Midway, because it would pose a threat to the safety of Hawaii, would virtually compel the enemy fleet to react with all its available strength. This would set the scene for the "decisive fleet engagement in the Pacific" which had been the focal point of Japanese naval strategy and of fleet training and preparation for so many years.

From the standpoint of relative strength, there was every reason for confidence in a Japanese victory if the enemy rose to the challenge. The enemy's surface combat strength, thanks to the destruction of his battleships in the Pearl Harbor attack, was limited mainly to carriers and cruisers, while Combined Fleet's striking power was even greater than at the start of hostilities. At the end of April 1942, Japan's superiority over the United States in aircraft carriers alone was nearly three to one. Against the four carriers believed currently available to the

U.S. Pacific Fleet—YORKTOWN, SARATOGA,[1] HORNET and
ENTERPRISE—Combined Fleet boasted seven large carriers and
four light carriers.

In view of this comfortable margin of superiority, Combined
Fleet decided that the objectives of the Midway operation could
safely be expanded to include the simultaneous capture of key
points in the western Aleutians. Permanent occupation of these
northern islands was not considered necessary as they were
thought to be of little use as air patrol bases during the greater
part of the year because of weather conditions. However, Combined Fleet strategists calculated that their temporary seizure,
in addition to permitting destruction of enemy military installations there, would serve to protect the northern flank of the
main Japanese thrust toward Midway and act as a diversion
which might throw the enemy forces off balance. The over-all
plan therefore called for landings on Adak, Kiska, and Attu,
with the invasion forces to withdraw in mid-September before
the onset of winter.

To carry out this gigantic two-pronged offensive, Combined
Fleet planned to commit the maximum strength that it could
muster. All the combat forces were to be thrown into the campaign with the exception of parts of the submarine fleet, which
were then either undergoing maintenance and repair or engaged
in commerce-raiding operations in the Indian Ocean, South
African waters and the Australia-New Zealand area, and some
surface elements indispensable to the local defense of the
southern occupied regions. Altogether, including transports,
auxiliaries and air strength, the Combined Fleet plan called for
the employment of over 200 ships, including no fewer than

---

[1] *Editors' Note:* Actually LEXINGTON. The Japanese believed that LEXINGTON
had been sunk by a Japanese submarine near Hawaii in January 1942. Actually
it was SARATOGA which was attacked, and though not sunk, she was badly damaged. The Japanese error led to their mistaking LEXINGTON for SARATOGA in the
Battle of the Coral Sea. See Chapter 6.

11 battleships, 8 carriers, 22 crusiers, 65 destroyers and 21 submarines; and approximately 700 planes. The ships participating
were to consume more fuel and cover a greater mileage in this
one operation than the peacetime Japanese Navy had ever done
in an entire year.

The task organization drawn up for the Midway operation
divided this massive strength into six major tactical forces under
the over-all command of Commander in Chief Combined
Fleet, Admiral Yamamoto. The designations and principal
components of these six forces were as follows:[2]

1. *MAIN FORCE*
Admiral Isoroku Yamamoto

a. MAIN BODY
Admiral Yamamoto

Battleships YAMATO (Combined Fleet flagship), NAGATO, MUTSU
Light carrier HOSHO (8 Type-96 bombers)
Light cruiser SENDAI
Nine destroyers
Seaplane carriers CHIYODA, NISSHIN (carrying midget submarines)

b. GUARD (Aleutians Screening) FORCE
Vice Admiral Shiro Takasu

Battleships HYUGA (flagship), ISE, FUSO, YAMASHIRO
Light cruisers OI, KITAKAMI
Twelve destroyers

2. *FIRST CARRIER STRIKING FORCE*
Vice Admiral Chuichi Nagumo

a. CARRIER GROUP[3]
Vice Admiral Nagumo

---

[2] *Editors' Note:* Complete and detailed list of all Japanese forces participating
in the Midway and Aleutians operations is given in Appendix 2.

[3] Carrier Division 5 (ZUIKAKU, SHOKAKU) was originally included in the
task organization but had to be dropped as a result of the Coral Sea battle, which
will be dealt with in Chapter 6, below.

Carrier Division 1
Vice Admiral Nagumo

Carriers AKAGI (flagship), KAGA
42 fighters, 42 dive bombers, 51 torpedo bombers

Carrier Division 2
Rear Admiral Tamon Yamaguchi

Carriers HIRYU (flagship), SORYU
42 fighters, 42 dive bombers, 42 torpedo bombers

b. SUPPORT GROUP
Rear Admiral Hiroaki Abe

Battleships HARUNA, KIRISHIMA
Heavy cruisers TONE (flagship), CHIKUMA

c. SCREENING GROUP
Rear Admiral Susumu Kimura

Light cruiser NAGARA (flagship)
Eleven destroyers

3. *MIDWAY INVASION FORCE*
Vice Admiral Nobutake Kondo

a. INVASION FORCE MAIN BODY
Vice Admiral Kondo

Battleships KONGO, HIEI
Light carrier ZUIHO (12 fighters, 12 torpedo bombers)
Heavy cruisers ATAGO (flagship), CHOKAI, MYOKO, HAGURO
Light cruiser YURA
Eight destroyers

b. CLOSE SUPPORT GROUP
Vice Admiral Takeo Kurita

Heavy cruisers KUMANO (flagship), SUZUYA, MIKUMA, MOGAMI
Two destroyers

c. TRANSPORT GROUP
Rear Admiral Raizo Tanaka

Twelve transports and three destroyer-transports carrying Midway
Landing Force (5,000 troops)

Light cruiser JINTSU (flagship)
Ten destroyers

d. SEAPLANE TENDER GROUP
Rear Admiral Ruitaro Fujita

Seaplane carrier CHITOSE (16 float fighters, 4 scout planes)
Seaplane carrier KAMIKAWA MARU (8 float fighters, 4 scout
   planes)
One destroyer and one patrol boat

e. MINESWEEPER GROUP
Captain Sadatomo Miyamoto

Four minesweepers
Three submarine chasers
One supply ship and two cargo ships

4. *NORTHERN (ALEUTIANS) FORCE*
Vice Admiral Moshiro Hosogaya

a. NORTHERN FORCE MAIN BODY
Vice Admiral Hosogaya

Heavy cruiser NACHI (flagship)
Two destroyers

b. SECOND CARRIER STRIKING FORCE
Rear Admiral Kakuji Kakuta

Light carrier RYUJO (flagship) (16 fighters, 21 torpedo bomb-
   ers)
Carrier JUNYO (24 fighters, 21 dive bombers)
Heavy cruisers MAYA, TAKAO
Three destroyers

c. ATTU INVASION FORCE
Rear Admiral Sentaro Omori

Light cruiser ABUKUMA (flagship)
Four destroyers
One minelayer
One transport carrying Army Landing Force (1,200 troops)

d. KISKA INVASION FORCE
Captain Takeji Ono

Light cruisers KISO (flagship), TAMA
Auxiliary cruiser ASAKA MARU
Three destroyers
Three minesweepers
Two transports carrying Naval Landing Force (1,250 troops)

e. SUBMARINE DETACHMENT
Rear Admiral Shigeaki Yamazaki

Submarines I-9 (flagship), I-15, I-17, I-19, I-25, I-26

5. ADVANCE (SUBMARINE) FORCE
Vice Admiral Teruhisa Komatsu

Light cruiser KATORI (flagship, at Kwajalein)

a. SUBMARINE SQUADRON 3
Rear Admiral Chimaki Kono

Submarine tender YASUKUNI MARU (flagship, at Kwajalein)
Submarines I-168, I-169, I-171, I-174, I-175

b. SUBMARINE SQUADRON 5
Rear Admiral Tadashige Daigo

Submarine tender RIO DE JANEIRO MARU (flagship, at Kwajalein)
Submarines I-156, I-157, I-158, I-159, I-162, I-165, I-166

c. SUBMARINE DIVISION 13
Captain Takeharu Miyazaki

Submarines I-121, I-122, I-123

6. SHORE-BASED AIR FORCE
Vice Admiral Nishizo Tsukahara

a. MIDWAY EXPEDITIONARY FORCE
Captain Chisato Morita

36 fighters (transported by carriers)
10 land bombers (at Wake)
6 flying boats (at Jaluit)

b. 24TH AIR FLOTILLA
Rear Admiral Minoru Maeda

Chitose Air Group
Captain Fujiro Ohashi
36 fighters, 36 torpedo bombers (at Kwajalein and Wake)

1st Air Group
Captain Samaji Inouye
36 fighters, 36 torpedo bombers (at Aur and Wotje)

14th Air Group
Captain Daizo Nakajima
18 flying boats (at Jaluit and Wotje)

The carefully coordinated timetable on which these various forces were to operate was centered on "N" Day,[4] 7 June, the date fixed for the main landing on Midway. A combination of two factors was responsible for the selection of this date. The first was the time needed to repair, overhaul and resupply the ships of the Nagumo Force and Vice Admiral Kondo's Second Fleet, which had returned to the homeland only in the latter part of April after completing their first-phase missions in the southern area. Since these preparations would take several weeks, it was estimated that the invasion date could not be set earlier than the first part of June. The second factor was the need of selecting a date when there would be adequate moonlight to facilitate night movements. The seventh day of June was the last day until almost one month later when the moon age would be right for the landing operations, and Combined Fleet was strongly opposed to postponing the Midway attack until July.

To meet the attack deadline, the various surface forces and transport groups were to sortie between 26 and 29 May, the

[4] *Editors' Note:* "N day," as used here, is the Japanese equivalent of the American term "D day." The Japanese varied the letter in different operations. For example, they used "X day" in the Pearl Harbor operation.

Northern Force from Ominato Naval Base, on the northern end of Honshu, and the Midway Invasion Force, except Vice Admiral Kondo's Main Body, from Saipan and Guam. Kondo's ships as well as Vice Admiral Nagumo's First Carrier Striking Force and the Main Force under Admiral Yamamoto were to sortie from Hashirajima Anchorage in the western Inland Sea and head direct for the battle area. En route the Main Force was to split into its two components, Admiral Yamamoto's Main Body continuing toward Midway while Vice Admiral Takasu's Guard Force would veer off to the northeast to screen the Aleutians invasion.

Since one of the objectives of the Aleutians attack was to create a diversion for the main thrust against Midway, the initial blow was to be struck in the northern area. On 4 June, N minus 3, Rear Admiral Kakuta's Second Carrier Striking Force, operating as part of the Northern Force, was to launch a neutralizing air strike against Dutch Harbor, the major enemy strongpoint in the Aleutians. The initial landings on Adak and Kiska Islands were to follow on 6 June, N minus 1. The Adak landing was to be carried out by the Attu Invasion Force, which was to withdraw after destroying military installations and mining the bays and harbors. It was then to carry out a landing on Attu, its main objective, on 12 June, N plus 5. The landing operations were to be screened by Kakuta's Carrier Striking Force, Vice Admiral Hosogaya's Northern Force Main Body, Vice Admiral Takasu's Guard Force, and an element of the Submarine Force detached to Northern Force command.

The same general pattern of attack was to be followed against Midway. On 5 June, N minus 2, the First Carrier Striking Force was to launch a preinvasion air strike on Midway from a point 250 miles northwest of the island, aimed at destroying enemy air strength, defensive installations, and any surface forces in the vicinity. On 6 June, N minus 1, Rear Admiral Fujita's Sea-

plane Tender Unit was to occupy tiny Kure Island, 60 miles
northwest of Midway, so that it might be used as a seaplane base
for direct support of the Midway landing.

While these preliminary operations were in progress, the
Transport Group carrying the Midway Landing Force, with
its escorting naval units, would move in toward the objective,
and at dawn on 7 June simultaneous landings would be made
on Sand and Eastern Islands, which together compose Midway
Atoll. Close-in support of the landing would be provided by
Rear Admiral Kurita's Support Group of heavy cruisers, while
Vice Admiral Kondo's Invasion Force Main Body would stand
off to the south or southwest of Midway to screen that flank
of the operation.

Any major enemy fleet reaction was expected to come only
after the Midway landing. Consequently, the Combined Fleet
plan provided that by 7 June the Japanese forces would move
into positions of readiness for the all-important decisive battle
phase of the operation. They were to remain in these positions
for seven days after the occupation of Midway unless the enemy
attacked sooner. The forces primarily relied upon to meet and
crush the enemy fleet were (1) Admiral Yamamoto's Main
Force Main Body, (2) Vice Admiral Takasu's Guard Force,
(3) Vice Admiral Nagumo's First Carrier Striking Force, (4)
Rear Admiral Kakuta's Second Carrier Striking Force, and (5)
elements of Vice Admiral Komatsu's Submarine Force. These
forces were to be deployed as follows:

Yamamoto Force: 600 miles northwest of Midway

Takasu Force: 500 miles north of Yamamoto Force

Nagumo Force: 300 miles east of Yamamoto Force

Kakuta Force: 300 miles east of Takasu Force

Submarine Forces: To establish three cordon lines by 2
June, N minus 5, disposed as follows, in order to detect the approach of enemy forces:

Cordon "A" (Submarine Squadron 3) between lat. 19°30′
N, and 23°30′ N, on long. 167° W.

Cordon "B" (Submarine Squadron 5) between lat. 29° 30′ N, long. 164°30′ W, and lat. 26°10′ N, long. 167° W.

Cordon "C" (1-9, 1-15, 1-17 of Submarine Squadron 1) between lat. 49° N, long. 166° W, and lat. 51° N, long. 166° W.

Alternative tactical methods were provided to meet different situations, but, in general, if a substantial enemy force advanced west of 160 degrees West Longitude, it was to be attacked first by the carriers and submarines, with the surface combat forces to come up and give support as circumstances might require. If the enemy advance developed north of 40 degrees North Latitude, the attack was to be made by the Second Carrier Striking Force and 1st Submarine Squadron, supported by the Takasu Force; and if south of that line, by the First Carrier Striking and 3rd and 5th Submarine Groups, supported by the Yamamoto Force. However, if the enemy fleet advanced in full strength, the Japanese northern and southern forces would unite and engage it in decisive battle, the Takasu Force rejoining Admiral Yamamoto's Main Body and the First and Second Carrier Striking Forces merging into one force under Vice Admiral Nagumo's command.

Although the principal role in the air phases of the Midway operation was of necessity assigned to the carrier forces, Vice Admiral Tsukahara's shore-based air command was given an important supporting part. Its main strength was to redeploy to island bases in the Pacific in advance of the operation and carry out extensive searches and patrols in conjunction with the assembly and movement of the surface forces to and from the battle areas. After the occupation of Midway, part of its strength was to be based there to defend the island and conduct air patrols to the east.

The shore-based air forces, however, obviously could not extend their preinvasion searches as far as Hawaii, a full 2,000 miles distant from the nearest Japanese base at Wotje, in the

Marshall Islands. This posed a difficult and vital problem, for any important naval reaction to the Midway attack would most probably originate from the Hawaiian area, and it was therefore essential to ascertain the strength and movements of the enemy forces there just prior to the start of the invasion operations. The prewar Japanese intelligence net in Hawaii, which had contributed so effectively to the success of the Pearl Harbor attack, was of course no longer operative. Reconnaissance by submarines or by small submarine-borne seaplanes was possible, but the former was relatively ineffective owing to the limited range of observation and easy enemy air patrol interference, while the latter was considered unlikely to succeed against an area with strong air defenses such as Hawaii.

As a partial solution, Combined Fleet decided to resort to a special stratagem that had already worked successfully once before. This involved the use of the Navy's newest long-range aircraft, the 31-ton Kawanishi Type-2 flying boat with a speed of 235 knots and a range of 4,000 miles. Even this range was not enough for a non-stop flight from the Marshalls to Hawaii and back, but if the big planes put down once at an unoccupied atoll along the way and refueled from submarines spotted there in advance, they could fly on to Hawaii, execute their missions, and get back to base.

On 4 March, two months prior to the elaboration of the final Midway plan, this method had been successfully tried for the first time in what was known as "Operation K." Taking off from Wotje, two of these flying boats had put down at French Frigate Shoals, about 500 miles northwest of Hawaii, refueled from submarines waiting there, and then flown on to Oahu, where they made a night reconnaissance of Pearl Harbor, dropping a few bombs for psychological effect before heading back to base.

In view of the success of "Operation K," Combined Fleet incorporated provision in the Midway plan for a similar reconnaissance mission. Vice Admiral Tsukahara's Shore-Based Air Force was to dispatch two Type-2 flying boats to Wotje in time to execute the mission between 31 May and 3 June (East Longitude date). Vice Admiral Komatsu's Submarine Force was to cooperate by ordering some of its Kwajalein-based submarines to French Frigate Shoals to refuel the planes.

This lone air reconnaissance effort, however, would obviously not be enough. In addition, it would still be necessary to place considerable reliance on the Submarine Force to keep a continuing watch on enemy fleet movements. Combined Fleet concluded that the only effective method would be to set up submarine cordons covering the approaches toward the Midway and Aleutians invasion points. Accordingly, the Midway plan directed the Submarine Force to station two cordons of one squadron each to the northwest and west of Hawaii, about halfway between Hawaii and Midway, and a third cordon of one squadron farther north toward the Aleutians, all to be in position by 2 June, N minus 5. These cordons have already been mentioned in connection with the planned decisive battle dispositions of the Japanese forces.

After the conclusion of the Midway operation, most of the forces that had operated in that area were to proceed to Truk by about 20 June and start preparing for the Fiji-Samoa-New Caledonia operations slated to be launched in early July. Admiral Yamamoto's Main Force, however, was to return to the homeland by about the same date, possibly proceeding to Truk later to support the next operations. The Submarine Force was to continue operating against Hawaii, employing Midway as an advance base. Most of the Aleutians forces were to return to Ominato, where they would be reassigned missions of escorting supply convoys to Midway and the Aleutians and guarding the waters east of the homeland.

Such, in brief outline, was the Combined Fleet plan for the Midway operation. As soon as it had been issued, each of the subordinate fleet commands involved in the operation earnestly began studying and planning for its own assigned mission. These studies, however, made it readily apparent that the plan could be considered satisfactory only from the viewpoint of those who persisted in regarding the battleship, with its big guns, as the main striking force of the Fleet. Despite the important roles assigned to the carrier and submarine forces, they were still to act primarily as an advance guard and shield for the battleships, softening up the enemy so that the battleships could step in to deliver the decisive blow.

CHAPTER 6 Preparations for Battle

1. BELATED CONSULTATIONS

By the end of April, a substantial part of the naval forces which were to take part in the Midway operation were already assembled in the Inland Sea. Except Carrier Division 5, detached to participate in the impending invasion attempt against Port Moresby, the Nagumo Force had returned to home waters on 22 and 23 April, ending its long voyage from the Indian Ocean. Vice Admiral Kondo's Second Fleet, which had already reached home on 17 April only to be ordered to sortie again the next day in pursuit of the enemy task force that launched the Doolittle raid, also was back in port after a futile week at sea.

The focal point of the assembly of forces was Hashirajima Anchorage in Hiroshima Bay. There, on board the giant Combined Fleet flagship YAMATO, Admiral Yamamoto and his staff were hurriedly putting the finishing touches to the Midway operation plan and organizing the start of battle preparations. The telephone cable linking the flagship with the shore hummed with a constant stream of messages as the Fleet Headquarters maintained close liaison with the Naval General Staff in Tokyo and made arrangements with the Kure Naval Base for ship repairs, maintenance and supply.

Vice Admiral Nagumo and Vice Admiral Kondo, neither of whom had previously been consulted regarding the Midway operation, now had their first opportunity to study the Combined Fleet plan. So far as the First Air Fleet commander and his staff were concerned, the reaction was almost one of indifference. They seemed to care little where the next operation was directed. The Nagumo Force had run up a brilliant record of

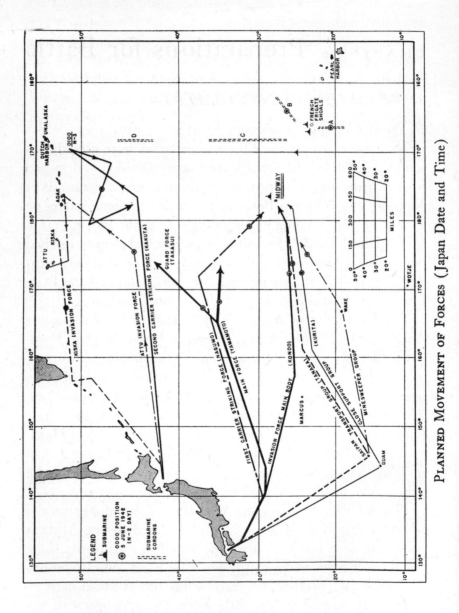

PLANNED MOVEMENT OF FORCES (Japan Date and Time)

achievement in the first-phase operations, and the headquarters was fully confident of its ability to carry out any mission which Combined Fleet assigned.

Beneath the headquarters level, the reception was more enthusiastic. Rear Admiral Tamon Yamaguchi, Commander Carrier Division 2, had for a time advocated that the next operation be aimed at Ceylon with a view to the eventual extension of Japanese control over the whole Indian Ocean area. However, after learning of the Midway plan, he became one of its staunchest supporters. From the outset of the war, Yamaguchi, who had onced served as Naval Attaché in Washington, had fervently believed that the United States Fleet must be challenged in decisive battle at the earliest opportunity. Since this was one of the central objectives of the Midway operation, it naturally won his complete approval. As for the flying officers of the Nagumo Force, they had every reason to welcome the Midway venture, for to them it meant a chance to destroy the American carrier force, which they regarded as their special foe.

The attitude of Vice Admiral Kondo and his staff, however, was quite different. On 1 May, the Second Fleet commander boarded YAMATO for his first meeting with Admiral Yamamoto since the start of the war. After a brief discussion of the first-phase operations, the conversation turned to the Midway plan. Vice Admiral Kondo frankly voiced misgivings, emphasizing in particular that the assault on Midway would have to be carried out without shore-based air support, while the enemy would be able to employ not only substantial shore-based air strength but also carrier forces which as yet had not been seriously damaged. Because of this grave disadvantage, he argued that it would be wiser to launch invasion operations against New Caledonia in order to sever the supply line between the United States and Australia.

Admiral Yamamoto, however, brushed aside Kondo's objections with the assertion that the Midway plan had been agreed upon between Combined Fleet Headquarters and the Naval General Staff after careful study on both sides, and could not be changed. He added that in spite of the risks involved in the Midway operation, there was no reason to fear defeat if surprise were successfully achieved.

Vice Admiral Kondo then turned to the Combined Fleet Chief of Staff, Rear Admiral Ugaki, and asked if the Fleet Headquarters was not concerned over the difficulty of keeping Midway supplied after its capture. Unless this could be done, he asserted, its occupation would be pointless. To this, Ugaki's far from reassuring reply was that if it eventually became impossible to continue supplying the occupation forces, they could be evacuated after completely destroying military installations. With this the discussion ended. It was quite apparent that Combined Fleet Headquarters, regardless of all objections, had no intention of backing down from its decision to carry out the Midway operation.

After returning to his own flagship, Vice Admiral Kondo related the substance of his talks in YAMATO to his Chief of Staff, Rear Admiral Kazutaka Shiraishi, and Senior Staff Officer, Captain Kuranosuke Yanagizawa. Yanagizawa regretfully remarked that at the very least he would like to see the staging point for the Midway invasion forces changed from Saipan to Truk in order to lessen the danger of premature enemy discovery. Second Fleet representatives later pressed this proposal during the Combined Fleet briefing conferences on the Midway plan, but to no avail. Combined Fleet was not in the mood to accept even minor changes.

2. TESTING THE BATTLE PLAN

On the same day that Vice Admiral Kondo communicated his doubts concerning the Midway venture to Admiral Yamamoto, Combined Fleet Headquarters initiated a four-day series of war games designed to test various operations already planned or tentatively contemplated for the second phase of the war. Staged on board flagship YAMATO under the direction of Combined Fleet Chief of Staff Rear Admiral Ugaki, the games were attended by a majority of the commanders and staff officers of the forces which were to take part in the Midway operation. Those who had returned only a short while earlier from the southern area were conspicuous by the deep tan of their complexions, a result of six months spent under the tropic sun. Their eyes sparkled with excitement as they assembled to study the roles they would play in the forthcoming operations.

The invasion of Midway was the starting point of the games, but it was only the beginning. Not since the war games of November 1941, which had rehearsed the Pearl Harbor attack and the southern invasions, had such a grandiose program of offensive operations been tested. The over-all hypothetical plan formulated by Combined Fleet Headquarters as a basis for the games was briefly as follows:

1. In early June the main strength of Combined Fleet will capture Midway, and a part of its strength will seize the western Aleutians.

2. After completion of these operations, most of the battleship strength will return to the homeland and stand by, while the remainder of the Midway invasion naval forces will assemble at Truk to resume operations early in July for the capture of strategic points in New Caledonia and the Fiji Islands.

3. The Nagumo Force will then carry out air strikes against Sydney and other points on the southeast coast of Australia.

4. Following the above, the Nagumo Force and other forces assigned to the New Caledonia-Fiji Islands operations will reassemble at Truk for replenishment. Sometime after the beginning of August, operations will be launched against Johnston Island and Hawaii, employing the full strength of Combined Fleet.

Except for the staff of Combined Fleet Headquarters, all those taking part in the war games were amazed at this formidable program, which seemed to have been dreamed up with a great deal more imagination than regard for reality. Still more amazing, however, was the manner in which every operation from the invasion of Midway and the Aleutians down to the assault on Johnston and Hawaii was carried out in the games without the slightest difficulty. This was due in no small measure to the highhanded conduct of Rear Admiral Ugaki, the presiding officer, who frequently intervened to set aside rulings made by the umpires.

In the tabletop maneuvers, for example, a situation developed in which the Nagumo Force underwent a bombing attack by enemy land-based aircraft while its own planes were off attacking Midway. In accordance with the rules, Lieutenant Commander Okumiya, Carrier Division 4 staff officer who was acting as an umpire, cast dice to determine the bombing results and ruled that there had been nine enemy hits on the Japanese carriers. Both AKAGI and KAGA were listed as sunk. Admiral Ugaki, however, arbitrarily reduced the number of enemy hits to only three, which resulted in KAGA's still being ruled sunk but AKAGI only slightly damaged. To Okumiya's surprise, even this revised ruling was subsequently cancelled, and KAGA reappeared as a participant in the next part of the games covering the New Caledonia and Fiji Islands invasions. The verdicts of the umpires regarding the results of air fighting were similarly juggled, always in favor of the Japanese forces.

The value of the games also was impaired by the fact that the participating staff officers from several major operational commands, including the Nagumo Force and the shore-based Eleventh Air Fleet, had had little time to study the operations to be tested. The result was that they could only play out their parts like puppets, with the staff of Combined Fleet Headquarters pulling the strings. The lack of preparation was illustrated by an incident which occurred during the Midway invasion maneuvers. There, the somewhat reckless manner in which the Nagumo Force operated evoked criticism, and the question was raised as to what plan the Force had in mind to meet the contingency that an enemy carrier task force might appear on its flank while it was executing its scheduled air attack on Midway. The reply given by the Nagumo Force staff officer present was so vague as to suggest that there was no such plan, and Rear Admiral Ugaki himself cautioned that greater consideration must be given to this possibility. Indeed, in the actual battle, this was precisely what happened.

Following the conclusion of the war games on 4 May, two additional days were devoted to study and briefing conferences concerning the Midway operation. Various recommendations were advanced for making changes in the operational plan, but for the most part they got nowhere. In particular, almost all the participating fleet commanders from Vice Admiral Kondo on down the line strongly urged postponement of the invasion date in order to allow more time for battle preparations. Rear Admiral Ugaki, however, asserted that this was impossible because a postponement, unless it were for an entire month, would mean that there would be inadequate moonlight for night maneuvering off the invasion beaches.

One problem raised by the staff of the Nagumo Force was the inadequacy of the radio communications equipment carried by flagship AKAGI. This, of course, was a weakness common to all carriers because of the necessity of keeping the radio masts small and unobtrusive so as not to interfere with the take-off and landing of aircraft. Rear Admiral Kusaka, Chief of Staff of the Nagumo Force, pointed out during the study conferences that AKAGI might fail to intercept enemy radio messages vitally important to forming an estimate of enemy movements and intentions. To remedy this, two alternatives were recommended. The first was that Admiral Yamamoto's flagship YAMATO, instead of leading the battleship main strength, which would necessitate maintaining radio silence, should operate independently and relay all important radio intercepts to the Nagumo Force. The second provided that YAMATO should operate directly with the carriers, Admiral Yamamoto assuming direct command of the Nagumo Force. Neither recommendation was accepted.

This was only one example of the general failure of the Combined Fleet Midway plan to provide for adequate support of the Nagumo Force. For air searches the Force would have to rely entirely on its own planes. To defend itself against air attack, it would have to depend largely on its own combat air patrol because the Force itself lacked enough screening units to throw up an effective barrage of antiaircraft fire. Obviously, the battleship groups, which were to be deployed 300 miles behind the carrier forces, would be incapable of rendering any assistance in case the latter got into trouble. In fact, it was difficult for Nagumo's staff to see how the battleships, if disposed so far to the rear, would serve any useful purpose whatever in the over-all operation.

Basically, the trouble lay in the fact, pointed out earlier, that the Midway plan rested on the obsolete concept, still dominant in Combined Fleet Headquarters, that battleships rather than carriers constituted the main battle strength of the Fleet. Instead of employing the battleships to screen and reinforce the carriers, it was the carriers which were placed in the supporting role. The fallacy of this concept was to be driven home with tragic force.

A week before the war games of 1-4 May, the need of a thoroughgoing fleet reorganization designed to place paramount emphasis on carrier air power rather than surface gun power had been strongly urged by Commander Genda and other officers of the Nagumo Force at a conference held on board YAMATO to review the first-phase operations. Rear Admiral Yamaguchi had specifically proposed that the entire mobile surface strength of Combined Fleet be reorganized into three task fleets, each of which would have a nucleus of three or four carriers with adequate numbers of battleships, cruisers and destroyers to screen them. Combined Fleet already had plenty of screening ships and, by the latter part of 1942, was also expected to have enough carriers to form three such task fleets. Two of them could be organized immediately, each well-balanced and with powerful carrier strength. Combined Fleet agreed to this proposal in principle, but actually no action was taken to put it into effect prior to the Midway operation.

The war games and study conferences thus ended with many officers in the operational forces dissatisfied over various aspects of the Midway plan, and with numerous important problems left unsolved. Some officers privately whispered that Combined Fleet Headquarters seemed seriously to underestimate enemy capabilities. None dared voice this accusation openly during the conferences, however, and to a considerable extent the operational commands themselves were guilty of overconfidence. This was certainly true of the Nagumo Force. We were so sure of our own strength that we thought we could smash the enemy Fleet singlehanded, even if the battleship groups did nothing to support us.

At the conclusion of the study conferences, Admiral Yamamoto called upon all Combined Fleet forces to devote their fullest energies to the successful prosecution of the forthcoming operations. He said in part:

"As a result of the smooth progress of the first-phase operations, we have established an invincible strategic position. This position, however, cannot be maintained if we go on the defensive. In order to secure it tenaciously, we must keep on striking offensively at the enemy's weak points one after another. This will be the central aim of our second-phase operations."

3. BATTLE OF THE CORAL SEA[1]

Even while the Midway operation was being studied and rehearsed, developments which were to influence it profoundly were taking place nearly 3,000 miles away on the northeastern approaches to Australia. There, Vice Admiral Shigeyoshi Inouye's Fourth Fleet had launched the long-planned invasion moves toward Tulagi in the Solomons and Port Moresby in southeastern New Guinea, which on 7 May precipitated the Battle of the Coral Sea.

As originally planned in January, the Tulagi and Port Moresby invasions were to have been carried out shortly after the occupation of Lae and Salamaua in early March. However, the appearance in the southeast area of an American naval force estimated to consist of two fleet carriers, four heavy cruisers, four light cruisers, and more than a dozen destroyers had led Combined Fleet to defer the operation until Fourth Fleet could be reinforced with a carrier division from the Nagumo Force and some additional heavy cruisers. These reinforcements, consisting mainly of Carrier Division 5 (ZUIKAKU, SHOKAKU) and Cruiser Division 5 (MYOKO, HAGURO), finally reached Fourth Fleet's home base at Truk just before the end of April. In addition, Combined Fleet released the light carrier SHOHO to Fourth Fleet command for the operations.

Since both Carrier Division 5 and Cruiser Division 5 were scheduled to take part in the later Midway operation, Vice Admiral Inouye lost no time in getting started. His operational plan called for the seizure of Tulagi on 3 May, with the main assault on Port Moresby to be carried out a week later. The invasion convoys, staging out of Rabaul, were to be covered by two principal surface forces—one a Close Covering Group composed of light carrier SHOHO, four heavy cruisers, and a destroyer, commanded by Rear Admiral Aritomo Goto; the

[1] *Editors' Note:* East longitude date, Zone minus 11 time.

other a Carrier Striking Force made up of ZUIKAKU and SHO-
KAKU, the two heavy cruisers of Cruiser Division 5, and six
destroyers, commanded by Vice Admiral Takeo Takagi. Under
Takagi, carrier air operations were to be commanded by Rear
Admiral Chuichi Hara, Commander Carrier Division 5. The
two forces sortied from Truk on 30 April and 1 May, respectively.

The Tulagi landing was successfully carried out on 3 May
according to plan, and the next day the Port Moresby invasion
force embarked from Rabaul in fourteen transports escorted by
one light cruiser and six destroyers. It had barely gotten under
way, however, when enemy carrier aircraft delivered a severe
attack on the Tulagi beachhead, sinking or damaging a number
of small Japanese naval craft offshore. This gave warning of the
presence of an enemy task force in the vicinity, and Vice Admiral Takagi's Carrier Striking Force, which was still some distance north of the Solomons, promptly headed south at high
speed to locate and engage the enemy. The Port Moresby
convoy, not yet in danger, continued on its way, closely covered
by Rear Admiral Goto's force.

By the morning of 6 May, the Takagi Force had skirted
around the southeastern extremity of the Solomons and entered
the Coral Sea, but it was not until the next day that it finally
made contact with the enemy. At dawn on the 7th, search planes
were launched from the carriers, and shortly thereafter one of
them radioed back that it had sighted an enemy task force, including one carrier, about 160 miles south of the Japanese position. The entire attack strength of ZUIKAKU and SHOKAKU—
a total of 78 bombers, torpedo planes and fighters—immediately took off to attack, but when they reached the reported
enemy position, they found that the "task force" actually was
only a large oiler escorted by a single destroyer. The two ships,
later identified as NEOSHO and Sims, were subjected to a fierce
attack, which sank the destroyer and left the oiler heavily

damaged and afire, with its crew abandoning ship.

Only a short while after the attack groups had taken off and headed for their objective, Rear Admiral Hara, commanding the air operations, received reports from search planes of the

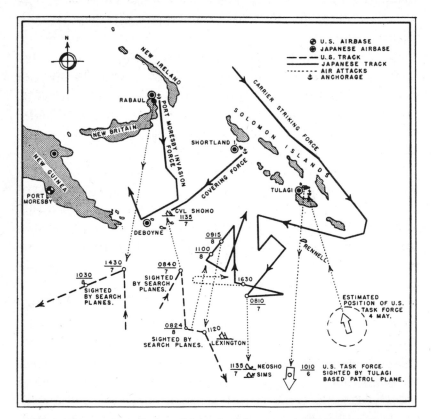

BATTLE OF THE CORAL SEA, 5-7 MAY 1942 (East Longitude Date, Zone minus 11 Time)

Goto Force strongly indicating that the earlier sighting report had been erroneous and placing the enemy carrier group to the southeast of the Louisiade Archipelago. It was too late, however, to divert the attack, and a precious opportunity to strike the first blow at the enemy carriers was lost.

The failure proved costly for the Japanese forces, for while the ZUIKAKU and SHOKAKU air units were busy attacking NEOSHO and SIMS, planes from the enemy carriers discovered a much more worthwhile target. Vice Admiral Inouye, commanding the over-all Japanese operations from Rabaul, had already ordered the Port Moresby Transport Group to retire northward until the threat from the enemy carriers was eliminated. It was executing this order, covered by Rear Admiral Goto's force when, at 1100 on the 7th, a force of nearly 100 American bombers and torpedo planes spotted the Covering Group and delivered a fierce attack. The enemy aircraft concentrated almost entirely on light carrier SHOHO, which was heavily hit and went to the bottom at 1135.

By the time the attack groups of ZUIKAKU and SHOKAKU were ready to take off again, it was late afternoon and Rear Admiral Hara felt that it would be too risky to send his full strength against the enemy carriers as the pilots would have to find their way back and land in darkness. Still he was eager to strike as quickly as possible and therefore decided to launch part of his strength for a dusk attack, using only picked crews trained in night operations. At 1630 a force of 27 bombers and torpedo planes took off and headed for the enemy's estimated position. It failed, however, to spot the carriers and, instead, had the misfortune to run into an enemy fighter patrol, losing several planes in the ensuing dogfight. The remaining planes turned back and on their way passed right over the enemy carriers without being able to attack because they had already jettisoned their bombs and torpedoes.

Before dawn the next day, 8 May, the Takagi Force again sent out float planes to look for the enemy, and at 0824 they radioed back that they had spotted the American carrier group bearing 205 degrees, 235 miles from the Japanese force. The group was reported to include two carriers and one other large unit, probably a battleship. ZUIKAKU and SHOKAKU immediately launched their full attack strength, aggregating about 70 bombers and torpedo planes. At 1120 the attack groups arrived over the target and began their assault against strong antiaircraft fire and fighter opposition.

The attack was highly effective, though not the total success that the reports of the returning fliers led Admirals Takagi and Hara to believe. According to these reports, both enemy carriers —one mistakenly identified as SARATOGA (actually LEXINGTON) and the other correctly as YORKTOWN—had been sent to the bottom, and a battleship or cruiser had been damaged. The actual results, not known to the Japanese until much later, were that LEXINGTON, though not sunk in the attack, was so heavily damaged that she had to be abandoned and finished off by torpedoes from her destroyer escort later the same day, while YORKTOWN sustained a single bomb hit which, though it caused considerable damage, did not put her out of action.

In the meantime the Takagi Force also underwent attack by the air groups of the American carriers. The enemy planes, which were on their way at the same time that Japanese planes headed for LEXINGTON and YORKTOWN, appeared over the Takagi Force at 1050 and continued attacking until 1220. ZUIKAKU managed to elude the attack by heading into a rain squall which hid her from the enemy pilots, but SHOKAKU, absorbing the full fury of the assault, sustained three direct bomb hits which rendered her incapable of continuing flight operations. Consequently SHOKAKU was ordered to withdraw, and ZUIKAKU had to recover the planes of both carriers.

The tide of battle now appeared to have veered strongly in favor of the Japanese, for despite the loss of SHOHO and damage to SHOKAKU, ZUIKAKU remained unharmed, whereas both of the American carriers were believed to have been eliminated. This seemed to present an excellent opportunity for the Takagi Force to continue the offensive and complete the enemy's destruction. At about 1700 on the 8th, however, Vice

Courtesy Shizuo Fukui

CARRIER *Shokaku*

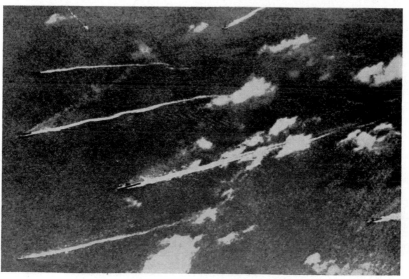

Official Japanese Navy Photo

UNITED STATES WARSHIPS AT THE BATTLE OF CORAL SEA,
8 MAY 1942. CARRIER *Lexington* IN CENTER

The Battle of the Coral Sea. Japanese Carrier *Shokaku* Immediately After a
Torpedo Hit Scored by U. S. Navy Planes

Admiral Inouye at Rabaul suddenly ordered the Striking Force to break off the action and retire, following this up a short while later with a further order postponing the Port Moresby invasion and directing the Transport Group to put back to Rabaul. The reason for the Fourth Fleet commander's decision apparently was his estimate that, although the American carrier group had been crushed, the carrier air strength remaining on the Japanese side was insufficient to protect the invasion force against land-based air assault.

When reports of Admiral Inouye's action reached Combined Fleet Headquarters late on the 8th, Admiral Yamamoto, highly displeased at Inouye's failure to exploit the advantage gained in the carrier battle of that morning, dispatched a strongly-worded order to the Fourth Fleet Commander directing that every effort be made to complete the destruction of the enemy force. Takagi was consequently ordered to head south again and reestablish contact, but two days of searching for the enemy proved fruitless, and his force finally retired from the battle area on the night of 10 May.

A tally of Japanese losses in the Battle of the Coral Sea showed light carrier SHOHO, destroyer KIKUZUKI, and three small naval units sunk, carrier SHOKAKU damaged, some 77 planes lost, and a total of 1,074 men killed or wounded. On the other hand, actual losses inflicted on the enemy, as learned after the war, were carrier LEXINGTON, oiler NEOSHO and destroyer SIMS sunk, carrier YORKTOWN damaged, 66 planes lost, and 543 killed or wounded. Thus, if the Coral Sea battle can be said to have been a Japanese victory, it was a victory only by the narrowest numerical margin, even without taking into account the thwarting of the Port Moresby invasion. Certainly, the actual outcome was a far cry from the sweeping triumph which was announced to the Japanese nation over the radio to the stirring accompaniment of the Navy March.

Rather than upset the time schedule already fixed for later

operations, Combined Fleet now decided on an indefinite post-ponement of the move against Port Moresby and ordered Carrier Division 5 and Cruiser Division 5 to return to the homeland immediately to prepare for the Midway invasion. On 17 May SHOKAKU reached Kure, having the unenvied distinction of being the most heavily damaged Japanese warship to put in at that naval base since the beginning of hostilities. The fact that hits by only three medium bombs had rendered her incapable of flight operations was a striking lesson in carrier vulnerability. Furthermore, a survey of her damages showed that at least one month would be required to complete repairs, which meant that she could not participate in the Midway operation.

Carrier Division 5 flagship ZUIKAKU, which followed SHOKAKU into port a few days later, had escaped physical damage, but because of heavy losses of flying personnel, it was soon apparent that she also would not be available for the Midway operation. Even if aircraft and air crew replacements were promptly provided, only a week now remained before the sortie of the Nagumo Force, and it would clearly be impossible to give the replacement personnel enough shipboard training to enable the carrier to function effectively in battle. Thus, the Coral Sea "victory" had far-reaching consequences for the Midway operation. The elimination of ZUIKAKU and SHOKAKU deprived the Nagumo Force of one-third of its air striking power—possibly the margin that made the difference between victory and defeat.

The unexpected exclusion of Carrier Division 5 from the Midway forces, however, did not diminish the optimism with which Combined Fleet Headquarters, or the Nagumo Force for that matter, viewed the impending operation. As the two American carriers involved in the Coral Sea battle were both believed to have been sunk, the ratio of carrier strength available for the Midway contest still appeared to be overwhelmingly in Japan's favor. The Nagumo Force, with the battle-tested carriers AKAGI, KAGA, SORYU and HIRYU still at its disposal, was fully confident of its ability to crush any enemy force that might be thrown against it. Even the Naval General Staff, which originally had opposed the Midway venture as too risky, now seemed to have little apprehension regarding the outcome.

These calculations were, of course, proven wrong by later events. YORKTOWN had not been sunk in the Coral Sea nor was she even damaged badly enough to keep her from participating in the next battle. The full story, as it became known to the Japanese after the war, showed that YORKTOWN hastened back to Pearl Harbor, where repair crews, by working around the clock for two straight days, succeeded in making her ready for sea in time to join the forces sent to forestall the Midway invasion. This achievement was in striking contrast to our own lackadaisical effort, as a result of which neither SHOKAKU nor ZUIKAKU was able to participate in the Midway operation.

4. FINAL PREPARATIONS

After the conclusion of the war games and staff conferences on board YAMATO during the first week of May, the flagship weighed anchor and proceeded from Hashirajima to Kure in order to load supplies and effect minor repairs. The harbor of the naval base seethed with tremendous activity. Ships kept arriving and departing in a never-ending procession, and small craft plied incessantly between the shore and warships moored in the harbor, shuttling supplies. Although the beginning of summer was almost at hand, RYUJO and JUNYO, the two carriers assigned to Vice Admiral Hosogaya's Northern Force, were conspicuously loading quantities of heavy winter clothing and equipment. It was easy for their crews, as well as personnel of the base, to guess that a part of the forces would be operating in Arctic waters.

On 18 May Colonel Kiyonao Ichiki, commander of the

Army detachment which was to participate in the Midway landing, went on board YAMATO with his staff to confer with Admiral Yamamoto and to be briefed on the operational plan. This virtually completed the briefing of all the participating forces, and on the 19th YAMATO returned to Hashirajima to make final sortie preparations. The next day Admiral Yamamoto issued an order which finally fixed the tactical grouping of the fleet forces as already outlined in the preceding chapter. The order also contained an estimate of enemy strength in the Midway, Hawaii, and Aleutians areas as follows:

> *Midway Area:* About 24 patrol flying boats, 12 Army bombers and 20 fighters. Several patrol boats stationed around Midway, and a number of submarines evidently operating to the west of the island.[2]
>
> *Hawaii Area:* About 60 patrol flying boats, 100 Army bombers and 200 fighters. Naval combat strength—2 or 3 carriers, 2 or 3 escort carriers, 4 or 5 heavy cruisers, 3 or 4 light cruisers, about 30 destroyers and 25 submarines.
>
> *Aleutians Area:* No enemy naval and air strength or important military installations except at Dutch Harbor.

Supplementing the above estimate, it was judged on the basis of Japanese intelligence that Midway was defended by a force of about 750 Marines abundantly equipped with coastal defense guns and antiaircraft artillery. The air strength based on the island, it was estimated, could rapidly be reinforced from Hawaii and might possibly be doubled as soon as the Japanese intention to attack became known. Intelligence indicated that the enemy's flying boats were conducting regular day and night patrols over a semicircular arc westward of Midway to a distance of 600 miles.

The Combined Fleet estimate of enemy carrier strength in the Hawaiian Islands was based principally on the calculation that HORNET and ENTERPRISE, which were known to have been

---

[2] *Editors' Note:* Actual American defensive strength in the Midway area is described in Chapter 8, Section 1: American Situation and Preparations.

involved in the Tokyo raid of 18 April, were now back at Pearl
Harbor. A possible third carrier was added to allow for the
eventuality that one of the two carriers believed sunk in the
Battle of the Coral Sea might only have been damaged and
have succeeded in making it back to Hawaii, or that WASP,
whose whereabouts was not known, might be in the Hawaiian
area. RANGER was definitely believed to be operating in the
Atlantic. LEXINGTON (actually SARATOGA) was believed to have
been sunk by a Japanese submarine near Hawaii in January
1942, but there were subsequent reports that she had gotten
back to the United States West Coast and was undergoing
repairs. That was all the enemy's carrier strength except for
newly-built escort carriers, a few of which were considered
likely to be at Hawaii. These, however, because of their inferior
speed, were not regarded as augmenting the enemy's effective
strength for fleet combat.

Despite the 20 May estimate, there were some indications
that the enemy might be caught with even fewer than the two
or three carriers which Combined Fleet anticipated might be
available in the Hawaiian area to oppose the Japanese invasion
of Midway. On 18 May a patrol plane of the South Seas Force
had spotted an enemy task force with two carriers to the east of
the Solomons, which suggested that HORNET and ENTERPRISE
had again sortied from Pearl Harbor to operate in the southwest
Pacific. This seemed to be confirmed by subsequent radio intelligence indicating the presence of an enemy carrier force to
the south of the Solomons and also by a reported raid on Tulagi
by enemy carrier planes a short while later.[3] Should this enemy
force continue operating in the Solomons area, it appeared

---

[3] *Editors' Note:* The carriers sighted by the Japanese patrol plane east of the
Solomons on 18 May were, indeed, ENTERPRISE and HORNET, which had sped out
from Pearl Harbor in the hope of assisting Task Force 17 in the Coral Sea
operations. By this time, however, the two carriers and their escorts had already
turned back under urgent orders to return to Pearl Harbor, and the subsequent
Japanese conjectures that this force might still be operating in the vicinity of the
Solomons were without foundation.

likely that the Americans would have virtually no carrier strength available at Hawaii to throw against the Midway invasion force. The invasion would then be easy, but the hope of luring the enemy fleet into decisive battle would be gone.

May 20th also saw the departure from Yokosuka and Kure of the Transport Group carrying the Army and Navy landing forces for Midway. The transports headed for the assembly point at Saipan, where they arrived on 24 May, Rear Admiral Takeo Kurita's Support Force of heavy cruisers simultaneously arriving at nearby Guam in preparation for covering the advance of the invasion convoy on Midway. Various units of Vice Admiral Hosogaya's Northern Force likewise began moving out of the western Inland Sea after the 20th, heading for Ominato, the staging point for the Aleutians invasion. Slowly the massive battle forces were getting into motion.

Forces which were to proceed direct from the Inland Sea to the battle area still had a week to wait. Admiral Yamamoto decided not to let this time go to waste, and on 21 May the Main Force, the Kondo Force, and Vice Admiral Nagumo's First Carrier Striking Force went out through Bungo Strait into the open sea and for two days engaged in fleet maneuvers —the biggest undertaken since before the outbreak of war, and the last ever to be staged in the open sea by the Imperial Navy.

On 25 May, back in Hashirajima Anchorage, the Midway and Aleutians operations were once more rehearsed in tabletop maneuvers held on board YAMATO. The assembled commanders and staff officers also listened to a detailed report of the Coral Sea battle given by Vice Admiral Takagi, who had commanded the Japanese force in that engagement. Now everything was ready for the big sortie. Force commanders and staff officers assembled at Hashirajima gathered on board YAMATO and joined Admiral Yamamoto in toasting the success of the forthcoming operation with cups of *sake* bestowed by his Majesty the Emperor.

CHAPTER 7

Heading for Battle

1. SORTIE OF FORCES

The stage was now set for the launching of the Midway Operation. At each of the three take-off points—Ominato on northern Honshu, Hashirajima in the western Inland Sea, and Saipan and Guam in the Marianas—the forces were poised and ready to head for their objectives.

Rear Admiral Kakuji Kakuta's Second Carrier Striking Force, assigned to the Aleutians prong of the offensive, was the first to sortie. Flying his flag in light carrier RYUJO, Kakuta took his force out of Ominato harbor at noon on 26 May, transited Tsugaru Strait and set an easterly course across the northern Pacific. Late the same night the force encountered a dense and seemingly endless fog, which made it difficult to keep formation, since not one of the ships was equipped with radar and strict radio silence was in force. Even so, the fog was not entirely unwelcome, for it lessened the danger of discovery by enemy submarines known to be lurking in the waters east of Hokkaido. For this the officers and men were grateful, but at the same time they fervently hoped that the fog would be gone by 4 June, when the carriers were to launch their strike against Dutch Harbor.

The following morning, 27 May, saw the departure of the Nagumo Force from Hashirajima Anchorage. As related in the opening chapter, the 21 ships of the Force threaded their way through Bungo Strait at about noon and by nightfall were well into the Pacific, forging southeastward in circular cruising disposition. There was no indication that we had been discovered by enemy submarines, and I turned in for the night with a comfortable feeling that all was going well. My own luck, however, was not to hold.

I had barely dropped off to sleep when I was suddenly awakened by sharp abdominal pains. Commander Tamai, AKAGI's Chief Surgeon, was quickly summoned, and after a careful examination he announced that it was appendicitis and he would have to operate immediately. This was a hard blow, for it meant that I would be a helpless spectator of the exciting events about to begin. I asked Tamai if he couldn't possibly treat me so that I could keep going for another ten days without an operation, but he was adamant. Commander Genda joined in urging me to follow the surgeon's advice. The appendectomy was performed that night as AKAGI sped on her way, and I awoke early the next afternoon in the ship's sick bay to find the sharp pain of the night before reduced to a dull ache, the aftermath of Tamai's surgery. A corpsman who came in to see how I was getting on told me that our noon position had been 430 miles south of Tokyo, and that we were now headed east.

Meanwhile, the other forces were also sortieing according to plan. From Ominato, Vice Admiral Hosogaya's Northern Force Main Body and the Attu and Kiska Invasion Forces departed on the 28th. Far to the south, the transports carrying the Midway landing forces, escorted by Rear Admiral Tanaka's light cruiser flagship, JINTSU, and 12 destroyers, together with seaplane carrier CHITOSE, tender KAMIKAWA MARU and other units, sortied from Saipan during that same evening. In order to deceive any enemy submarines that might be lurking in the vicinity, the invasion convoy first took a westerly course and skirted around to the south of Tinian before heading eastward. Rear Admiral Kurita's Support Group of heavy cruisers sortied almost simultaneously from Guam and took a parallel course about 40 miles to the southwest of the invasion convoy.

Last to sortie were the Main Body of the Midway Invasion

PHASES OF ATTACK ON *Shokaku* DURING THE
BATTLE OF THE CORAL SEA

LOADING TRANSPORT FROM TUG FOR MIDWAY OPERATION

Force under Vice Admiral Kondo and the Main Force under direct command of Admiral Yamamoto. Kondo's ships began moving out of Hashirajima during the early morning of 29 May, light cruiser YURA and seven destroyers of Destroyer Squadron 4 leading the way, followed by Cruiser Divisions 4 (ATAGO, CHOKAI) and 5 (MYOKO, HAGURO), Battleship Division 3 less its 2nd Section (HIEI, KONGO), light carrier ZUIHO and one destroyer. Admiral Kondo flew his flag in heavy cruiser ATAGO. After passing through Bungo Strait, the Force headed eastward.

Admiral Yamamoto's Main Force of 32 ships sortied on the heels of the Kondo Force. Light cruiser SENDAI and 20 destroyers under Commander Destroyer Squadron 3, Rear Admiral Shintaro Hashimoto, were in the van, followed by Cruiser Division 9 (light cruisers KITAKAMI and OI) under Rear Admiral Fukuji Kishi, Battleship Division 1 (YAMATO, NAGATO, MUTSU) directly under Admiral Yamamoto, and Battleship Division 2 (ISE, HYUGA, FUSO, YAMASHIRO) under Vice Admiral Takasu. Light carrier HOSHO and one destroyer brought up the rear.

It was five months since the battleship group had last sortied from home waters. Throughout the first-phase operations in the southern area, it had remained in the Inland Sea training rigorously for what it hoped would be a major role in the anticipated decisive battle against the American Fleet. The officers and men of the big battlewagons were still confident that their massive firepower would win the battle when it came. Now, at last, it looked as if they were going to have their chance to prove it, and the morale of the crews was high. The strength of the Force was greater than ever by reason of the addition of YAMATO, armed with the heaviest guns afloat, now making her maiden sortie.

As the Main Force headed for Bungo Strait, destroyers patrolling outside the strait suddenly reported sighting two

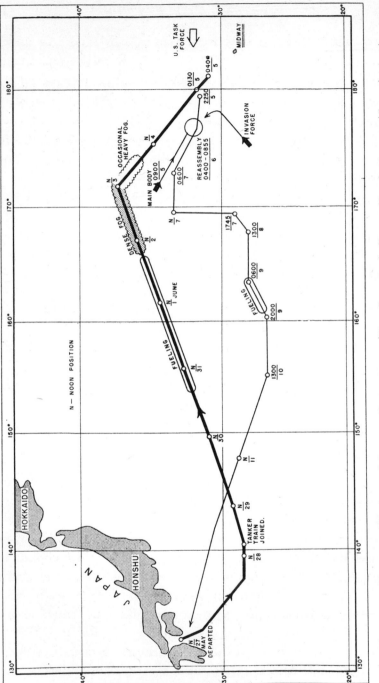

TRACK OF NAGUMO FORCE IN MIDWAY OPERATION (East Longitude Dates, Zone minus 9 (Japan) time)

enemy submarines. Radio intelligence had also reported a total
of six enemy submarines operating in waters close to the homeland, and four more operating to the northeast of Wake Island.
Antisubmarine operations by surface units and planes from Kure
Naval Base were immediately intensified, and all ships of the
Kondo and Yamamoto forces were ordered to proceed under
strict antisubmarine alert. Both forces passed through the
danger area happily without mishap.

After reaching the open sea, the Main Force shifted its
cruising disposition, the battleships forming two parallel
columns with YAMATO, NAGATO and MUTSU on the right and
ISE, HYUGA, FUSO and YAMASHIRO on the left. Between the
two columns light carrier HOSHO took position and engaged
in launching and recovering antisubmarine patrol planes. Light
cruiser SENDAI and 20 destroyers formed a circular screen
around the battleship group at a distance of 1,500 meters. Light
cruisers KITAKAMI and OI were stationed on the rear flanks,
10,000 meters apart, to guard against tracking enemy submarines. The force proceeded southeast at a speed of 18 knots,
zigzagging at intervals of five to ten minutes.

2. *ADMIRAL NAGUMO*

As I lay in AKAGI's sick bay convalescing from the operation
I had undergone on the night of our sortie, my thoughts naturally centered on the momentous operation in which our Fleet
was engaged. I thought especially of the heavy burden of responsibility resting on the shoulders of our own commander,
Admiral Nagumo, whose force was spearheading the attack.
Would he measure up to this responsibility?

My first acquaintance with Admiral Nagumo dated back to
1933. I was then a Lieutenant and Chief Flying Officer of
heavy cruiser MAYA, assigned to Cruiser Division 4, Second
Fleet. Besides MAYA, the division comprised flagship CHOKAI,

TAKAO, and ATAGO, Japan's newest heavy cruisers. Nagumo, then a captain, was Commanding Officer of TAKAO.

My duties brought me into frequent contact with Captain Nagumo, a capable, intelligent and energetic officer who was rated high among the many able captains in the Fleet. He belonged to what Navy officers called the "Red Brick Group." This meant that he had already served a tour of duty in the Navy Ministry, the curious designation coming from the fact that the Navy Ministry building was made of red brick. He had also served in the Naval General Staff, on the staff of Combined Fleet, and as an instructor at the Naval War College. His command of a heavy cruiser followed the normal course for promotion to flag rank. He would get a battleship the following year and eventually would become a Fleet Commander.

In the Combined Fleet tactical organization prevailing at that time, the Second Fleet constituted the Advance Force. Consequently, the emphasis in our training was primarily on torpedo attacks and night engagements. Captain Nagumo, an expert in torpedo warfare, was the right man in the right place. As a junior officer who job was simply to fly planes, I looked up to him with a feeling of awe and admiration because of the outstanding way he discharged his exacting duties. Every aspect of his leadership impressed me. His speeches at maneuver conferences were always logical and enlightening, and one could not help respecting his extraordinary ability. Candid, yet openhearted and considerate, he was always willing to assist the younger officers. We held him in high esteem and placed complete confidence in him.

At this time sentiment in favor of abrogating the Washington Naval Limitation Treaty was rapidly mounting in the Navy. In our eyes, the attitude of the central authorities seemed weak-kneed, and Captain Nagumo was leading an active movement against it. He busily visited the commanding officers of other ships and urged them to join in pressing for early abrogation of the treaty. As a result of his efforts, a recommendation was drafted and, after being signed by many officers, was forwarded to the central authorities through Fleet Headquarters as representing the opinion of the Fleet. This particularly pleased the young officers who always favored a firm policy, whatever it might be. My impressions of Captain Nagumo at that time convinced me that he would be a great naval leader.

Our paths did not cross again until 1941, by which time Nagumo had risen to Vice Admiral in command of First Air Fleet. I was assigned as a wing leader on carrier AKAGI. In the intervening years Nagumo's reputation had continued to rise, especially during his command of Destroyer Squadron 1 as a Rear Admiral. Serving under him again revived my memories of seven years earlier, and I was happy to be a member of his command.

It was not long, however, before I noted that Nagumo had changed, and I began to feel dissatisfied with his apparent conservatism and passiveness. It might have been because he was now commanding an air arm, which was not his specialty. Personally he was as warmhearted and sympathetic as ever, but his once-vigorous fighting spirit seemed to be gone, and with it his stature as an outstanding naval leader. Instead he seemed rather average, and I was suddenly aware of his increased age.

In directing operations he no longer seemed to take the initiative, and when plans were being developed, he most often merely approved the recommendations of his staff. Commander Genda, his Operations Officer, once summed up the situation to me in these words:

"Whenever I draft a plan, it is approved almost without consideration. This might appear to make my job easier, but it doesn't. On the contrary, it is disquieting to see my own plans approved without any check from above, and then issued as formal orders. I am self-confident, but not so self-confident that

I don't realize that anyone can make mistakes. Often I am puzzled over how to resolve an important problem. When I consider that a stroke of my pen might sway the destiny of the nation, it almost paralyzes me with fear.

"If I were serving under a commander like Admiral Onishi or Admiral Yamaguchi, my plans would be thoroughly studied from every possible angle and returned to me with comments and opinions. I would then feel more sure and more free to propose ideas that might be extreme."

I understood exactly what Genda meant and was in complete sympathy with him. Unfortunately, such passiveness was not peculiar to Nagumo alone. It was a common failing in the Japanese Navy. Fleet commanders generally were inclined to leave all details to their staffs and content themselves with controlling only the broad outline of affairs. Thus, the personality of the commander was rarely reflected in the execution of operations. This tendency to rely excessively on the staff was promoted by the fact that, under the Japanese Navy system, officers whose seniority put them in line for a fleet command were often given one for which their special qualifications did not suit them. The appointment of Nagumo, whose specialty was torpedo warfare, to command the First Air Fleet was an example. A commander's shortcomings in special fields were supposed to be compensated for by the specialists on his staff. The result was that the influence of the staff officers naturally became very great.

This did not mean, however, that staff officers trespassed on the authority of their superiors. Final responsibility for an operation always rested with the commander, and every action was presumed to have been taken by his decision. Indeed, Nagumo, passive though he was, did not always leave everything to his subordinates. There were occasions when he disregarded their advice and chose his own course of action.

3. DEVELOPMENTS, 30-31 MAY

The end of 29 May found the various Japanese forces forging ahead toward their objectives without any hitch other than the fog still plaguing the Kakuta Force. On the 30th, however, the weather also began to deteriorate over that part of the Central Pacific now being traversed by the Yamamoto and Kondo Forces. In the afternoon the Yamamoto Force encountered rain and increasingly strong winds which caused the destroyers and cruisers to ship occasional seas over their bows, making navigation difficult. The formation cut its speed to 14 knots, and zigzagging was discontinued.

It was not only the weather that was ominous. YAMATO's radio crew, which was keeping a close watch on enemy communications traffic, intercepted a long urgent message sent by an enemy submarine from a position directly ahead of the Japanese Transport Group. The message was addressed to Midway. It was in code, and we could not decipher it, but it suggested the possibility that the Transport Group had been discovered. If so, it would be logical for the enemy to surmise that the transports were almost certainly heading for Midway to attempt an invasion, since so large a convoy sailing east-northeast from Saipan could hardly be taken as merely a supply force going to Wake Island. Admiral Yamamoto's staff officers, however, were not greatly concerned. They nonchalantly took the view that if the enemy had guessed our purpose and now sent his fleet out to oppose the invasion, the primary Japanese objective of drawing out the enemy forces to be destroyed in decisive battle would be achieved.

Bad weather continued in the central Pacific on 31 May. Not only the Yamamoto and Kondo Forces, but also Vice Admiral Nagumo's carriers, which were a few hundred miles farther east, encountered strong winds and occasional rain. Meanwhile, YAMATO's radio intelligence unit observed further signs of

enemy activity, especially of aircraft and submarines, in both the
Hawaii and Aleutians vicinities. Admiral Yamamoto and his
staff surmised that the activity around Hawaii might presage
a sortie by an enemy task force, and they waited eagerly for
reports of the flying boat reconnaissance which was to have been
carried out over Hawaii on this date.

The two Type-2 flying boats assigned to this mission, designated the second Operation "K," had duly moved up to Wotje
and were scheduled to take off at 2400 May 30 (Tokyo time)
to reach French Frigate Shoals by 1430 (1730 local time)
shortly before sunset, refuel there from submarines and take
off within an hour and a half for Hawaii. If all went well, they
would arrive over Hawaii at 2045 (0115 May 31, local time).
After completing their reconnaissance, they would fly non-stop
back to Wotje, reaching there about 0920 (Tokyo time) on
1 June. Vice Admiral Komatsu, Commander Submarine Force,
had assigned six submarines to the operation. Three of them
were to refuel the flying boats at French Frigate Shoals. Another was to take station on a line between Wotje and French
Frigate Shoals, about 550 miles from the latter, to serve as a
radio picket ship. The fifth was to lie off Keahole Point, on
the island of Hawaii, as a rescue boat in case of mishap, and the
sixth was to be stationed 80 miles southwest of Oahu for
patrol and weather observation.

The carefully laid plan, however, had already gone awry.
On 30 May I-123, one of the fueling subs, reached French
Frigate Shoals and, to its dismay, found two enemy ships lying
at anchor.[1] It urgently radioed this information back to Kwaje-
lein, adding that there appeared to be little prospect of carrying out the refueling operation at the Shoals as planned. Vice
Admiral Goto, 24th Air Flotilla commander at Kwajalein,
who was responsible for directing the second Operation "K,"

---

[1] *Editors' Note:* These were probably seaplane tenders THORNTON and BALLARD,
which had been stationed at French Frigate Shoals.

accordingly ordered a 24-hour postponement, instructing I-123 to keep watching the Shoals in the hope that the enemy ships would depart.

This forlorn hope was blasted the following day when I-123 reported that she had sighted two enemy flying boats near the entrance to the Shoals. This made it apparent that the enemy was already using the Shoals as a seaplane base, and there consequently was no alternative to complete abandonment of Operation "K."

These disappointing developments were promptly communicated to Admiral Yamamoto in YAMATO. The failure of Operation "K" meant that there was no way of ascertaining what enemy strength actually was present at Pearl Harbor. Nevertheless, Combined Fleet Headquarters still hoped that, if an enemy force did sortie from that base to oppose the Midway invasion, the submarine cordons scheduled to be established by Vice Admiral Komatsu's command between Hawaii and Midway by 2 June would suffice to provide advance warning as well as knowledge of the enemy's strength.

4. DEVELOPMENTS, 1-2 JUNE

The first of June found the Yamamoto Force still surrounded by dark, forbidding weather, although the rain had ceased. Low-lying clouds made visibility so poor that it was barely possible from YAMATO's bridge to make out the phantom shapes of the destroyer screen 1,500 meters away.

It was now time for the Main Force to rendezvous with its tanker train and refuel. The oilers were not found at the prearranged rendezvous point, however, and HOSHO launched planes to look for them. The search proved unsuccessful because of poor visibility, but at this point the tanker train radioed its position to YAMATO, making it possible to effect a rendezvous. At the same time, because radio silence had been broken, it had to be assumed that the enemy was now aware of the position of the Main Force.

Evidence that the enemy had already discovered or, at the very least, strongly suspected the Japanese advance toward Midway mounted sharply during the day. Radio intelligence disclosed a marked intensification of communications traffic out of Hawaii, and 72 out of 180 intercepted messages were "urgent," indicating an unusually tense situation. A chance encounter 500 miles north-northeast of Wotje between a Japanese patrol plane from that island and an American flying boat, which exchanged brief machine-gun bursts, also showed that the enemy had extended his Midway-based air patrols out to a radius of 700 miles. There were still further reports to the effect that enemy submarines had been sighted about 500 miles northeast and north-northeast of Wake Island, which almost certainly indicated the existence of an American submarine patrol line some 600 miles southwest of Midway.

By this time the Midway transport convoy had reached a point about 1,000 miles to the west of Midway and was proceeding on a northeast course. Advancing at a rate of 240 miles in 24 hours, the convoy would enter the 700-mile patrol radius of American planes from Midway on 3 June, two days before the date set for the preinvasion air strike on the island by the Nagumo Force. It looked as if the transports were advancing too fast for their own safety.

Cloudy weather, with occasional rain, persisted in the vicinity of the Yamamoto Force on 2 June. Fueling operations, which had started the preceding day after the delayed rendezvous with the tankers, were resumed in the morning but had to be discontinued again when visibility became so poor that the ships could no longer maneuver safely.

Still another hitch now developed in the operation plan. Owing to overhaul delays which had postponed their departure from the homeland, the submarines of Squadron 5 assigned to the "B" cordon line scheduled to be established on 2 June to the northwest of Hawaii failed to reach their assigned positions. Boats of Submarine Squadron 3 assigned to the "A" cordon line to the west of Hawaii were also unable to reach their stations because of delays resulting from the miscarriage of Operation "K." Actually it was not until 4 June that the submarines arrived on station.

With the submarine cordons not yet established, Admiral Yamamoto and his staff remained completely in the dark regarding enemy task force activities. During 2 June, however, submarine I-168, reconnoitering the Midway area, sent in a few bits of information regarding the situation there. The report stated that no ships had been observed other than a picket ship south of Sand Island; that the enemy appeared to be flying intensive air patrols to the southwest, probably to a distance of 600 miles; that a strict alert seemed to be in force, with numerous aircraft on defensive patrol day and night; and that many construction cranes were visible on the island, suggesting that installations were being expanded. This turned out to be the only significant reconnaissance report sent in by a submarine during the Midway operation, despite the great reliance placed on them by Combined Fleet Headquarters.

During the 2nd the Nagumo Force, cruising some 600 miles ahead of the Yamamoto Force, entered an area enveloped in thick mist. Clouds hovered low over the ocean, and light rain began to fall. Fog seemed likely to follow. Already visibility was so restricted that neighboring ships in the formation could scarcely see each other.

Vice Admiral Nagumo in flagship AKAGI was as much in the dark about enemy fleet movements and intentions as Combined Fleet Headquarters. Indeed, because of AKAGI's limited radio-receiving capacity, coupled with the radio silence being observed by the advancing Japanese forces, he lacked much of the information which had been received by Admiral Yamamoto in the Fleet flagship and which strongly suggested that the enemy was already aware or highly suspicious of a Japanese advance toward Midway and was preparing to counter it. This was precisely the situation which Rear Admiral Kusaka, Nagumo Force Chief of Staff, had feared might develop. Prior to the sortie, he had repeatedly requested that YAMATO relay all important radio intelligence information to AKAGI, but it was apparent that Admiral Yamamoto and his staff still hoped that surprise had not been lost and felt it advisable to continue radio silence.

Thus, as 2 June ended, the Japanese forces were steadily approaching their objectives through adverse weather. Thus far there was no certain indication that any of them had actually been detected by the enemy, and every man from Commander in Chief Combined Fleet on down hoped that the precious advantage of surprise was still in Japanese hands.

5. DEVELOPMENTS—3 JUNE

By dawn on 3 June the mist which the Nagumo Force had encountered the previous afternoon had become a heavy blanket of fog. Steaming at fog navigation quarters, adjoining ships in the formation were often unable to see each other across their scant 600-yard intervals. Powerful searchlights were turned on, but they scarcely showed through the gloom.

The task of maintaining zigzag courses through this endless veil, with only momentary and infrequent glimpses of consorting ships, was arduous and nerve-wracking. Yet it had to be done, for we were entering waters patrolled by enemy submarines. While the fog was advantageous in keeping us hidden from prying scout planes, this benefit was canceled by the increased hazards of navigation. Moreover, the fog would not hamper the enemy's radar-equipped submarines, yet it prevented us from launching antisubmarine patrol planes. To cope

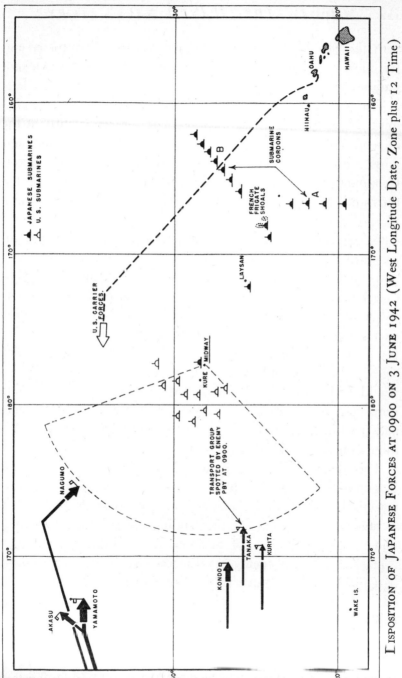

Disposition of Japanese Forces at 0900 on 3 June 1942 (West Longitude Date, Zone plus 12 Time)

with these and other problems that beset us, all ships were at full alert and double watches were posted at submarine lookout stations.

The starboard side of AKAGI's bridge was occupied by Admiral Nagumo and his entire staff. They stared silently at the impenetrable curtain surrounding the ship, and each face was tense with anxiety. Captain Aoki and his Navigation Officer, Commander Miura, on the other side of the bridge, devoted their entire energies to keeping the ship on course and maintaining position in the formation. From time to time they leaned out of the window in an effort to peer through the all-encompassing fog.

A change in course was scheduled for 1030, and it had to be executed if our timetable was to be carried out. Yet, prior to execution of such a course change in heavy fog, confirmation would have to be communicated to all ships in the formation lest some stray and become lost. With visibility so limited, flag signals obviously could not be employed, and even searchlights would be ineffective to transmit the required orders. Nothing remained but to use radio, which was sure to reveal our presence and position to the enemy—a matter of deep concern to Admiral Nagumo and his staff.

This distressing situation served to bring out the fact that Nagumo had been assigned two tactical missions which were essentially incompatible. The assignment to attack Midway on 5 June in preparation for the landing operation put his force under rigid limitations of movement. The other mission—to contact and destroy enemy naval forces—required that Nagumo be entirely free to move as the situation required, and it also made it absolutely essential to keep our whereabouts secret while searching for the enemy.

A decision obviously had to be made as to which of these missions should be given precedence. Nagumo's staff had pondered this problem hypothetically for a long time, but now the Task Force Commander faced a situation requiring a definitive choice. And still there was not a scrap of information about enemy naval forces. In this critical situation the senior member of the staff, Captain Oishi, was the first to speak up.

"The Combined Fleet operation order gives first priority to the destruction of enemy forces. Cooperation with the landing operation is secondary. But the same order specifically calls for our air attack on Midway Island on 5 June. This means that the air attack must be carried out exactly as scheduled, provided that no enemy task forces arc located by the time we are ready to launch.

"If we do not neutralize the Midway-based air forces as planned, our landing operations two days later will be strongly opposed and the entire invasion schedule will be upset."

With his usual directness Admiral Nagumo voiced the question in everyone's mind, "But where is the enemy fleet?"

In answer Oishi continued, "We know nothing of the enemy's whereabouts because we failed to reconnoiter Pearl Harbor. But if his forces are now in Pearl Harbor, we shall have plenty of time to prepare to meet them should they sortie following our strike at Midway. They will have over 1,100 miles to cover.

"Even if they are already aware of our movements and have sortied to meet us, they cannot be far out from base at this moment and certainly can't be near us. I think, therefore, that the first thing for us to do is to carry out the scheduled raid on Midway."

At this, Chief of Staff Kusaka turned to the Intelligence Officer and asked if radio intercepts had given any indication of enemy movements. Informed that nothing had been picked up, Kusaka asked if any information had been received from Combined Fleet flagship YAMATO. Receiving another negative response, he addressed a suggestion to Admiral Nagumo. "Since we must maintain the schedule at all cost, would you

approve the use of our low-powered, inter-fleet radio for sending the order to change course?"

The Commander assented to this as the only feasible solution, and the order was sent accordingly by medium-wave
transmitter. A reduced-power transmission would reach out to
the fringe of our force and, it was hoped, not farther. This
method was not entirely safe, but it had worked on occasion in
the past, thanks to enemy carelessness. In this case, however,
the message was received clearly even by YAMATO, which was
600 miles to the rear. Inasmuch as an enemy task force was
then only a few hundred miles distant—a fact of which we were
totally unaware—it was highly probable that it, too, intercepted this signal.[2]

From the first, the planners of the Midway operation calculated that the enemy naval forces would be lured out by the
strike on Midway Island and not before. We had not the slightest idea that the enemy had already sortied, much less that a
powerful enemy force was lying in wait, ready to pounce upon
us at any moment.

Dense fog still hung over the Nagumo Force throughout
the afternoon and on into the night. In contrast to the tenseness
prevailing on AKAGI's bridge, her wardroom hummed with the
lusty chatter and laughter of carefree flyers whose only job
was to jump into their planes and roar off at a moment's notice.
Everything was ready for the scheduled air raid two days hence,
and no flight missions had been ordered because of the adverse
weather. The pilots consequently had nothing to do and passed
their time playing cards.

Meanwhile, the weather around the Yamamoto Force, 600
miles astern, improved somewhat in the afternoon, and refueling, which had been suspended on the preceding day, was resumed.

[2] *Editors' Note:* Probable, but not actual. This transmission was not picked
up by the Americans.

LIGHT CARRIER *Ryujo*

VICE ADMIRAL KAKUJI KAKUTA

The worst thing about the persistent fog was that it cloaked enemy movements in complete secrecy. As previously mentioned, the plan for a flying boat reconnaissance of Pearl Harbor on 31 May, using French Frigate Shoals as a refueling point, had been thwarted. Nor did our submarines provide any information. The sole remaining source of information was radio intelligence. As early as 30 May, such intelligence picked up by Admiral Yamamoto's flagship YAMATO had pointed to brisk enemy activity in the Hawaii area, especially of patrol planes. This strongly suggested the possibility of a sortie by an enemy force from the Hawaiian base, but Combined Fleet sent no warning whatever to Admiral Nagumo!

Admiral Nagumo and his staff were deeply chagrined when they learned after the battle that because of this radio intelligence Combined Fleet Headquarters had suspected an enemy sortie. Why did Combined Fleet not transmit this vital information to the Carrier Striking Force so that any danger of its being taken by surprise might be averted?

There were two reasons behind this unfortunate failure. Firstly, Combined Fleet Headquarters thoughtlessly believed that AKAGI, closer to the enemy than YAMATO, would naturally have obtained the same information, and that Admiral Nagumo was formulating his decisions accordingly. Secondly, they feared that radio communication between the two forces would reveal their positions to the enemy.

At any rate, Admiral Yamamoto's failure to issue necessary precautionary instructions to the forces under his command was an important cause of the Midway fiasco. He was to blame for being too much preoccupied with the idea of "radio silence." It is easy to imagine what angry and bitter emotions must have welled up in Rear Admiral Kusaka when he went on board YAMATO after the battle to report on the near annihilation of the Nagumo Force and there learned for the first time of Combined Fleet's negligence. Well might he have said, "My

God! How often I told them not to let this happen! If only they had let us know in time. . .!"

Combined Fleet Headquarters, however, was not alone to blame. The Naval General Staff back in Tokyo was also partially responsible, for it again sent a radio to Combined Fleet concerning enemy fleet activity in the Solomon Islands area. The message carried the strong implication that the movement of the Japanese forces toward Midway was not yet suspected by the enemy.

The Naval General Staff had originally opposed the Midway operation, but once having given its approval, it was responsible for the whole operation even more than was Combined Fleet Headquarters. With the decisive battle only a few days off, it was engaged in gathering all available intelligence regarding enemy activity. What particularly attracted the attention of the intelligence staff was indications that an American carrier task force still was operating in the Solomons area. If this were true, as the Naval General Staff believed, it constituted powerful evidence that the enemy did not yet suspect our intention, for if he did, he would obviously have called all his scarce remaining carriers back from the Southwest Pacific. Even after intercepting a number of "Urgent" calls from American radios in the Hawaii-Midway area, the Naval General Staff still stuck fast to its first conclusion. This was perhaps due to the inherent Japanese tendency toward wishful thinking, which permeated our actions throughout the war.

The storm of battle was about to break, and for the first time in six months, Fate did not seem to be smiling upon us. No change, however, was made in the operational plan. All forces plunged onward through the boundless fog like stagecoach horses driven blindly forward by a cracking whip.

CHAPTER 8

Gathering Storm

1. AMERICAN SITUATION AND
PREPARATIONS[1]

If Admiral Yamamoto and his staff were vaguely disturbed by
the persistent bad weather and by lack of information concerning the doings of the enemy, they would have been truly dismayed had they known the actual enemy situation. Post-war
American accounts make it clear that the United States Pacific
Fleet knew of the Japanese plan to invade Midway even before
our forces had sortied from home waters. As a result of some
amazing achievements by American intelligence, the enemy had
succeeded in breaking the principal code then in use by the
Japanese Navy. In this way the enemy was able to learn of
our intentions almost as quickly as we had determined them
ourselves.

In early May the enemy knew that another major operation
was being planned by the Japanese Fleet, to be carried out by
the end of that month or early in June. The precise objective
of this operation was not known at first, but by the middle of
May the enemy had not only learned that the Japanese target
was Midway but also had ascertained with considerable accuracy the makeup of forces to be employed. Admiral Chester
W. Nimitz, Commander in Chief U.S. Pacific Fleet, personally
visited the island in early May and took steps toward strength-
ening the garrison forces and adding to the defense facilities
and fortifications.

By early June, Midway plane strength had been augmented
by the arrival of 16 Marine Corps dive bombers, 7 Wildcat
fighters, some 30 Navy patrol flying boats, and 18 B-17s and

[1] *Editors' Note:* West longitude date, Hawaii (Zone plus 9½) time.

4 B-26s from the Army.[2] More than 2,000 garrison troops were deployed ashore, and many antiaircraft batteries were installed. A number of motor torpedo boats were also brought in to be employed for short-range coastal patrol and night attack missions. In addition, three submarine patrol arcs were set up at distances of 100, 150, and 200 miles from Midway, with a total of 20 submarines on stations by 4 June.

The United States Pacific Fleet was determined to oppose the invasion of Midway with all the strength that it could muster. On this point the calculations of Combined Fleet had been entirely correct. Midway was so important to the safety of Hawaii that the American Fleet could not let it be taken without a battle.

Advance knowledge of Japanese intentions was an important advantage, but nevertheless the prospects confronting the American forces were hardly promising. The Japanese forces to be committed were overwhelmingly superior, and the American carrier situation was critical. LEXINGTON had just been sunk in the Battle of the Coral Sea, and in the same engagement YORKTOWN had sustained damage which made it problematical whether she could get back to Pearl Harbor for repair in time to participate in Midway's defense. SARATOGA was still at San Diego, where she had undergone repairs for torpedo damage inflicted by a Japanese submarine on 11 January some 500 miles southwest of Oahu. This left only HORNET and ENTERPRISE which, after returning from the raid on the Japanese homeland in April, had been ordered out to the Southwest Pacific to join in the operations in the Coral Sea. Accordingly, Pacific Fleet Headquarters urgently ordered Task Force 16 (centered around HORNET and ENTERPRISE) and 17 (including damaged YORKTOWN) to return at once to Pearl Harbor. Task Force 16 arrived on 26 May (27th, Japan date), coincident with the sortie of the Nagumo Force from the Inland Sea, and Task

[2] *Editors' Note:* These additions brought the total count of planes on Midway to around 120.

Force 17 came in early in the afternoon of the following day. YORKTOWN went immediately into drydock where repair crews swung into action in a furious race against time.

After refueling and hasty battle preparations, Task Force 16, now commanded by Rear Admiral Raymond A. Spruance, sortied from Pearl Harbor on 28 May (29th in Japan), just as the Yamamoto and Kondo Forces were leaving Hashirajima, and headed for the waters northeast of Midway. In addition to HORNET and ENTERPRISE, the Task Force contained five heavy cruisers, one light cruiser, and nine destroyers. By after-noon of the next day repairs to YORKTOWN had miraculously been completed. She then fueled, took on a quickly organized air complement and sortied in the morning of 30 May with two heavy cruisers and six destroyers as Task Force 17, Rear Ad-miral Frank J. Fletcher in command. These two forces were to rendezvous on 3 June, refuel and then proceed under Fletcher's over-all command to a point northeast of Midway by the morning of the next day.

In the light of these facts, it is obvious that the second Op-eration "K," on which Combined Fleet had placed so much reliance, would have been of no avail even if it had been carried out. The flying boats, which were to arrive over Pearl Harbor at 0115 31 May, would have been too late to catch either Spruance's or Fletcher's forces. Indeed, execution of the re-connaissance as planned might have had worse results than no reconnaissance at all, for the complete absence of carrier strength at Pearl Harbor might have led Admiral Yamamoto to the mistaken conclusion that the enemy forces were still where they had last been reported, in the Southwest Pacific. This delusion would have been furthered by the fact that, on 1 June, Admiral Yamamoto received from the Naval General Staff in Tokyo a dispatch which gave its considered judgment that an enemy carrier force was still operating in the vicinity of the Solomon Islands!

And what about the submarine cordons? As far as can be

determined from the American records available to the author, it appears possible, though by no means certain, that the sortie of the American forces toward Midway might have been detected had the Japanese submarines been on station by the scheduled date of 2 June. By the 4th, however, when they actually did move into position, the enemy carrier groups were to the north of Midway, well beyond the cordon lines, waiting to strike at the flank of the unsuspecting Japanese forces.

The trouble, of course, lay in the fact that the entire Japanese invasion plan, including the provisions for the flying boat reconnaissance of Pearl Harbor and the submarine cordons, was based on the assumption that tactical surprise would be achieved and that enemy fleet reaction would not get under way until after the assault on Midway had begun. Combined Fleet planners completely failed to provide for the contingency that the enemy might somehow learn of our intentions in advance and thus be able to deploy his forces for an ambush attack.

This failure must be ascribed, more than anything else, to the arrogant over-confidence engendered by our early victories. We were accustomed to success and so sure of our superior strength that no thought was given to the possibility that things might not go exactly as we had planned.

The enemy, too, was confident despite the heavy odds in our favor. In a message to the officers and men of Task Forces 16 and 17 on the eve of their sortie from Pearl Harbor, Admiral Nimitz declared that "the coming operation will give you a chance to deal a mighty blow to the enemy." Admiral Spruance, on 3 June, also issued the following exhortation to his command:

> An attack for the purpose of capturing Midway is expected. The attacking force may be composed of all combat types, including four or five carriers, transports and train vessels. If the presence of Task Forces 16 and 17 remains unknown to the

enemy, we should be able to make surprise flank attacks on the enemy carriers from a position northeast of Midway. Further operations will be based on the result of these attacks, damage inflicted by Midway forces, and information of enemy movements. The successful conclusion of the operation now commencing will be of great value to our country. Should our carriers become separated during attacks by enemy aircraft, they will endeavor to remain within visual touch.

From the first day of June, Midway-based planes patrolled in search of the Japanese invasion forces, covering a semicircle to the west to a radius of 600 miles. Their searches were, of course, hampered by the fog through which the Japanese forces were approaching. But the Americans, whom we believed to be unknowing and unprepared, were in reality apprised of our intentions and standing by in full readiness to attack when the time was right.

The curtain was now ready to lift on a battle that would teach us a tragic lesson.

2. *JAPANESE TRANSPORTS DISCOVERED* [3]

The steady rain which had been falling on the Main Force finally let up on 3 June (Japan 4 June), but the sky still looked sullen and threatening. At 0800, according to plan, Admiral Yamamoto ordered Vice Admiral Takasu's Guard Force to break off from the Main Body and proceed to cover the Aleutians operations. Takasu was to reach a point 500 miles south of Kiska Island by 6 June, at which time Admiral Yamamoto's Main Body would be in its planned position 500 miles farther south. The plan provided for the two forces to rejoin in case of a concerted enemy counterattack in either area.

[3] *Editors' Note:* Up to this point the movements of the Japanese forces have been narrated in Japan date and time. Beginning here and extending through the account of the battle, local time and West Longitude date are used. This section is related in Midway (Zone plus 12) time.

Within an hour after the split-up of the Main Force, Admiral Yamamoto received a sudden message from Admiral Tanaka's flagship JINTSU, which was in direct escort of the Midway transport convoy, reporting that the convoy had been discovered at 0900 by an enemy search plane over 600 miles west of the target island. Tanaka reported that the enemy flying boat had clung tenaciously to the transports until heavy antiaircraft fire from JINTSU's companion warships forced it to break off the contact.

This development altered the entire aspect of the operation. A part of our forces had now been definitely discovered and, in all probability, its location had been reported. It was clear that action could be expected—and soon.

It came that afternoon when a flight of nine bomb-laden B-17s attacked the transport convoy. Fortunately no hits were scored, and the transports proceeded on their way. Everyone in the convoy breathed a deep sigh of relief. Early in the morning of the 4th, however, other enemy planes came and made a low-level attack. One released a torpedo which hit the bow of AKEBONO MARU, a tanker at the rear of the transport column. The resulting explosion was powerful enough to kill 11 men and wound 13, but it must have been a partial dud since material damage to the ship was negligible. She was slowed down only momentarily and did not lose her place in the formation.

As reports of these developments were flashed to YAMATO in rapid succession, signs of concern began to show on the faces of Yamamoto's staff. Just a short time before they had been beaming with optimism over the prospects of the forthcoming battle, but now things were looking less rosy. They had not expected that the transports would be discovered before Nagumo had launched his attack against Midway. Or perhaps it would be more accurate to say that the discovery was contrary to their hopes rather than their expectations.

The Midway operation plan had provided for the slow transports to be sent out well ahead of the Carrier Striking Force. Thus they were especially susceptible of premature discovery by the enemy. One way to avoid this danger would have been to advance the departure of the Nagumo Force by one day, so that American air strength at Midway could be neutralized before the convoy came within range of the island's search planes. Combined Fleet planners had actually considered this modification and proposed it to Admiral Nagumo. But he had counterproposed that the departure of the transports be delayed one day instead. Admiral Yamamoto rejected this suggestion because the landing had been planned for the last favorable day of the lunar phase and could not be postponed. Hence, with some misgivings, the original plan was adhered to.

3. ACTION TO THE NORTH, 3 JUNE 1942 [4]

By the time that detection of the Midway transport convoy had foreshadowed the opening of battle to the south, the Japanese diversionary thrust against the Aleutians was already under way.

Rear Admiral Kakuta's Second Carrier Striking Force, spearheading the northern thrust, reached its scheduled launching position for the strike on Dutch Harbor in the very early hours of 3 June. Sunrise was at 0258, and all preparations to take off were completed 45 minutes earlier to take advantage of the long northern twilight. But the sky, to the disappointment of the crews, did not show first light as expected.

On the bridge of flagship Ryujo, Captain Tadao Kato, in a heavy fur coat, was giving last-minute orders to the attack unit commanders. Not only was the enemy situation unknown, but the fliers, who had never operated in the northern Pacific before, did not even know what sort of weather conditions to

[4] *Editors' Note:* Aleutian (Zone plus 10) time.

expect. Rear Admiral Kakuta anxiously patted the shoulder of the staff Aviation Officer, Lieutenant Commander Masatake Okumiya, to attract his attention amidst the roar of the plane engines warming up on the flight deck, and inquired what he thought about launching the attack.

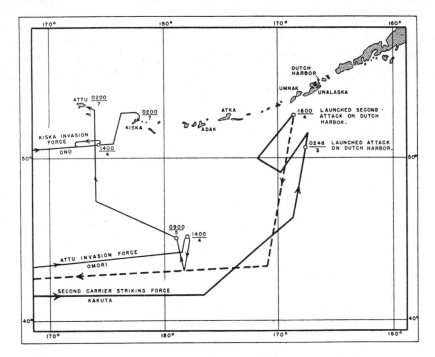

MOVEMENTS OF ALEUTIANS ATTACK FORCES, 3-7 JUNE 1942
(West Longitude Date, Zone plus 10 Time)

"Please, Sir, we will have to wait a little longer," Okumiya replied. He looked at his watch to find that it was 0228, but still the sky had not begun to brighten. Kakuta's senior staff officer, Commander Masanori Odagiri, who had been staring skyward for several minutes, commented that there seemed to be a fog. His observation proved correct and served to explain the continuing darkness.

With aircraft carrier RYUJO in the lead, the task force was approaching Dutch Harbor at 22 knots. The mercury stood at 7 degrees below zero Centigrade.

Lieutenant Commander Okumiya frowned as he thought of the handicaps under which the attack was being executed. For one thing, the fliers were provided with maps of the Dutch Harbor area copied from a chart over 30 years old. The only other guide the Japanese had was a single photograph almost as old as the map. Many shoreline portions of the target island were shown on the map by dotted lines, indicating unsurveyed places. The island was actually unknown to us even in outline. Could the pilots find such a target in bad weather? Failure to locate the targets would mean that there would also be difficulty in getting back to the carriers, and some of the planes might get lost. But this was war. The Japanese forces had come so far for the sake of victory, and there must be no lack of resolution now. Despite the fog, the attack must be launched at the first increase in visibility. Okumiya glanced at the sky with growing impatience.

At 0238 the shapes of the other ships in the formation began gradually to come into sight. The Admiral seemed anxious to order the planes off immediately, but his staff officers still remained silent. By 0243 light carrier JUNYO, 1,000 meters distant, became clearly visible and Okumiya shouted, "Sir, we can launch now!" The Admiral nodded and looked toward the Signal Officer, Lieutenant Commander Okada, who ordered, "Squadrons, take off for attack!" Blinker signals flashed from the flagship.

Planes rose methodically from the flight decks into the misty haze. From RYUJO eleven bombers and six fighters took off, from JUNYO twelve dive bombers and six fighters, all planes under command of Lieutenant Yoshio Shiga. A cloud ceiling of only 500-700 feet made formation flight impossible, so the planes headed independently for Dutch Harbor, some 180 miles to the northwest. The day had dawned, but still the sun failed to appear. One of the RYUJO bombers crashed into the icy sea while taking off, but prompt action by an escorting destroyer resulted in the miraculous rescue of the entire crew.

The attack planes were barely out of sight when enemy scouts began to fly over the Kakuta Force. A flying boat maintained close contact through the fog and dropped bombs before finally withdrawing, but there were no hits.

Lieutenant Masayuki Yamagami's group from RYUJO managed to weave through breaks in the clouds and reach Dutch Harbor despite the weather. Luckily the clouds directly over the target lay wide agape. But there were no enemy planes or ships to be seen. At 0407 the bombers attacked a radio station and oil tanks, while fighters strafed a flying boat moored in the water. All planes got back to the carrier except one fighter, which was hit while strafing and made a forced landing on the southern shore of Aktan Island, 20 miles northeast of Dutch Harbor. The pilot's neck was broken in the landing. Five weeks later an American Navy search party found the plane, which was only superficially damaged.

JUNYO's planes, led by Lieutenant Shiga, encountered an enemy flying boat on their way to the target. The escorting fighters shot it down, but the resultant delay, coupled with the bad weather, kept Shiga's group from reaching Dutch Harbor, and it returned without attacking any land targets.

The opening attacks thus fell short of anticipated results. Aerial photographs taken during the attack, however, provided a real surprise. They showed Dutch Harbor to be far better equipped than had been imagined. There were modern warehouses, barracks, wharves, and fuel storage tanks, with a network of excellent connecting roads. The well-developed roadways alone bore eloquent testimony to the strategic value of these enemy installations.

On their way back from Dutch Harbor, Yamagami's planes

radioed in that they had spotted five enemy destroyers at anchor in Makushin Bay, on the northern coast of central Unalaska Island. Rear Admiral Kakuta, who was noted for his promptness in engaging any enemy that appeared, ordered an attack on the destroyers with all available planes. Not only the squadrons of the two carriers, but even seaplanes from heavy cruisers TAKAO and MAYA, were ordered to take part. A total of 24 planes actually headed for the target, but foul weather along the way forced most of them to turn back.

Soon after the planes took off on this second mission, the weather closed in again, and even neighboring ships occasionally could not see one another. The attack planes, unable to keep formation, returned in scattered small groups crawling just above the sea. Most of their engines were wheezing and coughing because of the freezing cold as they returned over the carriers. The men in the ships held their breath as they watched the planes stagger down onto the flight deck one after another. Once all the carrier planes were on board, the Kakuta Force continued to advance until it was some 100 miles from the enemy shore.

Meanwhile, the four Type-95 two-seater reconnaissance seaplanes ("Daves" or "Petes") from TAKAO and MAYA had continued their daring advance through the stormy weather. They were intercepted by enemy fighters, however, and a dogfight ensued in which two of them were downed and the other two suffered some damage, though they managed to return near their ships. Both the crippled planes broke up in the water the moment they landed, but the injured crewmen were rescued.

Thus ended the first day's operations in the northern area. It was now clear that the Americans had air bases on or near Unalaska, but their location was as completely unknown as that of the hidden stars beyond the thick fog. The Dutch Harbor attack had inflicted little actual damage on the enemy. More important, it proved entirely ineffective in achieving its diversionary objective, since the Americans were already well aware that the main Japanese attack was directed at Midway.

4. FALSE ALARMS

Far to the south, the submarine elements assigned to the "A" and "B" cordon lines between Midway and the main Hawaiian Islands at last took up their stations during 3 June, two days behind schedule. Each submarine remained submerged during the day and surfaced at night, never relaxing its lookout for enemy forces coming from the direction of Pearl Harbor. But they had arrived too late. The enemy ships had already passed the positions of the cordons and moved far to the west.

Meanwhile, the afternoon of the 3rd found the Nagumo Force heading southeast for Midway at 24 knots. The Force was cruising in a compact ring formation with the four carriers in the center. The perimeter was formed by battleships HARUNA and KIRISHIMA, heavy cruisers TONE and CHIKUMA, light cruiser NAGARA, and 12 destroyers.

Suddenly, at 1940, heavy cruiser TONE hoisted an urgent signal reporting approximately 10 enemy planes sighted on bearing 260°. Three AKAGI fighters took off immediately to intercept, but as they encountered no enemy planes and as no air attack came, it was concluded that TONE's report had been erroneous.

After this brief alarm the Force continued on undisturbed until 0230, 4 June. Then one of AKAGI's lookouts reported: "What appears to be the light of an enemy contact plane sighted on starboard beam, bearing 070°. Above the clouds. Approaching." Every man on the bridge strained his eyes in the reported direction, but nothing was in sight. Nevertheless, Captain Aoki, who had not once left the bridge since departing from the homeland, instantly ordered General Quarters, and all hands hurried to their stations. Stars, both bright and dim, blinked through the scattered clouds and gained motion from the roll of the ship. After half a minute of futile watching and waiting, the captain called the lookout and asked if he still saw the reported light. A slight pause preceded the reluctant reply, "No, Sir, I have lost it."

The captain then cautioned all lookouts against mistaking stars for moving lights due to the motion of the ship. "Make sure of your sightings before reporting," he ordered.

Mumbled responses indicated that the lookouts understood the warning, and again there was silence. The captain was about to secure the ship from General Quarters when the same lookout suddenly shouted another warning:

"Light sighted in the same direction! It is not a star!"

An antiaircraft alert order was immediately flashed to all ships of the Force. But again all efforts to confirm the presence of an enemy plane proved vain.

Now zero-hour for launching the strike on Midway was rapidly approaching. Promptly at 0245, AKAGI's loudspeakers barked an order turning out air crews assigned to the attack. Maintenance men were already preparing the planes for take-off, and there was a deafening roar of motors starting and warming up.

The noise and pre-takeoff excitement throughout the ship roused Commander Genda, Staff Operations Officer, who had been confined to sick bay shortly after our departure because of a high fever which, it was feared, betokened pneumonia. Now, unwilling to miss the launching of the attack, he made his way to the bridge. There he encountered Admiral Nagumo, who placed an arm around his shoulder and asked how he was feeling.

"I am very sorry, Sir, to have been absent so long. I have a slight temperature but am feeling much better now." Genda's feverish eyes betrayed that he was much sicker than he was willing to admit, but they also sparkled with fighting spirit.

Genda's appearance on the bridge was a moving inspiration to every man present. For more than six months he had played a leading role in planning and directing the successful operations of the Nagumo Force. It bolstered the morale of everyone to see him again at Admiral Nagumo's side, ready for battle.

With his attack groups about to take off for Midway, Admiral Nagumo still was without information of enemy fleet activity. Wartime records disclose that just prior to launching the attack, Admiral Nagumo estimated—or, rather, misestimated—the enemy situation as follows:

1. The enemy fleet will probably come out to engage when the Midway landing operations are begun.

2. Enemy air patrols from Midway will be heavier to westward and southward, less heavy to the north and northwest.

3. The radius of enemy air patrols is estimated to be approximately 500 miles.[5]

4. The enemy is not yet aware of our plan, and he has not yet detected our task force.

5. There is no evidence of an enemy task force in our vicinity.

6. It is therefore possible for us to attack Midway, destroy land-based planes there, and support the landing operation. We can then turn around, meet an approaching enemy task force, and destroy it.

7. Possible counterattacks by enemy land-based air can surely be repulsed by our interceptors and antiaircraft fire.

Such was the sad misjudgment under which Admiral Nagumo, through no fault of his own, led the proud Japanese Carrier Striking Force into a battle that would see it smashed beyond repair.

[5] *Editors' Note:* This estimate appears strange in view of the encounter mentioned earlier between Japanese and American patrol planes 700 miles from Midway on 30 May (1 June, Japan time). Evidently Admiral Nagumo was unaware of this contact.

BOMBING OF DUTCH HARBOR, 4 JUNE 1942

VICE ADMIRAL CHUICHI NAGUMO

CHAPTER 9

The Nagumo Force
Fights

1. SEARCH FOR THE ENEMY

At about 0300 on the morning of 4 June the noisy drone of
plane engines warming up roused me from slumber. I got out of
bed and attempted to stand, but my legs were still unsteady.
The sound of engines alternately hummed and then rose to a
whining roar. AKAGI was preparing to launch her planes for
the attack on Midway.

Unable to resist the desire to be topside at take-off time, I
slipped out of the sick bay. The watertight doors of every
bulkhead had been closed, leaving only a small manhole in each
door open for passage. It was an arduous task to squeeze through
these small openings in my weakened condition, and cold sweat
soon ran down my forehead. I frequently felt exhausted and
dizzy and had to squat on the floor to rest.

The passageways were empty. All hands were at their stations.
Lights were dimmed for combat condition, and one could see
a distance of only a few feet. With great effort I finally climbed
the ladders up to my cabin just below the flight deck, clutch-
ing the handrails every step of the way. There I paused long
enough to catch my breath and put on a uniform before going
on to the flight control post. The first-wave attack planes were
all lined up on the flight deck. The warm-up was completed,
and the roar of the engines subsided. I found Commander
Masuda, Air Officer of AKAGI, in charge of flight preparations.

My colleagues expressed concern over my leaving bed, but
they understood when I explained that I could not bear to hear

the sound of the engines and remain below in sick bay. I looked up at the dark sky. The dawn still seemed far off. The sky was cloudy, and the weather, while not good, was not bad enough to prevent flying. The sea was calm.

I asked Lieutenant Furukawa when sunrise would be.

"At 0500, Sir," was the reply.

"Have search planes already been sent out?"

"No, Sir. They will be launched at the same time as the first attack wave."

"Are we using the single-phase search system?"

"Yes, Sir. As usual."

I recalled the attacks on Colombo and Trincomalee in the Indian Ocean, two months earlier, when single-phase search had been employed. It had not been a wise tactic. In both instances, the searches had spotted enemy surface forces while our attack groups were away hitting the enemy bases, and this had caused our carriers some anxious moments. With this in mind, I inquired what plans had been made for the eventuality that our search planes might sight an enemy fleet during the Midway attack.

"No need to worry about that," Lieutenant Commander Murata replied. "After the first attack wave departs, the second wave, consisting of Lieutenant Commander Egusa's dive bombers, my torpedo bombers, and Lieutenant Commander Itaya's Zeros, will be available to attack any enemy surface force that might be discovered."

"I see. Well, that's a good team, and we can just hope that the enemy fleet does come out so we can destroy it. What searches are scheduled?"

Furukawa explained them to me on the map board. "There are seven lines extending east and south, with Midway lying within the search arc. We are using one plane each from AKAGI and KAGA, two seaplanes each from TONE and CHIKUMA, and one from HARUNA. The search radius is 300 miles for all planes except HARUNA's, which is a Type-95 and can do only half that."

Although the coverage appeared adequate, I still felt that a two-phase search would have been wiser. A single-phase search might be sufficient if we wished only to confirm our assumption that no enemy fleet was in the vicinity. However, if we recognized the possibility that this assumption might be wrong and that an enemy force might be present, our searches should have been such as to assure that we could locate and attack it before it could strike at us. For this purpose a two-phase dawn search was the logical answer.

As the term indicates, a two-phase search employs two sets of planes which fly the same search lines, with a given time interval between them. Since our planes were not equipped with radar at this time, they were completely reliant on visual observation and could search effectively only by daylight. Consequently, to spot an enemy force as soon as possible after dawn, it was necessary to have one set of planes (the first phase) launched in time to reach the end of their search radius as day was breaking. This meant that the areas traversed in darkness on their outbound flight remained unsearched. Hence, a second-phase search was required over these same lines by planes taking off about one hour later.

Men assigned to the first phase of such a search obviously had to be well trained in night flying. Nagumo had such pilots and could have used this method, but it would have required twice as many planes as a single-phase search. Despite the importance of conducting adequate searches, our naval strategists were congenitally reluctant to devote more than a bare minimum of their limited plane strength to such missions. Ten per cent of total strength was all they were willing to spare for search operations, feeling that the rest should be reserved for offensive use. But such overemphasis on offensive strength had proven detrimental to our purposes before this, and it would again.

Naturally enough, Admiral Nagumo was eager to devote maximum strength to the Midway attack and did not want to use any more planes for search than seemed absolutely necessary. Since he had no reason to suspect the presence of an enemy force in the area, he was satisfied that a single-phase search was adequate precaution against the unexpected.

Search planes from AKAGI and KAGA were launched at 0430, simultaneously with the departure of the first Midway attack wave. HARUNA's seaplane was also catapulted at this time. But the TONE and CHIKUMA planes, which were covering the center lines of the search pattern, were delayed. Watching the two cruisers, I noticed that the last of their search planes did not get off until just before sunrise, nearly half an hour behind schedule. It was later learned that TONE's planes had been held up by catapult trouble, while one of CHIKUMA's planes had a balky engine. This last plane was forced to turn back at 0635 when the engine trouble recurred and it ran into foul weather.

Although poorly advised, a one-phase search despatched half an hour before sunrise would still have been helpful if everything had worked out as planned. But the delay in launching TONE's planes sowed a seed which bore fatal fruit for the Japanese in the ensuing naval action. Reviewing the full story of the battle on both sides, we now know that the enemy task force was missed by CHIKUMA's search plane which, according to the plan, should have flown directly over it. The enemy force was discovered only when the belated TONE plane, on the line south of the CHIKUMA plane, was on the dog-leg of its search. Had Admiral Nagumo carried out an earlier and more carefully planned two-phase search, had the observer of the CHIKUMA plane been more watchful on the outward leg of his search, or had the seaplanes been catapulted on schedule, the disaster that followed might have been avoided.

The fundamental cause of this failure, again, lay in the Japanese Navy's overemphasis on attack, which resulted in inadequate attention to search and reconnaissance. In both the training and organization of our naval aviators, too much importance and effort were devoted to attack. Reconnaissance was taught only as part of the regular curriculum, and no subsequent special training was given. Also, there were no organic reconnaissance units of any appreciable size in the Japanese Navy. When reconnaissance missions were required, attack planes were usually refitted and assigned to perform them. There were no carrier-borne planes designed solely for search. In the Pearl Harbor attack, every carrier-borne bomber of Nagumo's six carriers was assigned to the attack, leaving for search only some ten-odd float planes from the accompanying battleships and cruisers. This had been perhaps the basic reason for Admiral Nagumo's decision to withdraw upon that occasion without exploiting his advantage. At the critical moment, when he had to decide whether to launch another attack on Pearl Harbor, he did not have the vital information which reconnaissance planes could have provided. The Nagumo Force continued to suffer from this same lack of aerial reconnaissance in every action that followed.

While searching for the British Fleet in the Indian Ocean earlier in the year, our search planes often lost their way, and the carriers had to send out radio signals on which they could home. This, however, also alerted the enemy to our position, and the result was an understandable reluctance on the part of Admiral Nagumo and his staff to send out search planes if it could possibly be avoided. This reluctance was still present in the Midway operation, and, coupled with the erroneous estimate of the enemy situation, was responsible for the inadequate search dispositions ordered by Admiral Nagumo.

One small step toward remedying the search weakness of the Nagumo Force had been taken prior to the sortie for Midway. After prolonged negotiations with the authorities, Nagumo had succeeded in getting two carrier based reconnaissance planes of a new type, on which experiments had just been completed. This type had been designed originally as a dive bomber, but was altered for use as a search plane. It was later designated the Type-2 carrier-borne reconnaissance plane or *Suisei* ("Judy") dive bomber, and there were high expectations for its success in reconnoitering enemy task forces. Two of these planes had been loaded on board SORYU before departure.

In the morning of 4 June Admiral Nagumo and his staff were still unaware that the Japanese Transport Group had been sighted and attacked by planes from Midway. AKEBONO MARU was the only ship hit and she was not damaged enough to hinder her progress, but the important thing was that the enemy was fully alerted to the presence of Japanese ships approaching in the direction of Midway. And we did not know that they knew.

2. *FIRST ATTACK WAVE LAUNCHED*

In the predawn darkness of 4 June, at a point 240 miles northwest of Midway, the first attack wave was about to take off from Admiral Nagumo's carriers for the strike on Midway. A southeasterly breeze and calm sea provided ideal launching conditions. The eastern sky was tinged with a faint glow which dimly outlined the horizon. It was 40 minutes before sunup when the loudspeakers barked out the command, "Aviators, assemble!" There was a quick scurry of pilots to the briefing room under the bridge. Too weary to follow, I remained alone at the flight control station. The fliers were soon back on deck running toward their planes. The Air Officer returned to the control post and began shouting a quick succession of orders.

"All hands to launching stations!"

"Start engines!"

"Captain, head full into the wind, and increase speed for a relative velocity of 14 meters."[1]

[1] *Editors' Note:* Wind speed per second; equivalent to 19.2 miles per hour.

Plane engines were started, and livid white flames spurted from exhaust pipes. The flight deck was soon a hell of ear-shattering noise.

Lieutenant Takehiko Chihaya, in full flying gear, stopped briefly at the flight control station and bade me good-bye. I wished him luck and watched him go nimbly down a ladder and jump into the cockpit of his lead dive bomber, waiting near the base of the bridge. The wing lights of his plane blinked on, indicating that he was ready, and soon the blue and red lights of all the planes glowed in the darkness.

"All planes ready, Sir," an orderly reported. Flood lights suddenly illuminated the flight deck, making day of the night. "Planes ready for take off, Sir," the Air Officer reported to the ship's captain.

AKAGI was steaming full into the wind with speed increased, and the wind gauge showed the required velocity. "Commence launching!" came the order from the bridge. Swinging a green signal lamp, the Air Officer described a big circle in the air.

A Zero fighter, leading the flock of impatient war birds, revved up its engine, gathered speed along the flight deck, and rose into the air to the accompaniment of a thunderous cheer from AKAGI's crew. Caps and hands waved wildly in the bright glare of the deck lights.

The first plane was followed by eight more Zeros. Then came the dive bombers, each carrying a 250-kilogram land bomb. The canopy of Chihaya's plane was open, and the young leader waved good-bye to the cheering hands on deck. The next instant the plane rose into the darkness with a loud roar. Soon all 18 dive bombers were in the air. Overhead a neat array of red and blue lights showed that the Zeros were in formation.

Some 4,000 meters to port, HIRYU was also launching planes. Thin streaks of light followed each other skyward from the floodlit deck. In 15 minutes the four carriers had launched a total of 108 planes. While forming up, they made a great circle over the Fleet and then headed off into the southeastern sky at 0445.

Over-all commander of the first attack wave was Lieutenant Joichi Tomonaga, personally leading 36 Type-97 level bombers from SORYU and HIRYU. To his left followed 36 Type-99 dive bombers from AKAGI and KAGA, led by Lieutenant Shoichi Ogawa, a KAGA squadron commander. Lieutenant Masaharu Suganami of SORYU led the fighter escort of 36 Zeros (nine from each carrier). One hundred and eight planes in all.

This was Tomonaga's first sortie of the Pacific War. He had reported to HIRYU just before her departure from the homeland. He was, however, a veteran of the Sino-Japanese war and a capable and experienced flier, well qualified to lead the attack. Lieutenant Ogawa, a gallant pilot, had been in every action of the Nagumo Force since Pearl Harbor. His skill and daring were unequalled in the Naval Air Corps. Lieutenant Suganami, like most of the pilots, was also a veteran of the Pacific War since the Pearl Harbor attack. Full of fighting spirit, he was a typical fighter pilot. All the other pilots were well trained, and most were experienced. They worked together well as a team. I watched their lights disappear into the darkness, regretting my illness and praying for their good luck.

The flight deck, which moments before had been filled with a deafening din, was now silent. There were no planes, no drone of engines. Only a few deck hands ran here and there, busily stowing various pieces of gear. But the stillness was again broken by the raucous loudspeaker as it blared out the order, "Prepare second attack wave!"

To the accompaniment of clanging bells, planes soon were being whisked up to the flight deck and rolled from the elevators to their line-up positions. The forward elevators brought up fighters; the midship and stern elevators delivered bombers. Maintenance crews wheeled torpedoes from the ammunition rooms and secured them to the planes. All hands worked feverishly. There was no time for rest as the first light of dawn was beginning to brighten the eastern sky.

It was 0500 when the crimson sun rose over the horizon. The flight deck was again filled with planes ready to attack in the event an enemy task force appeared. The dive bombers each carried one 250-kilogram bomb, and the level bombers each carried a torpedo. The second attack wave also totaled 108 planes—36 Type-99 dive bombers (18 each from HIRYU and SORYU), 36 Type-97 torpedo bombers (18 each from AKAGI and KAGA), and 36 Zero fighters.

The dive-bomber group was led by Lieutenant Commander Takashige Egusa, from SORYU, long the Navy's leading expert in dive-bombing. When Japan began girding herself for war, his dive-bomber group had trained vigorously with the aim of destroying the United States carrier fleet at one blow. They had had no opportunity for this in the Pearl Harbor attack because no aircraft carriers had been present that day. In the Indian Ocean operations that followed, however, they had demonstrated their proficiency by sending the British carrier HERMES as well as cruisers DORSETSHIRE and CORNWALL to the bottom. Now the opportunity they had waited for seemed near at hand. No wonder excitement ran high.

The leader of the torpedo-bomber group was Lieutenant Commander Shigeharu Murata, from AKAGI. When the Pearl Harbor operation had first been envisaged, an aerial torpedo attack was thought impossible because of the shallow harbor. It was through Murata's untiring and arduous efforts that this problem had been overcome, and he had led the torpedo planes to their brilliant successes in the Pearl Harbor strike. Now he hoped to display equal effectiveness on the open sea. Lieutenant Commander Shigeru Itaya, of AKAGI, who commanded the fighter escort group, was another veteran of long flying experience. One of the senior fighter pilots of the fleet, his brilliant war record had already established him as an ace.

Indeed, these three leaders were the best possible men for the job at hand, and their fliers were the elite of the naval air arm. In training, experience, and ability, there was no finer air combat team in the entire Japanese Navy. Admiral Nagumo had concluded that there was no enemy carrier group anywhere in the neighborhood of his force; yet he had prudently kept on hand his first-string team to pit against enemy carriers in case they should appear.

Thus, everything was in seeming readiness even for the unexpected. It remained only to give the signal if enemy ships were sighted, and the second attack wave would take care of the rest. Still, there was something disturbing about the situation. Since the search planes had set out only a short while earlier, it would probably be some time before we learned definitely from them whether or not an enemy force was in the vicinity. But this was not the only threat that might arise. It was also necessary to anticipate shore-based air attacks from Midway. Maneuvering as we were, within easy striking range of the island, with a full deckload of planes, we certainly presented an attractive target. Somehow we resembled a man walking through a lonely forest with a bag of gold on his shoulder, an inviting prey for the first robber who saw the chance to pounce upon him. Worried lest we be attacked in this vulnerable condition, I asked whether our fighter cover had taken off.

"Yes, Sir," was the reply. "After the first attack wave left, nine fighters were launched from KAGA. Another nine are now standing by on our flight deck."

A total of 18 fighter planes to protect the entire Striking Force! In the event of an enemy attack, they would be powerless to stop it. But we had already committed 36 fighters to the Midway attack, and another 36 were being held in reserve in the second attack wave. That left just 18 fighters as combat air patrol for our force of 21 ships.

I had a fear that we might lose flexibility by keeping half of our strength in stand-by reserve. Until an enemy fleet was discovered, or its absence confirmed, a full half of our striking strength had to be kept for immediate use. And because that readiness had to be maintained even though we should be attacked by land-based planes, our flexibility of operation seemed impaired from the very outset.

Weakened by my exertions and somewhat worried over the tactical situation of our Force, I suddenly felt dizzy and climbed down to my cabin beneath the flight deck to rest. My thoughts, however, were with Tomonaga and his fliers about to strike the first blow at Midway.

3. MIDWAY STRIKE

By 0445 the first attack wave had completed forming up over the Striking Force, and after climbing to 4,000 meters it sped off to the southeast. When still about 150 miles from the target, these planes were discovered by an enemy flying boat. Unsuspected, it shadowed them to within 30 miles of Midway where it moved high above the formation to drop a parachute flare, alerting enemy interceptors which were already in the air in anticipation of the strike.

Upon sighting the flare signal, enemy fighters swarmed to the attack. A savage air battle ensued from 0645 to 0710, but the tactical superiority of the Zero fighter again proved itself and the enemy challenge was successfully repulsed. Thanks to the effective protection of Lieutenant Suganami's fighters, every one of our level bombers and 36 dive bombers arrived safely over the target. Suganami's success in blocking the enemy fighters from making a single hit on the bombers was a feat almost without parallel in the Pacific War.

Meanwhile, Lieutenant Ogawa's dive bombers screamed down on their targets through fierce antiaircraft fire, releasing their 250-kilogram bombs at perilously low altitude. Simultaneously, 12 level bombers concentrated on an air strip on Eastern Island with 800-kilogram bombs dropped from an altitude of 3,500 meters. The rest of the bombers demolished hangars and other installations on Eastern and Sand Islands.

The absence of surprise sharply reduced the effectiveness of our attack. The fully alerted enemy had sent all of his planes aloft, some to intercept and attack, the others merely to take refuge. Finding no planes on the fields, Tomonaga's bombers attacked the hangars, which were easily destroyed, and the airstrip. But the loss of empty hangars was of little significance, and it was next to impossible for so few planes to effectively damage the airstrip.

Lieutenant Tomonaga was well aware that the primary objective of the strike was to neutralize enemy air strength based on Midway. Since the first attack obviously had not achieved this goal, he concluded that it would be necessary to strike again in order to destroy the enemy planes when they returned to the island. Accordingly, as his planes headed back to the carriers, he radioed: "There is need for a second attack. Time: 0700."

Japanese losses in the first-wave attack were negligible. Three level bombers and one dive bomber were shot down by enemy antiaircraft fire, and only two fighters failed to return.

Post-war American accounts fully confirm that Midway's defenders were ready and waiting for the attack. At about 0520, as recounted later, an enemy PBY had spotted our carrier force and radioed a warning back to Midway. Another PBY had sighted the Japanese air formation 150 miles from the target and followed it in. Radar stations on Midway also picked up the formation and traced its approach.

Shortly after 0600, every operational plane on the island took off, leaving the airstrips bare. The American fighters swiftly climbed for altitude so that they could pounce on the

Japanese formations from above. All antiaircraft batteries on the island were fully manned. When the PBY dropped its flare at a distance of 30 miles from the island to illuminate the attacking planes, the American interceptors dove into action from a 5,000-foot advantage. The strength of the Japanese force was exaggeratedly reported as 60 to 80 bombers and 50 Zero fighters.

According to the American account, the defenders thought that they had shot down 53 Japanese planes during the attack—10 by antiaircraft fire and the rest by aerial combat—whereas there were actually only five Japanese planes that failed to return to the carriers. On the other hand our fliers' claims of some 42 American planes destroyed were also exaggerated, though less flagrantly, since there were in all only 26 present. Of these only two returned undamaged to the island, and the rest were either destroyed or badly shot up.

The actual damage to Midway installations was, as we suspected, far from complete. However, the American account shows that the fuel supply system was so badly bombed that all subsequent fueling operations had to be carried out by hand. Some damage was done to the airstrip, and more than 20 casualties were suffered on the ground. The seaplane hangar and fuel storage tanks on Sand Island were destroyed.

4. SHORE-BASED AIR ATTACK

Back on AKAGI the departure of the Midway Attack Force had been followed by anxious waiting both for news of the strike itself and for enemy counteraction which had to be expected momentarily. For the latter we had not long to wait.

After descending from the flight deck, I had been in my bunk but a few minutes when a bugle sounded the alarm, "Air raid!" This was followed almost at once by the strident roar of interceptors taking off. I counted the planes as they raced down the deck directly overhead. Nine fighters took off. I shouted unheard encouragement to the pilots but was too feeble to rise from my bunk. A glance at my watch showed the time to be 0520.

The sudden quiet after the planes' take-off was broken shortly by the shattering bark of our antiaircraft guns. My weakness was again overcome by an insistent impulse to see what was happening, and I struggled up once more to the flight command post, where the Air Officer informed me that the target was a flying boat. An enemy PBY had sighted our force.[2] The time was 0525.

I asked a lookout if our fighters had shot down the PBY, and his negative reply surprised me. The Air Officer explained, "The PBY managed to elude them by a very cunning maneuver. It was first sighted to the south flying at about 4,000 meters. The pilot came directly overhead as if to bomb us. By the time our fighters got up to meet him, he had disappeared eastward into the clouds. We thought he had given up the contact, but he came back again. Our fighters still failed to catch him because of the clouds. Now he seems to be gone for good."

A report came from our radio monitors that a long message was being sent by an enemy plane, obviously nearby because the reception was very clear. It must be the PBY's report of our position. Now we were sure to be attacked. It was just a question of what would strike us, and how soon. Again worn out by my exertion, I collapsed on the deck, helpless and giddy. An officer placed a parachute pack under my head as a pillow, and I lay there watching the brightening sky and listening to the commotion about me.

At 0535 one of Tone's search planes, launched half an hour

[2] *Editors' Note:* This plane from Midway made the first U.S. contact with the Japanese carriers. It also reported the Japanese air attack force heading toward the island. The American carriers at this time were about 200 miles ENE of the Nagumo Force.

earlier, radioed that it had sighted an enemy flying boat 40 miles out, heading for our carriers. Either the PBY which had already spotted us was coming back to resume the contact, or another was moving in for the same purpose. All eyes on AKAGI's bridge searched the horizon, but for some minutes no flying boat came into sight.

Then, at 0542, a bridge-top lookout suddenly shouted, "Enemy flying boat, starboard beam, elevation 50°, above the clouds, visible at intervals!" Everyone fixed his gaze in the direction indicated, and the Air Officer called out, "There it is! Very high. Over 4,000 meters." A minute later fighters were roaring off AKAGI's deck to pursue the intruder.

During the next hour there was a confusing succession of reported contacts on our force both by individual flying boats and by small numbers of enemy planes of unidentified type. There was also a further radio warning from TONE's search plane at 0555 that 15 enemy planes were heading toward us. The formation upped its speed to 28 knots, and TONE, after sighting three planes overhead at 0643, began making smoke to provide concealment against attack. Since no attack took place during this entire period, however, some of the reported contacts must have been erroneous or on our own fighters patrolling overhead. But there was no question that enemy flying boats were shadowing us, skilfully maneuvering in and out of the clouds to elude pursuit.

Each time one of the persistent PBYs was sighted, now to starboard, now to port, AKAGI's harassed fighter director would shout orders to our combat air patrol to go after it. The enemy pilots, however, were so adept at weaving through the clouds that the fighters merely exhausted themselves to no avail. While our own movements were thus observed and reported continuously, there was still no warning from our own search planes of any enemy task force.

At 0700 Lieutenant Tomonaga's message recommending a

second strike against Midway was received on the bridge of flagship AKAGI. Still no enemy planes had yet attacked our Force, but almost immediately thereafter Tomonaga's recommendation was underlined by the first of a series of desperate shore-based air assaults which amply proved to Admiral Nagumo that enemy air strength on Midway had not been eliminated.

At 0705 a bugle sounded, "Air raid!" and all eyes in the flight command post turned toward the southern sky. I managed to pull myself up for a look and noticed that it had become a beautiful day. There was fairly heavy cloud cover at about 6,000 feet, but the air was clear and visibility good.

A destroyer in the van section of our ring formation suddenly hoisted a flag signal, "Enemy planes in sight!" Emitting a cloud of black smoke to underline the warning, she opened fire with her antiaircraft guns. Soon we spotted four planes approaching from 20 degrees to port. They looked like torpedo bombers, but before they could get close enough to permit confirmation, our fighters had pounced upon them and shot down three, causing loud cheers all around me. The last plane gave up the attack and withdrew with our Zeros in hot pursuit.

A bridge-top lookout was heard from a moment later: "Six medium land-based planes approaching, 20 degrees to starboard. On the horizon." Scanning the sky to starboard, sure enough, I saw the enemy planes flying in a single column. It looked as if the enemy had planned a converging attack from both flanks, but fortunately for us the timing was off.

Following the lead destroyers, our cruisers opened fire. Then battleship KIRISHIMA, to starboard of AKAGI, loosed her main batteries at the attackers. Still they kept coming in, flying low over the water. Black bursts of antiaircraft fire blossomed all around them, but none of the raiders went down. As AKAGI's guns commenced firing, three Zeros braved our own antiaircraft barrage and dove down on the Americans. In a moment's

TYPE 95 RECONNAISSANCE SEAPLANE—"DAVE"

TYPE 97 (TORPEDO) BOMBER—"KATE"

HIGH-SPEED RECONNAISSANCE PLANE, LATER DESIGNATED TYPE 2
CARRIER-BASED RECONNAISSANCE PLANE AND
DIVE BOMBER—"JUDY"

PLANES READY FOR TAKE-OFF FROM JAPANESE CARRIER

"KATE"   "VAL"
FROM *Soryu*   FROM *Hiryu*

PLANES TAKING OFF FROM CARRIER DECK

time three of the enemy were set aflame and splashed into the water, raising tall columns of smoke. The remaining three planes kept bravely on and finally released their torpedoes. Free of their cargo, the attacking planes swung sharply to the right and away, except for the lead plane which skimmed straight over AKAGI, from starboard to port, nearly grazing the bridge. The white star on the fuselage of the plane, a B-26, was plainly visible. Immediately after clearing our ship, it burst into flames and plunged into the sea.

About this time several torpedoes passed to port of AKAGI, trailing their pale white wakes. AKAGI had maneuvered so skilfully that not one torpedo scored, and everyone breathed a deep sigh of relief.

This attack actually consisted of six torpedo planes (TBF Avengers) and four B-26s (Marauders), all armed with torpedoes, which had taken off unescorted from Midway at 0615. American accounts indicate that one TBF and two B-26s were all that returned from the attack.

Admiral Nagumo needed no further convincing that Midway should be hit again, and he felt that it would be safe to do so as no enemy surface force had yet been reported. Consequently, at 0715, just as the torpedo attack was ending, he ordered the planes of the second wave, which had been armed for an attack on enemy ships, to prepare instead for another strike on Midway. This meant that the torpedo-laden level bombers on AKAGI and KAGA had to be de-armed and reloaded with bombs.[3] The ones already on the flight deck were taken down to the hangar one after another, and the re-arming began. Flying crews and maintenance men worked furiously at the arduous task.

[3] *Editors' Note:* Only AKAGI and KAGA were affected because, as described earlier, the torpedo bomber group of the second attack wave was composed of planes from these two carriers, with HIRYU and SORYU providing the dive bomber group. The torpedo bombers of HIRYU and SORYU had gone out with the first attack wave, in which the dive bomber group had come from AKAGI and KAGA.

There was only a brief respite before the Nagumo Force was attacked again. Just before 0800 an AKAGI lookout reported that enemy bombers were attacking HIRYU. Dark geysers of water were seen rising up around the carrier, and in the next instant identical columns were rising around SORYU. But there was no black smoke to indicate a direct hit on either ship. When the curtains of water settled, the two carriers were still steaming ahead, evidently unharmed.

I consulted an aircraft recognition chart and found that SORYU's attackers were B-17s, the latest model United States Army bomber. There were fourteen in all. A study of postwar American sources shows that these planes took off from Midway before dawn to attack the Japanese transport convoy but were diverted to the carriers. After dropping their bomb loads of more than four tons per plane from an altitude of 20,000 feet, they returned safely to base and optimistically reported having scored four hits on two carriers.

I was chagrined to see that none of our fighters pursued the B-17s. Recalling the reported toughness of these big planes, however, I realized that the 20-mm. guns of our fighters would have had a hard time knocking them down anyway. Meanwhile, the "Forts" roared defiantly away. Our antiaircraft fire concentrated on them but registered no hits.

About this time all Zeros of our second attack wave were sent up to augment our combat air patrol. At 0800 a lookout reported a group of small planes coming from the direction of Midway. The lead destroyers of our screen sent up a billow of smoke and opened fire on them.

Their attack method was puzzling as they came in too high for torpedo attack and too low for dive-bombing. They approached in shallow dives, heading straight for HIRYU. There were 16 planes in all, widely scattered. They were jumped by 10 or more Zeros, which sent one after another spinning into the sea. Even when half of them had been shot down, the re-

maining planes bravely held their course and finally released
bombs which seemed certain to hit the carrier. But when the
bomb splashes and smoke cleared, HIRYU was still intact, steaming on as gallantly as ever. It struck me as strange that the
American planes had not employed their customary, highly
effective hell-diving technique in this attack.

This was explained in postwar accounts of the American side
of the action. The leader of these 16 Marine Corps dive
bombers (SBDs) had taken off from Midway about an hour
before, knowing full well that his pilots were not experienced
in dive-bombing. Accordingly, upon sighting the carriers, he
decided on a glide bombing attack. Half of these planes never
returned to their base, and six of the ones that did were damaged
beyond repair.

We had by this time undergone every kind of air attack by
shore-based planes—torpedo, level bombing, dive-bombing—
but were still unscathed. Frankly, it was my judgment that the
enemy fliers were not displaying a very high level of ability,
and this evaluation was shared by Admiral Nagumo and his
staff. It was our general conclusion that we had little to fear
from the enemy's offensive tactics. But, paradoxically, the very
ineffectiveness of the enemy attacks up to this time contributed
in no small measure to the ultimate American triumph. We
neglected certain obvious precautions which, had they been
taken, might have prevented the fiasco that followed a few
hours later. The apparently futile sacrifices made by the enemy's
shore-based planes were, after all, not in vain.

As the glide-bombing attack ended, a destroyer on the far
side of our ring formation made a smoke signal that it had
spotted more enemy planes. Almost 100 were counted. The
destroyer opened fire on them but stopped abruptly after a
few rounds upon recognizing that it was our first attack wave
returning from Midway. The time was 0830.

Owing to the independent evasive maneuvering of our ships

during the enemy air attacks and the peripatetic movements of the carriers while launching and recovering fighter planes, our once compact cruising disposition had become widely dispersed. It was therefore desirable to take advantage of the lull in the attacks to re-form, but now the recovery of Tomonaga's planes was of greater urgency. With the veteran fliers we had at this time, speedy recovery operations on board the carriers even under stringent battle conditions were little more than child's play. Given fifteen minutes from the time the ship turned into the wind, a carrier's whole complement of planes could put down on her deck with expert skill.

No time was lost in getting the recovery underway. On each carrier the order was given, "Clear the deck to recover planes!" AKAGI again became a hive of activity. The uncomplaining crews egged on by exhortations to "Hurry it up!" fell to their jobs with tremendous energy. In a matter of minutes the flight deck was clear, and at 0837 a signal streamed from the yard-arm, "Commence landing!" The returning planes orbited and swooped to the deck in rapid succession. By shortly after 0900 all four carriers had recovered their planes.

Three of our crippled bombers circled once over HIRYU before coming in to land. Lieutenant Commander Masu Kawa-guchi, in charge of recovery operations, instantly summoned a surgeon to the command post. One of the planes had to land on a single wheel. Lieutenant Hiroharu Kadono, the pilot, lost consciousness the moment his plane jolted to a halt. He had been hit in the leg by a machine-gun bullet when enemy fighters attacked the formation near the target. Despite the pain of his wound, he flew on with the formation, made the attack, and managed to return to the carrier.

Lieutenant Tomonaga's plane was hit in the left wing fuel tank, but he too managed to get back. His report included an account of the gallant death of Lieutenant Rokuro Kikuchi, a bomber pilot from HIRYU, whose plane had been fatally hit by antiaircraft fire over the island. Kikuchi had opened the canopy, waved goodbye to his comrades, then closed it firmly, and plunged headlong to the ground.

5. AMERICAN CARRIERS SIGHTED

Already about an hour before Tomonaga's Midway strike planes got back to the carriers, however, there had been a development which completely altered the battle situation confronting Admiral Nagumo. TONE's No. 4 search plane, which had been launched a full half hour behind schedule, finally reached its 300-mile search limit on course 100° at 0720, and it then veered north to fly a 60-mile dog-leg before heading back. Eight minutes later its observer suddenly discerned, far off to port, a formation of some 10 ships heading southeast. Without waiting until it could get a closer look, the plane immediately flashed a message to the Nagumo Force: "Ten ships, apparently enemy, sighted. Bearing 010°, distant 240 miles from Midway. Course 150°, speed more than 20 knots. Time, 0728."

This vital message was received by the flagship only after several minutes' delay occasioned by the relaying of the message through TONE.[4] When it reached Admiral Nagumo and his staff on AKAGI's bridge, it struck them like a bolt from the

[4] *Editors' Note:* Documentary evidence is both contradictory and inconclusive as to the exact time this message was received. The Nagumo Force official report states, in its narrative summary of the operation, that the message was only received "at about 0500" (0800, Midway time). This, however, is clearly shown to be inaccurate by entries in the detailed action log contained in the same document, these entries establishing that, at 0745 and again at 0747, as related immediately following, Admiral Nagumo dispatched orders indicating prior receipt of the TONE search plane report. The action log also shows that other messages from the TONE plane, where both sending and receipt times were given, were received either simultaneously with their sending or, in a few cases, with a delay of not more than ten minutes evidently caused by relaying of the messages. *First Air Fleet Detailed Battle Report No. 6, 15 June 1942, pp. 6, 18-32.* Equivalent references in English translation of this document, U.S. Navy ONI Publication OPNAV P32-1002, *The Japanese Story of the Battle of Midway*, are pp. 7, 13-16.

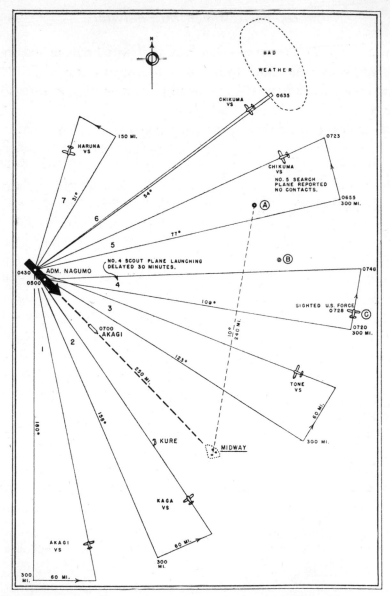

NAGUMO FORCE DAWN SEARCHES, 4 JUNE 1942 (West Longitude Date, Zone plus 12 Time).

Editors' Note: Original chart in Japanese text showed only generalized position of U.S. forces WNW of plane (C). Their position as reported by the plane is shown at (A), while (B) is their position as supplied from American sources. It is probable that the plane's calculations were grossly in error and that the plane was off its scheduled course.

blue. Until this moment no one had anticipated that an enemy surface force could possibly appear so soon, much less suspected that enemy ships were already in the vicinity waiting to ambush us. Now the entire picture was changed.

Lieutenant Commander Ono, the Staff Intelligence Officer, quickly plotted the enemy's reported position on the navigation chart and measured off the distance between it and our force. The enemy was just 200 miles away! This meant that he was already within striking range of our planes, but if he had carriers, we were also within *his* reach. The big question now was what composed the enemy force. Above all, did it contain any carriers?

The complete lack of information in the search plane report on the make-up of the enemy force caused both concern and irritation to Admiral Nagumo, Chief of Staff Kusaka and the other staff officers. "Ten ships, apparently enemy" was not a very illuminating description. Obviously, the ships could only be enemy, but what types were present? At 0747, a peremptory order was flashed to the TONE plane, "Ascertain ship types and maintain contact."

Two minutes before this, Admiral Nagumo had already taken another action made imperative by the sighting of the enemy. Since 0715 AKAGI and KAGA, whose torpedo bombers had been held back in the second attack wave, had been hurriedly rearming them with 800-kilogram bombs in place of torpedoes for another strike on Midway. The rearming had by this time been more than half completed. Now, however, it was urgently necessary to maintain readiness to meet the enemy fleet in case further information from the TONE plane confirmed it to be a real threat to the Nagumo Force. Therefore, at 0745, Admiral Nagumo ordered the rearming of the two carriers' torpedo bombers to be immediately suspended and directed his whole Force to prepare for a possible attack on enemy ships.

At 0758 the TONE search plane radioed that the enemy had

changed course to 080°, but again the ship types were not mentioned. The staff were now fuming with angry impatience, and at 0800 another dispatch went out ordering the search plane to report the composition of the enemy force immediately.

Finally, at 0809, the reply came in: "Enemy ships are five cruisers and five destroyers."

"Just as I thought," Ono said triumphantly, "there are no carriers." He handed the message to the Chief of Staff. Kusaka's reaction was that, if the enemy force was without carriers, it could safely be taken care of later, and the Nagumo Force could first finish destroying enemy air strength based on Midway.

The relief inspired by the 0809 message, however, was short-lived. At 0820 the TONE plane was heard from again, and this time it reported, "Enemy force accompanied by what appears to be aircraft carrier bringing up the rear."

This information electrified everyone. But there was still a residue of doubt because of the words "appears to be." The identification was not certain. And if the enemy force did include a carrier, why hadn't carrier-type aircraft yet joined in the attacks on the Nagumo Force? So reasoned the optimists.

At 0830 still another message came in from the TONE plane. It reported: "Two additional enemy ships, apparently cruisers, sighted. Bearing 008°, distant 250 miles from Midway. Course 150°, speed 20 knots."

From the size of the enemy force Admiral Nagumo now concluded that it must contain at least one carrier. It was therefore essential, he decided, to attack these ships before launching another strike on Midway. However, serious obstacles stood in the way of an immediate attack. Not only had the greater part of AKAGI's and KAGA's torpedo bombers already been rearmed with bombs by the time Admiral Nagumo ordered the rearming suspended at 0745, but in addition all Zeros of the second attack wave fighter escort had been sent aloft to reinforce our

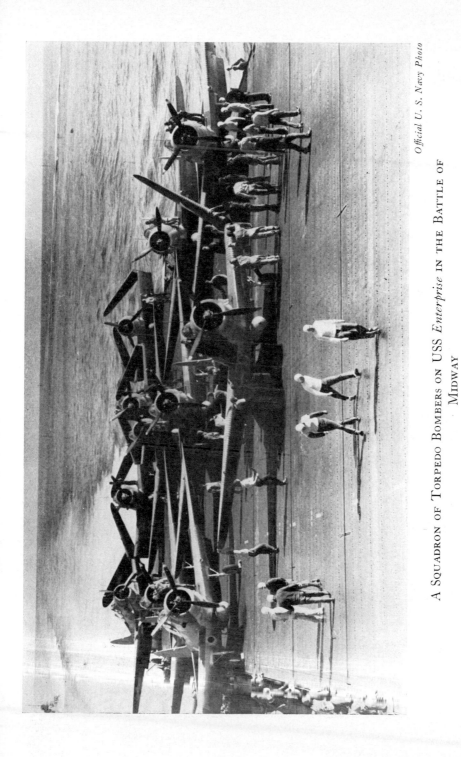

A SQUADRON OF TORPEDO BOMBERS ON USS *Enterprise* IN THE BATTLE OF
MIDWAY

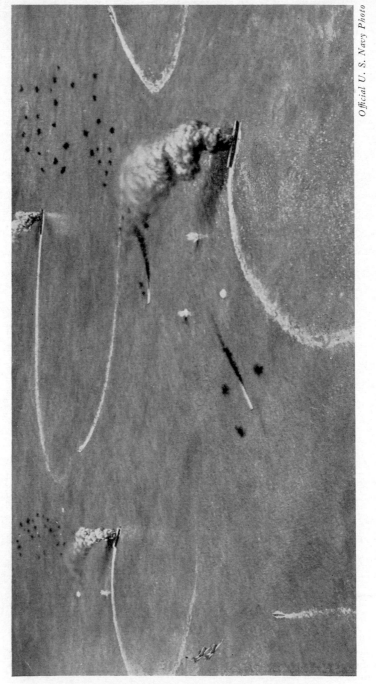

Bel Geddes Model of U. S. Dive-Bomber Attack on *Akagi*, *Kaga* and *Soryu*

combat air patrol against the repeated attacks by enemy shore-based planes. As a result, the only planes that were actually armed appropriately for an attack on enemy ships and lined up on the flight decks ready for take-off were the 36 dive bombers of HIRYU and SORYU.

Admiral Nagumo's dilemma was a difficult one, indeed. If he launched the dive bombers for a forestalling attack on the enemy task force, they would have no fighter protection and losses might be severe. Also, there was the question of whether to use the torpedo bombers now lined up on the flight decks of AKAGI and KAGA but already rearmed with 800-kilogram bombs.[5] These bombs, though less effective than torpedoes against a ship target, could still inflict severe damage if hits were scored. But the torpedo bombers required fighter protection far more, even, than the dive bombers. To bomb effectively, they must maintain a straight and level course, which gives no opportunity for evasive maneuvering. Without protective escort, they would be easy prey for nimble enemy fighters.

As Admiral Nagumo pondered his course of action, the return of Tomonaga's planes from the Midway strike made a quick decision imperative. Some of the planes were in distress and the fighter escorts were running low on fuel, so that their recovery could not be long delayed without risking added losses. Either the carriers' decks must be cleared by launching the dive and torpedo bombers to attack the enemy without fighter cover, or the planes must be moved to make way for the recovery, thus making it impossible to launch an attack until some time later.

Rear Admiral Yamaguchi, the aggressive commander of CarDiv 2, chose this moment to make an urgent recommendation to Admiral Nagumo. In his flagship, HIRYU, which was

[5] *Editors' Note:* As their rearming was completed, these planes had again been brought up to the flight decks of the two carriers, apparently remaining there when further rearming was suspended. Such planes as had not yet been changed over from torpedoes to bombs evidently remained below on the hangar deck.

maneuvering at some distance from AKAGI, he had anxiously been following the successive sighting reports from TONE's search plane, and Admiral Nagumo's failure to order prompt offensive action against the enemy task force struck him as unwise and dangerous. He now addressed a signal to his superior, relayed by destroyer NOWAKI. The signal read: "Consider it advisable to launch attack force immediately."

In Admiral Nagumo's judgment, however, the risks involved in sending out an attack force without fighter protection were too great. The slaughter of the unescorted American planes which had attacked his ships within the past hour and a half was, after all, pretty convincing proof of that. A wiser course, he thought, was first to recover both the Midway strike planes and the second wave fighters which had been diverted to combat air patrol, then to reorganize his forces while temporarily retiring northward to avoid further air attack, and finally, when all preparations were complete, to turn around and destroy the enemy task force by an all-out attack.

Nagumo's reasoning was logical enough. His force was well balanced and appeared greatly superior in strength. Therefore, it would be easy to destroy the enemy if all his striking power were thrown into a single, massive attack. Such strategy was orthodox, but it had one flaw—neglect of the time factor. Victory in battle does not always go to the stronger; it often goes to the side which is quicker to act boldly and decisively to meet unforeseen developments, and to grasp fleeting opportunities.

By his decision, taken shortly after 0830, to recover the Midway strike before doing anything else, Admiral Nagumo virtually committed himself to the second, more cautious plan of action. On board AKAGI, when the order was given to clear the deck for recovery, the weary maintenance crews began once more to lower the torpedo bombers to the hangar deck. There, the orders now were to switch back from bombs to torpedoes.

Flight Officer Masuda, whose light-heartedness and good nature seemed to prevail under any circumstances, greeted these instructions with amazingly cheerful astonishment. "Here we go again!" he exclaimed. "This is getting to be like a quick-change contest."

While the returning planes came down one after another on the flight deck, the work of rearming the torpedo bombers on the hangar deck below proceeded furiously. The crew, clad only in tropical shorts and half-sleeved shirts, hastily unloaded the heavy bombs, just piling them up beside the hangar because there was no time to lower them to the magazine. There would be cause to recall and regret this haphazard disposal of the lethal missiles when enemy bombs later found their mark in AKAGI.

At 0855, as the recovery operations neared completion, Admiral Nagumo acted to put the rest of his plan into execution. A blinker signal sent out to all ships ordered: "After completing recovery operations, Force will temporarily head northward. We plan to contact and destroy enemy task force."

Simultaneously with this order, Admiral Nagumo dispatched a radio to Admiral Yamamoto in YAMATO and to Vice Admiral Kondo, commanding the Midway Invasion Force, to inform them of the critical new developments. The message said: "Enemy force of one carrier, five cruisers and five destroyers discovered at 0800, bearing 010°, distant 240 miles from Midway. We will head for it."[6]

[6] *Editors' Note:* The inaccuracies and omissions in this message are interesting. By telescoping together the various TONE search plane reports and giving a single median time of 0800, it could have led Admiral Yamamoto, had he not also received these reports, to believe that the enemy force had first been discovered a half hour later than it actually was. This undoubtedly bears a close relation to the obviously inaccurate statement in the narrative portion of the Nagumo Force official action report, referred to earlier, with regard to the time of receipt of the TONE plane's 0728 message.

The message is further inaccurate in that the sighting position given is the position as of 0728, when the enemy was first spotted, and not as of 0800; and also in that it fails to mention the two additional cruisers reported by the TONE plane at 0830, 25 minutes before this message was dispatched.

Finally, it is curious that the message concludes, "We will head for it" (the enemy force) without mentioning the temporary northward retirement while preparing to attack. In this connection, the ONI translation of the Nagumo Force

By 0918 the recovery of the last plane of the Midway Attack Force as well as the second wave fighters on combat air patrol had been completed. Course was set at 030°, and the force sped on at 30 knots to lessen the danger from Midway-based air and at the same time achieve a position of advantage over the enemy fleet.

During all this feverish activity and excitement, I had remained prostrate on the deck at the flight command post, a helpless spectator of events. Our success in beating off the much-feared attacks by enemy shore-based planes had led me to share the prevailing optimism. Then, someone had told me of the sighting of the enemy task force, but I did not learn until after the operation the details of the discussions on AKAGI's bridge which led up to Admiral Nagumo's final decision to defer action until he could mount an all-out attack.

Unaware of these deliberations, I felt relieved that our second attack wave had not yet been committed to Midway, at the same time regretting the hasty rearming of our torpedo bombers for a land attack. At least, I thought, the dive-bomber group from HIRYU and SORYU was ready to attack the enemy, and I expected that it would be ordered off the carriers momentarily. This expectation—and hope—waned as the recovery of the first attack wave got underway with no sign that the dive bombers had yet taken off. It gave way to dismayed surprise when I learned of Admiral Nagumo's order issued at 0855, indicating that no attack would be launched until we had time to reorganize our forces while temporarily retiring northward.

Looking back on this critical moment, which ultimately was to decide the battle, I can easily realize what a difficult choice faced the Force Commander. Yet, even now, I find it hard to justify the decision he took. Should he not have sacrificed every

---

report translates the above-quoted part of the message, "We *are heading* for it," But as the vagaries of Japanese syntax allow either a present or future meaning of the verb, it appears fairer to Admiral Nagumo to choose the future rendition as given in this account.

other consideration in favor of sending the dive bombers immediately against the enemy ships? Should he not have dispatched the torpedo bombers also, even though armed with bombs? He could have launched them to orbit until enough fighters could be recovered, refueled and launched again to provide escort. The planes back from Midway could have been kept in the air at least until the bombers had cleared. Damaged planes, if unable to remain aloft any longer, could have crash-landed in the sea, where destroyers would have rescued their crews.

"Wise after the event," the saying goes. Still, there is no question that it would have been wiser to launch our dive bombers immediately, even without fighter protection. In such all-or-nothing carrier warfare, no other choice was admissible. Even the risk of sending unprotected level bombers should have been accepted as necessary in this emergency. Their fate would probably have been the same as that of the unescorted American planes which had attacked us a short while before, but just possibly they might have saved us from the catastrophe we were about to suffer.

6. ENEMY CARRIER PLANES ATTACK

As the Nagumo Force proceeded northward, our four carriers feverishly prepared to attack the enemy ships. The attack force was to include 36 dive bombers (18 "Vals" each from HIRYU and SORYU) and 54 torpedo bombers (18 "Kates" each from AKAGI and KAGA, and nine each from HIRYU and SORYU). It proved impossible, however, to provide an adequate fighter escort because enemy air attacks began again shortly, and most of our Zeros had to be used to defend the Striking Force itself. As a result, only 12 Zeros (three from each carrier) could be assigned to protect the bomber groups. The 102-plane attack force was to be ready for take-off at 1030.

After TONE's search plane reported the presence of a carrier in the enemy task force, we expected an attack momentarily and were puzzled that it took so long in coming. As we found out after the war, the enemy had long been awaiting our approach, was continuously informed of our movements by the flying boats from Midway, and was choosing the most advantageous time to pounce. Admiral Spruance, commanding the American force, planned to strike his first blow as our carriers were recovering and refueling their planes returned from Midway. His wait for the golden opportunity was rewarded at last. The quarry was at hand, and the patient hunter held every advantage.

Between 0702 and 0902 the enemy launched 131 dive bombers and torpedo planes. At about 0920 our screening ships began reporting enemy carrier planes approaching. We were in for a concentrated attack, and the Nagumo Force faced the gravest crisis of its experience. Was there any escape? An electric thrill ran throughout the fleet as our interceptors took off amid the cheers of all who had time and opportunity to see them.

Reports of approaching enemy planes increased until it was quite evident that they were not from a single carrier. When the Admiral and his staff realized this, their optimism abruptly vanished. The only way to stave off disaster was to launch planes at once. The order went out: "Speed preparations for immediate take off!" This command was almost superfluous. Aviation officers, maintenance crews, and pilots were all working frantically to complete launching preparations.

The first enemy carrier planes to attack were 15 torpedo bombers.[7] When first spotted by our screening ships and combat air patrol, they were still not visible from the carriers, but they soon appeared as tiny dark specks in the blue sky, a little above the horizon, on AKAGI's starboard bow. The distant wings

---

[7] *Editors' Note:* These planes were of the valiant VTB-8 (Lt. Cdr. J. C. Waldron) from HORNET. All 15 planes were shot down, and the sole survivor was Ens. G. H. Gay, who was rescued from the water by a Navy Catalina next day.

flashed in the sun. Occasionally one of the specks burst into a spark of flame and trailed black smoke as it fell into the water. Our fighters were on the job, and the enemy again seemed to be without fighter protection.

Presently a report came in from a Zero group leader: "All 15 enemy torpedo bombers shot down." Nearly 50 Zeros had gone to intercept the unprotected enemy formation! Small wonder that it did not get through.

Again at 0930 a lookout atop the bridge yelled: "Enemy torpedo bombers, 30 degrees to starboard, coming in low!" This was followed by another cry from a port lookout forward: "Enemy torpedo planes approaching 40 degrees to port!"

The raiders closed in from both sides, barely skimming over the water. Flying in single columns, they were within five miles and seemed to be aiming straight for AKAGI. I watched in breathless suspense, thinking how impossible it would be to dodge all their torpedoes. But these raiders, too, without protective escorts, were already being engaged by our fighters. On AKAGI's flight deck all attention was fixed on the dramatic scene unfolding before us, and there was wild cheering and whistling as the raiders went down one after another.

Of the 14 enemy torpedo bombers which came in from starboard, half were shot down, and only 5 remained of the original 12 planes to port. The survivors kept charging in as AKAGI opened fire with antiaircraft machine guns.

Both enemy groups reached their release points, and we watched for the splash of torpedoes aimed at AKAGI. But, to our surprise, no drops were made. At the last moment the planes appeared to forsake AKAGI, zoomed overhead, and made for HIRYU to port and astern of us. As the enemy planes passed AKAGI, her gunners regained their composure and opened a sweeping fire, in which HIRYU joined. Through all this deadly gunfire the Zeros kept after the Americans, continually reducing their number.

Seven enemy planes finally succeeded in launching their

torpedoes at HIRYU, five from her starboard side and two from port. Our Zeros tenaciously pursued the retiring attackers as far as they could. HIRYU turned sharply to starboard to evade the torpedoes, and we watched anxiously to see if any would find their mark. A deep sigh of relief went up when no explosion occurred, and HIRYU soon turned her head to port and resumed her original course. A total of more than 40 enemy torpedo planes had been thrown against us in these attacks, but only seven American planes had survived long enough to release their missiles, and not a single hit had been scored. Nearly all of the raiding enemy planes were brought down.[8]

Most of the credit for this success belonged to the brilliant interception of our fighters, whose swift and daring action was watched closely from the flagship. No less impressive was the dauntless courage shown by the American fliers, who carried out the attack despite heavy losses. Shipboard spectators of this thrilling drama watched spellbound, blissfully unaware that the worst was yet to come.

As our fighters ran out of ammunition during the fierce battle, they returned to the carriers for replenishment, but few ran low on fuel. Service crews cheered the returning pilots, patted them on the shoulder, and shouted words of encouragement. As soon as a plane was ready again, the pilot nodded, pushed forward the throttle, and roared back into the sky. This scene was repeated time and again as the desperate air struggle continued.

7. *FIVE FATEFUL MINUTES*

Preparations for a counter-strike against the enemy had continued on board our four carriers throughout the enemy torpedo attacks. One after another, planes were hoisted from the

[8] *Editors' Note:* Of the total 41 torpedo planes from the three American carriers, only six actually returned from the attack.

Fire and Damage on USS *Yorktown* (CV-5) During Battle of Midway

BATTLE OF MIDWAY, JUNE, 1942. THE USS *Yorktown* (CV-5) MANEUVERS TO AVOID
ANOTHER TORPEDO ATTACK

hangar and quickly arranged on the flight deck. There was no time to lose. At 1020 Admiral Nagumo gave the order to launch when ready. On AKAGI's flight deck all planes were in position with engines warming up. The big ship began turning into the wind. Within five minutes all her planes would be launched.

Five minutes! Who would have dreamed that the tide of battle would shift completely in that brief interval of time?

Visibility was good. Clouds were gathering at about 3,000 meters, however, and though there were occasional breaks, they afforded good concealment for approaching enemy planes. At 1024 the order to start launching came from the bridge by voice-tube. The Air Officer flapped a white flag, and the first Zero fighter gathered speed and whizzed off the deck. At that instant a lookout screamed: "Hell-divers!" I looked up to see three black enemy planes plummeting toward our ship. Some of our machine guns managed to fire a few frantic bursts at them, but it was too late. The plump silhouettes of the American "Dauntless" dive bombers quickly grew larger, and then a number of black objects suddenly floated eerily from their wings. Bombs! Down they came straight toward me! I fell intuitively to the deck and crawled behind a command post mantelet.

The terrifying scream of the dive bombers reached me first, followed by the crashing explosion of a direct hit. There was a blinding flash and then a second explosion, much louder than the first. I was shaken by a weird blast of warm air. There was still another shock, but less severe, apparently a near-miss. Then followed a startling quiet as the barking of guns suddenly ceased. I got up and looked at the sky. The enemy planes were already gone from sight.

The attackers had gotten in unimpeded because our fighters, which had engaged the preceding wave of torpedo planes only a few moments earlier, had not yet had time to regain altitude.

Consequently, it may be said that the American dive bombers' success was made possible by the earlier martyrdom of their torpedo planes. Also, our carriers had no time to evade because clouds hid the enemy's approach until he dove down to the attack. We had been caught flatfooted in the most vulnerable condition possible—decks loaded with planes armed and fueled for an attack.

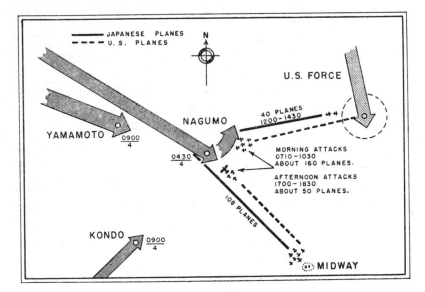

AIR ACTION, 4 JUNE 1942

Looking about, I was horrified at the destruction that had been wrought in a matter of seconds. There was a huge hole in the flight deck just behind the amidship elevator. The elevator itself, twisted like molten glass, was drooping into the hangar. Deck plates reeled upward in grotesque configurations. Planes stood tail up, belching livid flame and jet-black smoke. Reluctant tears streamed down my cheeks as I watched the fires spread, and I was terrified at the prospect of induced explosions which would surely doom the ship. I heard Masuda yelling, "Inside! Get inside! Everybody who isn't working! Get inside!"

Unable to help, I staggered down a ladder and into the ready room. It was already jammed with badly burned victims from the hangar deck. A new explosion was followed quickly by several more, each causing the bridge structure to tremble. Smoke from the burning hangar gushed through passageways and into the bridge and ready room, forcing us to seek other refuge. Climbing back to the bridge I could see that KAGA and SORYU had also been hit and were giving off heavy columns of black smoke. The scene was horrible to behold.

AKAGI had taken two direct hits, one on the after rim of the amidship elevator, the other on the rear guard on the portside of the flight deck. Normally, neither would have been fatal to the giant carrier, but induced explosions of fuel and munitions devastated whole sections of the ship, shaking the bridge and filling the air with deadly splinters. As fire spread among the planes lined up wing to wing on the after flight deck, their torpedoes began to explode, making it impossible to bring the fires under control. The entire hangar area was a blazing inferno, and the flames moved swiftly toward the bridge.

Because of the spreading fire, our general loss of combat efficiency, and especially the severance of external communication facilities, Nagumo's Chief of Staff, Rear Admiral Kusaka, urged that the Flag be transferred at once to light cruiser NAGARA. Admiral Nagumo gave only a half-hearted nod, but Kusaka patiently continued his entreaty: "Sir, most of our ships are still intact. You must command them."

The situation demanded immediate action, but Admiral Nagumo was reluctant to leave his beloved flagship. Most of all he was loathe to leave behind the officers and men of AKAGI, with whom he had shared every joy and sorrow of war. With tears in his eyes, Captain Aoki spoke up: "Admiral, I will take

care of the ship. Please, we all implore you, shift your flag to
NAGARA and resume command of the Force."

At this moment Lieutenant Commander Nishibayashi, the
Flag Secretary, came up and reported to Kusaka: "All passages
below are afire, Sir. The only means of escape is by rope from
the forward window of the bridge down to the deck, then by
the outboard passage to the anchor deck. NAGARA's boat will
come alongside the anchor deck port, and you can reach it by
rope ladder."

Kusaka made a final plea to Admiral Nagumo to leave the
doomed ship. At last convinced that there was no possibility
of maintaining command from AKAGI, Nagumo bade the Captain good-bye and climbed from the bridge window with the
aid of Nishibayashi. The Chief of Staff and other staff and
headquarters officers followed. The time was 1046.

On the bridge there remained only Captain Aoki, his Navigator, the Air Officer, a few enlisted men, and myself. Aoki
was trying desperately to get in touch with the engine room.
The Chief Navigator was struggling to see if anything could
be done to regain rudder control. The others were gathered on
the anchor deck fighting the raging fire as best they could. But
the unchecked flames were already licking at the bridge. Ham-
mock mantelets around the bridge structure were beginning to
burn. The Air Officer looked back at me and said, "Fuchida, we
won't be able to stay on the bridge much longer. You'd better
get to the anchor deck before it is too late."

In my condition this was no easy task. Helped by some
sailors, I managed to get out of the bridge window and slid
down the already smoldering rope to the gun deck. There I was
still ten feet above the flight deck. The connecting monkey
ladder was red hot, as was the iron plate on which I stood.
There was nothing to do but jump, which I did. At the same
moment another explosion occurred in the hangar, and the resultant blast sent me sprawling. Luckily the deck on which I

landed was not yet afire, for the force of the fall knocked me out momentarily. Returning to consciousness, I struggled to rise to my feet, but both of my ankles were broken.

Crewmen finally came to my assistance and took me to the anchor deck, which was already jammed. There I was strapped into a bamboo stretcher and lowered to a boat which carried me, along with other wounded, to light cruiser NAGARA. The transfer of Nagumo's staff and of the wounded was completed at 1130. The cruiser got under way, flying Admiral Nagumo's flag at her mast.

Meanwhile, efforts to bring AKAGI's fires under control continued, but it became increasingly obvious that this was impossible. As the ship came to a halt, her bow was still pointed into the wind, and pilots and crew had retreated to the anchor deck to escape the flames, which were reaching down to the lower hangar deck. When the dynamos went out, the ship was deprived not only of illumination but of pumps for combatting the conflagration as well. The fireproof hangar doors had been destroyed, and in this dire emergency even the chemical fire extinguishers failed to work.

The valiant crew located several hand pumps, brought them to the anchor deck, and managed to force water through long hoses into the lower hangar and decks below. Firefighting parties, wearing gas masks, carried cumbersome pieces of equipment and fought the flames courageously. But every induced explosion overhead penetrated to the deck below, injuring men and interrupting their desperate efforts. Stepping over fallen comrades, another damage-control party would dash in to continue the struggle, only to be mowed down by the next explosion. Corpsmen and volunteers carried out dead and wounded from the lower first aid station, which was jammed with injured men. Doctors and surgeons worked like machines.

The engine rooms were still undamaged, but fires in the

middle deck sections had cut off all communication between the bridge and the lower levels of the ship. Despite this the explosions, shocks, and crashes above, plus the telegraph indicator which had rung up "Stop," told the engine-room crews in the bowels of the ship that something must be wrong. Still, as long as the engines were undamaged and full propulsive power was available, they had no choice but to stay at General Quarters. Repeated efforts were made to communicate with the bridge, but every channel of contact, including the numerous auxiliary ones, had been knocked out.

The intensity of the spreading fires increased until the heat-laden air invaded the ship's lowest sections through the intakes, and men working there began falling from suffocation. In a desperate effort to save his men, the Chief Engineer, Commander K. Tampo, made his way up through the flaming decks until he was able to get a message to the Captain, reporting conditions below. An order was promptly given for all men in the engine spaces to come up on deck. But it was too late. The orderly who tried to carry the order down through the blazing hell never returned, and not a man escaped from the engine rooms.

As the number of dead and wounded increased and the fires got further out of control, Captain Aoki finally decided at 1800 that the ship must be abandoned. The injured were lowered into boats and cutters sent alongside by the screening destroyers. Many uninjured men leapt into the sea and swam away from the stricken ship. Destroyers ARASHI and NOWAKI picked up all survivors. When the rescue work was completed, Captain Aoki radioed to Admiral Nagumo at 1920 from one of the destroyers, asking permission to sink the crippled carrier. This inquiry was monitored by the Combined Fleet flagship, whence Admiral Yamamoto dispatched an order at 2225 to delay the carrier's disposition. Upon receipt of this instruction, the Captain returned to his carrier alone. He reached the anchor deck, which was still free from fire, and there lashed himself to an anchor to await the end.

Stand-by destroyer ARASHI received word at midnight that an enemy force was 90 miles to the east of AKAGI's and her own position. One hour later a lookout sighted several warships through the darkness, and the commander of the destroyer division, Captain K. Ariga, gave chase with all four of his ships, ARASHI, NOWAKI, HAGIKAZE, and MAIKAZE. He failed to catch up with or identify these shadows, however, and returned to stand by the carrier. It later turned out that the mysterious ships belonged to Rear Admiral Tanaka's Destroyer Squadron 2.[9]

When Admiral Yamamoto ordered the delay in disposing of AKAGI, it was because he saw no need for haste in this action since his force was then proceeding eastward to make a night attack on the enemy. Now, however, as defeat became apparent and the prospect of a night engagement grew dim, a quick decision became necessary. At 0350 on 5 June, Admiral Yamamoto finally gave the fateful order to scuttle the great carrier. Admiral Nagumo relayed the order to Captain Ariga, directing him to rejoin the force when his mission had been accomplished. Ariga in turn ordered his four destroyers to fire torpedoes at the doomed ship. NOWAKI's skipper, Commander Magotaro Koga, later described how painful it was for him to fire the powerful new Type-93 torpedo into the carrier, which was his first target of the war. Within 20 minutes all four destroyers had fired. Seven minutes later the sea closed over the mighty ship, and a terrific underwater explosion occurred, sending out shocks that were felt in each destroyer. The carrier's final rest-

---

[9] *Editorial Note:* DesRon 2 was part of Vice Admiral Kondo's Midway Invasion Force, assigned to direct escort of the Transport Group. When Kondo advanced eastward hoping to engage the enemy in surface battle during the night of 4 June, Destroyer-Squadron 2 was included in his forces, explaining its presence in this area.

ing place was at latitude 30° 30′ N, longitude 179° 08′ W.[10]
The time was 0455, just minutes before sunrise.

All but 263 members of the carrier's crew survived this last
of her great battles. Before the fatal torpedoes were fired,
AKAGI's navigator, Commander Y. Miura, had boarded the
carrier and persuaded Captain Aoki to give up his determination
to go down with the ship. Both men finally moved safely to
one of the destroyers.

KAGA, which had been hit almost simultaneously with AKAGI
in the sudden dive-bombing attack, did not last as long as the
flagship. Nine enemy planes had swooped down on her at 1024,
each dropping a single bomb. The first three were near-misses
which sent up geysers of water around her without doing any
damage. But no fewer than four of the next six bombs scored
direct hits on the forward, middle and after sections of the
flight deck. The bomb which struck closest to the bow landed
just forward of the bridge, blowing up a small gasoline truck
which was standing there and spreading fire and death throughout the bridge and surrounding deck area. Captain Jisaku Okada
and most of the other occupants of the ship's nerve center were
killed on the spot. The senior officer to survive the holocaust

---

[10] *Editors' Note:* The sinking positions of the Japanese carriers (scuttling position for HIRYU) given in this book are those shown on the action chart of the
Nagumo Force official action report (*First Air Fleet Detailed Battle Report No.
6, 15 June 1942*), previously cited. The action chart positions, except in the
case of KAGA, differ considerably from the sinking positions stated in the narrative
summary and ship damage table of this same document. The widest divergence is in
respect to the scuttling position of HIRYU, the chart position being 31° 38′ N,
178° 51′ W, and the position given in the narrative summary and ship damage
table being 31° 27′ 30″ N, 179° 23′ 30″ E. In view of these discrepancies in
the Battle Report, the American editors requested that the author make a thorough
check to determine, if possible, which positions are correct. The author did this,
consulting all available records as well as key participants still living, including
Commander Minoru Genda. His conclusion, independently supported by
American evidence, was that the chart positions are the correct ones. It is interesting to note that the original Japanese version of this book neatly avoided this
whole problem by nowhere giving the sinking positions, either textually or in
charts.

was Commander Takahisa Amagai, the Air Officer, who immediately took command of the carrier.

Furious fires broke out, seemingly everywhere. During the succeeding hours damage control crews fought desperately to check the spreading flames, but their efforts were largely unavailing, and there was scarcely a place of shelter left in the entire ship. Commander Amagai was forced to seek refuge on the starboard boat deck, where he was joined by many of the men. The carrier's doom seemed imminent.

Some three and a half hours after the bombing attack, a new menace appeared. The flame-wracked carrier now lay dead in the water and had begun to list. Commander Amagai, scanning the adjacent sea, suddenly discerned the telltale periscope of a submarine a few thousand meters from the ship. Minutes later, at 1410, Lieutenant Commander Yoshio Kunisada, a damage control officer, saw three white torpedo wakes streaking toward the carrier. They seemed sure to hit, and Kunisada closed his eyes and prayed as he waited for the explosions. None came. Two of the torpedoes barely missed the ship, and the third, though it struck, miraculously failed to explode. Instead, it glanced off the side and broke into two sections, the warhead sinking into the depths while the buoyant after section remained floating nearby. Several of KAGA's crew, who were swimming about in the water after having jumped or been blown overboard when the bombs struck the carrier, grabbed onto the floating section and used it as a support while awaiting rescue. Thus did a weapon of death become instead a life-saver in one of the curious twists of war.[11]

[11] *Editors' Note:* Details of the submarine attack on KAGA are from Cdr. Amagai, who survived the war and now resides at Tsuchiura, near Tokyo. When interrogated by the United States Strategic Bombing Survey in October 1945, this same officer gave an account which differed in some minor particulars. (Cf. USSBS, *Interrogations of Japanese Officials*, I, p. 2.) His recollection at the time of this interrogation was that he had been swimming in the water following KAGA's abandonment when the submarine made its attack. Later, however, in

KAGA's protecting destroyers, HAGIKAZE and MAIKAZE, were unaware of the submarine's presence until the torpedo attack occurred. Immediately they sped out to its suspected location and delivered a heavy depth-charge attack, the results of which were not known. The submarine failed to reappear, so the destroyers turned back to the crippled carrier and resumed rescue operations.

Meanwhile, uncontrollable fires continued to rage throughout KAGA's length, and finally, at 1640, Commander Amagai gave the order to abandon ship. Survivors were transferred to the two destroyers standing by. Two hours later the conflagration subsided enough to enable Commander Amagai to lead a damage-control party back on board in the hope of saving the ship. Their valiant efforts proved futile, however, and they again withdrew. The once crack carrier, now a burning hulk, was wrenched by two terrific explosions before sinking into the depths at 1925 in position 30° 20′ N, 179° 17′ W. In this battle 800 men of KAGA's crew, one-third of her complement, were lost.

SORYU, the third victim of the enemy dive-bombing attack, received one hit fewer than KAGA, but the devastation was just as great. When the attack broke, deck parties were busily pre-

---

view of documentary records establishing that the submarine attacked at 1410 and that his own order to abandon ship was not issued until 1640, he recognized that his previous USSBS statement must have confused the actual sequence of events. Further modifying his earlier testimony, Amagai explained that, although he saw the submarine's periscope before the attack, he personally did not observe the torpedoes coming at the ship. He said that Lieutenant Commander Kunisada, who at the time was lying on the exposed bulge of the listing carrier, did see them and reported the details to him (Amagai) after they both had transferred to one of the rescue destroyers. These minor changes do not affect the main point of Amagai's testimony; namely, that an enemy submarine tried to torpedo KAGA but failed to inflict any damage. This is corroborated by the action chart of the Nagumo Force official action report, which records a submarine torpedo attack on KAGA at 1110 June 5, Japan time (1410 June 4, Midway time), noting "no damage sustained." The report specifies "induced explosions in gasoline or bomb storage compartments" as the cause of KAGA's sinking.

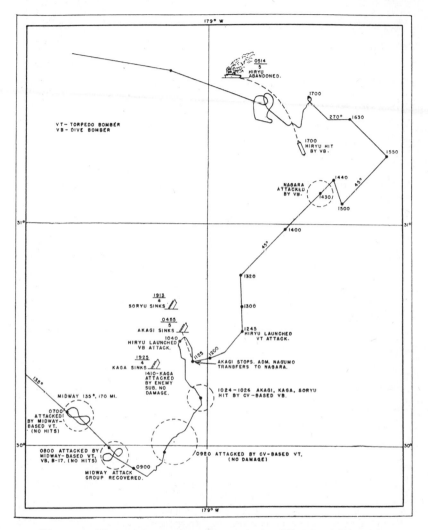

NAGUMO FORCE ACTION, 4 JUNE 1942 (Track of Flagship
Akagi up to 1125, *Nagara* thereafter)

paring the carrier's planes for take-off, and their first awareness
of the onslaught came when great flashes of fire were seen
sprouting from KAGA, some distance off to port, followed by
explosions and tremendous columns of black smoke. Eyes in

stinctively looked skyward just in time to see a spear of 13
American planes plummeting down on SORYU. It was 1025.

Three hits were scored in as many minutes. The first blasted
the flight deck in front of the forward elevator, and the next
two straddled the amidship elevator, completely wrecking the
deck and spreading fire to gasoline tanks and munition storage
rooms. By 1030 the ship was transformed into a hell of smoke
and flames, and induced explosions followed shortly.

In the next ten minutes the main engines stopped, the steering system went out, and fire mains were destroyed. Crewmen,
forced by the flames to leave their posts, had just arrived on
deck when a mighty explosion blasted many of them into the
water. Within 20 minutes of the first bomb hit, the ship was
such a mass of fire that Captain Ryusaku Yanagimoto ordered
"Abandon ship!" Many men jumped into the water to escape
the searing flames and were picked up by destroyers HAMAKAZE
and ISOKAZE. Others made more orderly transfers to the destroyers.

It was soon discovered, however, that Captain Yanagimoto
had remained on the bridge of the blazing carrier. No ship
commander in the Japanese Navy was more beloved by his men.
His popularity was such that whenever he was going to address
the assembled crew, they would gather an hour or more in
advance to insure getting a place up front. Now, they were
determined to rescue him at all costs.

Chief Petty Officer Abe, a Navy wrestling champion, was
chosen to return and rescue the Captain, because it had been
decided to bring him to safety by force if he refused to come
willingly. When Abe climbed to SORYU's bridge, he found
Captain Yanagimoto standing there motionless, sword in hand,
gazing resolutely toward the ship's bow. Stepping forward, Abe
said, "Captain, I have come on behalf of all your men to take
you to safety. They are waiting for you. Please come with me
to the destroyer, Sir."

When this entreaty met with silence, Abe guessed the Captain's thoughts and started toward him with the intention of carrying him bodily to the waiting boat. But the sheer strength of will and determination of his grim-faced commander stopped him short. He turned tearfully away, and as he left the bridge he heard Captain Yanagimoto calmly singing "Kimigayo," the national anthem.

At 1913, while her survivors watched from the near-by destroyers, SORYU finally disappeared into a watery grave, carrying with her the bodies of 718 men, including her Captain. The position of the sinking was 30° 38′ N, 179° 13′ W.

Not one of the many observers who witnessed the last hours of this great carrier saw any sign of an enemy submarine or of submarine torpedoes. There was a succession of explosions in the carrier before she sank, but these were so unquestionably induced explosions that they could not have been mistaken for anything else. It seems beyond doubt, therefore, that American accounts which credit U.S. submarine NAUTILUS with delivering the *coup de grâce* to SORYU have confused her with KAGA. Nor, as already related, did the submarine attack on KAGA contribute in any way to her sinking.[12]

[12] *Editors' Note:* Since NAUTILUS' claim to have finished off SORYU has hitherto been accepted in all U.S. accounts of the Midway battle, the American editors have carefully reexamined the available evidence and are satisfied that it overwhelmingly supports the accuracy of the story as given here, indicating KAGA rather than SORYU to have been the target of the NAUTILUS attack and further indicating this attack to have been ineffectual. The evidence, in addition to that already cited in footnote 11, p. 185, is summarized below:

(a) The time given in *First Air Fleet Detailed Battle Report No. 6* for the submarine attack on KAGA, 1410 4 June, Midway time, jibes quite closely with the time given in American accounts for NAUTILUS' attack on what she believed to be SORYU. According to the latter accounts, NAUTILUS fired her torpedoes between 1359 and 1405 at a range of 2,700 yards, which means that they would have reached the target a few minutes later. The Japanese battle report records no submarine attack on SORYU at any time.

(b) Records for destroyer HAGIKAZE confirm that, while she was standing by crippled KAGA on 4 June, she carried out a depth-charge attack on an enemy submarine. Records for destroyers HAMAKAZE and ISOKAZE, which were standing by SORYU, mention no encounter whatever with an enemy submarine.

8. HIRYU'S GALLANT FIGHT

When enemy bombs rendered AKAGI incapable of functioning as fleet flagship, temporary command of the Nagumo Force was automatically assumed by Rear Admiral Hiroaki Abe,

---

(c) As available Japanese records do not show either KAGA's position when she was attacked or that of SORYU at the same time, there is no possibility of comparison with the NAUTILUS attack position of 30° 13′ N, 179° 17′ W. *First Air Fleet Detailed Battle Report No. 6,* however, does show the sinking positions of the two carriers, and it is worth noting that KAGA's, at 30° 20′ N, 179° 17′ W, is closer to the NAUTILUS attack position than SORYU's at 30° 38′ N, 179° 13′ W. According to Commander Amagai, SORYU was not within sight of KAGA at the time of the sub attack. KAGA, it should also be remembered, had lost all propulsive power by this time.

(d) The only contradictory evidence on the Japanese side is provided by postwar United States Strategic Bombing Survey interrogations of two Japanese officers: Captain Hisashi Ohara, who was executive officer of SORYU in the Midway battle, and Rear Admiral Keizo Komura, who commanded heavy cruiser CHIKUMA. The interrogation of Captain Ohara (USSBS, *Interrogations of Japanese Officials,* I, p. 168) credits him with stating that there was a big explosion in SORYU in mid-afternoon, 4 June, and that submarine torpedoes were responsible. Rear Admiral Komura (*Ibid.,* II, p. 460) was quoted as saying that SORYU was torpedoed by an enemy submarine at about 1100 June 5 (1400 June 4, Midway time), that CHIKUMA attacked the submarine, lowered a boat to help rescue SORYU's survivors, and then left the scene to join HIRYU.

In view of the conflict between Ohara's testimony, as reported by USSBS, and documentary sources, the author asked him in March 1954 for a recapitulation of the events leading up to SORYU's sinking in the Midway battle. Ohara replied with a written statement completely at variance with the interrogation cited above. In it he affirmed, "No underwater torpedo attacks were observed throughout the battle. I myself did not see any at all, nor was any reported to me by members of the crew."

As for Komura's statement, information contained in *First Air Fleet Detailed Battle Report No. 6* clearly shows it to be confused and erroneous. The report shows that it was actually at 1112 June 4, Midway time, shortly after the dive-bombing attack, that CHIKUMA dispatched her cutter to assist SORYU, and that she thereafter did not remain in the area but immediately proceeded north with other ships to screen HIRYU. Consequently CHIKUMA could not possibly have observed a torpedo attack on SORYU at 1400, three hours later, even if there had been one.

(e) Contradictory evidence on the American side boils down to NAUTILUS' identification of her target as a "SORYU-class carrier." Actually, KAGA could easily have been mistaken for SORYU as the two ships were strikingly similar in appearance except for KAGA's 25-foot greater length. Both carriers had starboard islands, whereas AKAGI and HIRYU had them on the port side. Since NAUTILUS' skipper, Lieutenant Commander W. A. Brockman, Jr., had only hurried and in-

Commander Cruiser Division 8, in his own flagship, heavy cruiser TONE. At the same time command of air operations passed to Rear Admiral Tamon Yamaguchi, Commander Carrier Division 2, whose flagship, HIRYU, was the only carrier left undamaged after the devastating enemy attack.

Rear Admiral Yamaguchi was one of the ablest commanding officers in the Japanese Navy. At the Naval Academy he had graduated second in his class. But unlike many honor graduates whose ability in the classroom failed to translate itself into ability in battle, he was daring and far-sighted, a clear-thinking and resolute commander with a capacity for quick decision.

Although defeat now stared us starkly in the face, the battle had to be continued as long as we retained even a small part of our striking power. Rear Admiral Abe quickly ordered Rear Admiral Susumu Kimura, Commander Destroyer Squadron 10, to stand by the three stricken carriers with light cruiser NAGARA and six destroyers. NAGARA was to become the force flagship after taking on board Admiral Nagumo and his staff from the disabled AKAGI. Two destroyers were assigned to screen each of the carriers and stand by to rescue the crews in case any ships had to be abandoned. The rest of the Nagumo Force, centered around HIRYU, continued steadily north.

With no time to lose, Rear Admiral Yamaguchi immediately decided to launch an attack on the American carriers. The attack force, consisting of 18 dive bombers and 6 escorting Zero fighters, took off at 1040. It was commanded by Lieutenant Michio Kobayashi, a HIRYU squadron leader, who had been with the Nagumo Force in every campaign. The planes flew toward the enemy at an altitude of 4,000 meters. On the way groups of American carrier planes were sighted winging their way homeward, and Kobayashi signalled his pilots to follow stealthily behind. Two of his covering fighters, however, in-

---

termittent periscope glimpses of his target, it is not surprising that he mistook KAGA for the smaller but otherwise similar SORYU. It is to be noted that Commander Brockman identified the two accompanying destroyers as cruisers.

discreetly pounced on the enemy torpedo bombers, reducing Kobayashi's escort to only four Zeros. When still some distance from their target, his planes were intercepted by enemy fighters who took a heavy toll. Nevertheless, eight planes got through to make the attack. Two of these were splashed by American cruiser and destroyer gunfire, but six bore in on the enemy carrier, scoring hits which started fires and raised billowing clouds of smoke.

Three Zeros and 13 dive bombers, including Kobayashi's, were lost in the attack. The five bomber pilots who returned brought back only fragmentary accounts which did not present a very coherent picture. A summary of their reports seemed to indicate that six bombs had been dropped, but the number of hits was not known or agreed upon. They claimed that about seven enemy planes had been shot down. One point of unanimity, however, was that an enemy carrier had been stopped and was sending up great columns of smoke. Admiral Yamaguchi concluded that it must have been hit by at least two 250-kilogram bombs and severely damaged.

What he did not know was that damage-control parties in the U.S. carrier YORKTOWN (for she had been the target) had worked so effectively that by 1400 the carrier was again able to make 18 knots under her own power.

At the first discovery of the American carrier force, Admiral Nagumo had ordered SORYU to launch her new high-speed reconnaissance plane to make contact with the enemy and confirm his strength. The plane had been launched promptly, but it had not sent in any radio reports. On his return the pilot found SORYU damaged and ablaze, so he landed on HIRYU's deck. Called before Admiral Yamaguchi, the pilot explained, "Radio trouble prevented my sending a message, so I hurried back to report that the enemy force contains three carriers— ENTERPRISE, HORNET, and YORKTOWN!"

This was startling news even though the number of planes in the first enemy strike had already made it plain that the

Bow View of Carrier *Hiryu* on Fire After Being Hit by
Dive Bombers in the Battle of Midway, 4 June 1942
(Photo by plane from light carrier *Hosho*)

BEL GEDDES MODEL OF FATAL ATTACK ON *Hiryu*, 4 JUNE

American force had more than the single carrier previously reported. HIRYU, now alone, faced three crack enemy carriers, only one of which had thus far suffered any damage. And one of these carriers was YORKTOWN, which we thought had been sunk, or at least very heavily damaged, in the Coral Sea battle!

Admiral Yamaguchi decided to launch another attack with all his remaining planes. Lieutenant Joichi Tomonaga, a HIRYU wing leader, was chosen to lead the 10 torpedo planes (one from AKAGI) and 6 fighters (two from KAGA) which were then available in HIRYU. The left wing fuel tank of Tomonaga's plane, damaged during the strike on Midway, had not yet been repaired. When his maintenance man mentioned this, Tomonaga merely smiled and said, "All right, don't worry. Leave the left tank as it is and fill up the other."

The man spoke again after a moment's hesitation, "Yes, Sir. But should we bring your plane to the starting line just the same?"

Fastening his flight suit, Tomonaga answered calmly, "Yes, and hurry it up. We're taking off." So the damaged plane was moved into position.

Several of Tomonaga's aviators begged him to exchange planes with them, but he cheerfully declined. Everyone knew that he would have insufficient fuel for the return flight, but no one mentioned it. It would have been no use, for clearly his mind was made up.

Preparations were completed at 1245, and the 16 planes rose from the flight deck to head for the enemy. Motionless as a statue, Admiral Yamaguchi watched the orderly take-off, led by a man who knew that he would not return. Every spectator stood grim and silent, crushed by this cruel aspect of war which allowed of no human feeling. One after another the planes roared off the deck. Hands were raised in silent farewell, and tears welled in every eye.

At 1426 the attack group spotted an enemy carrier with

several escorts some 10 miles ahead, and Tomonaga ordered his fliers to close for the attack. Protecting enemy fighters tried to intercept but were promptly engaged by the escorting Zeros while the torpedo planes bored in toward the carrier. At 1432 Tomonaga ordered his planes to break from their approach formation and split up to make runs on the target from various directions. Two minutes later he ordered the attack. Swooping from an altitude of 2,000 meters to within a hundred meters of the water, the planes headed straight for the American carrier. At 1445 a radio message reported two torpedo hits on this ship, which was identified half an hour later as being of the YORKTOWN class.

No further details of the attack were known until the surviving Japanese planes returned and were recovered by HIRYU at 1630. Only five torpedo bombers and three fighters—half of the number launched—got back to the carrier. The pilots claimed one hit on a carrier and reported severe damage to a SAN FRANCISCO-class cruiser, but later information indicated that the claimed hit on the cruiser had actually been a Japanese plane splashing into the water nearby. Eight enemy fighters were also reported to have been shot down.

Postwar American accounts show that around 1442 YORKTOWN actually received two torpedo hits, successfully evading two others which were aimed at her. The two hits, added to the damage inflicted by the earlier dive-bomber attacks, were enough to doom the ship.[13] But none of her escorts sustained any damage from this air attack.

As had been fully expected, Lieutenant Tomonaga's plane was not among those which came back. Lieutenant (jg) Toshiro

---

[13] *Editors' Note:* YORKTOWN'S captain ordered Abandon Ship within 15 minutes of the torpedo hits, but the carrier was still afloat two days later when Japanese submarine I-168 found her in the afternoon of 6 June and fired four torpedoes. Two hit YORKTOWN causing her to sink next morning at 0600, and one hit destroyer HAMMANN, engaged in salvage work alongside, causing her to sink within four minutes.

Hashimoto, who had flown with Tomonaga as observer in the first-wave attack on Midway but who was in a different plane in this attack, gave an eye-witness account of the finish of the gallant flight leader: "His plane, with its distinguishing yellow tail, was clearly discernible as he broke through the heaviest antiaircraft fire I have ever witnessed. He launched his torpedo, and then, in the next instant, his plane disintegrated. His assault on the carrier, in the face of that devastating gunfire, was tantamount to a suicide crash."

So ended the second raid by HIRYU planes and the last Japanese strike on American ships in the Battle of Midway. The aviators who made the attacks, as well as Rear Admiral Yamaguchi, who heard their reports, believed that the first and second attacks had hit different targets, and hence that two American carriers had been mortally damaged. The fact was, however, that YORKTOWN was the target both times. So speedily had repairs been effected after the first attack that Tomonaga's planes had mistaken her for another and undamaged ship.

9. ENEMY CARRIER PLANES STRIKE AGAIN

Having launched three air attacks, including the Midway strike, HIRYU was now almost devoid of planes. When the last returning plane of Tomonaga's group let down on the carrier's deck at 1630, HIRYU had left, out of all her planes, only six fighters, five dive bombers, and four torpedo bombers. The fliers, who had pursued the deadly struggle since dawn, were at the limit of exhaustion, and the ship's crew was in scarcely better condition. While her own planes were attacking the enemy, HIRYU had been the target of repeated and relentless enemy strikes. Since sunup no fewer than 79 planes had attacked, and the ship had successfully evaded some 26 torpedoes and 70 bombs. Nevertheless, despite his meager remaining air strength and the exhaustion of his men, Admiral Yamaguchi was still determined to fight back. He realized, however, that further daylight attack could not possibly succeed, and he decided to make a final attempt at twilight when his few planes would have a better chance of getting in to strike an effective blow at the enemy.

There was a lull in battle shortly before 1700, and the opportunity was taken to serve a meal to the crew, who were still at General Quarters. The fare was sweet rice balls, and everyone ate voraciously. But even during this brief respite, combat air patrol had to be maintained, making the most of the six remaining fighters. Preparations also went ahead for the planned dusk attack. In order to locate what was believed to be the enemy's only remaining carrier, Admiral Yamaguchi decided to send out a fast reconnaissance plane on search.

At 1703, just as this plane was ready to take off, a lookout shouted, "Enemy dive bombers directly overhead!" They had come in from the southwest so that the sun was behind them, and having no radar, we were unable to detect their approach. Thirteen planes singled out HIRYU as their target.

As the ship's antiaircraft batteries opened up, Captain Kaku, HIRYU's skipper, ordered full right rudder, and the ship swung lumberingly to starboard. This timely action enabled HIRYU to evade the first three bombs, but more enemy planes came diving in and finally registered four direct hits which set off fires and explosions. Columns of black smoke rose skyward as the carrier began to lose speed.

All four bomb hits were near the bridge, and the concussions shattered every window. The deck surface of the forward elevator was blasted upward so that it obstructed all forward view from the control area. Fire spread among the loaded planes on deck and cut off all passageway to the engine rooms. The doomed men below deck worked until they were overcome by the intense heat and suffocating smoke. Theirs was heroic courage and devotion to duty.

As the last of our carriers was hit and damaged, the enemy planes began devoting their attention to the screening ships as well. Battleship HARUNA had already been attacked at 1649 by four level bombers, and 19 minutes later she was attacked again by two dive bombers. All bombs fell short, and the battleship went unscathed. HARUNA escaped again at 1826 when attacked by land-based bombers. Heavy cruiser TONE was the target of three dive bombers at 1720, nine more at 1728, and then three land-based bombers at 1818, but no hits were scored. CHIKUMA eluded nine dive bombers at 1732, a single attack at 1745, and three land-based bombers at 1810.

HIRYU finally slowed to a halt at 2123 and began a list which increased to 15 degrees as she continued to ship water. Fire pumps were disabled, as was the steering system, but repairs were later effected on one of the pumps and it was worked vigorously to combat the flames. In the midst of these efforts enemy B-17s attacked but failed to make any bomb hits.

KAZAGUMO, flagship of Captain T. Abe, Commander Destroyer Division 10, was bravely and skillfully brought alongside the burning carrier to assist in fighting the fires and to supply the hard-working crew with food and drink. Destroyer YUGUMO stood guard nearby.

Two desperate attempts to gain access to the engine rooms were unsuccessful. Finally it became clear that there was no hope of saving the ship, and Admiral Yamaguchi sent a message to Admiral Nagumo, via destroyer KAZAGUMO, reporting that he was ordering HIRYU's crew to abandon ship. At 0230, 5 June, he directed Captain Kaku to summon all hands topside. To the 800 or so men who responded, he gave these final instructions:

As Commanding Officer of this carrier division, I am fully

and solely responsible for the loss of HIRYU and SORYU. I shall remain on board to the end. I command all of you to leave the ship and continue your loyal service to His Majesty, the Emperor.

Admiral Yamaguchi's staff begged permission to remain with him on the flagship, but their pleas were firmly rejected, and with sad reluctance they made ready to transfer to KAZAGUMO, standing alongside. Before parting, the Admiral and his staff drank a silent farewell toast in water from a breaker near at hand. The senior staff officer, Commander Ito, asked if there were any messages the Admiral wished to entrust to him. There were none, but Yamaguchi took off his black deck cap and gave it to Ito as a memento. He then asked for a length of cloth which Ito was carrying, so that he might lash himself to the bridge structure and thus be sure of going down with the ship.

Captain Kaku himself was determined to stay and accordingly besought the Admiral to leave the ship. Yamaguchi smiled understandingly, but firmly rejected this proposal with a shake of his head. So the two commanding officers bade a last farewell to their subordinates as a brilliant moon shone down on the devastation of the carrier's deck.

Surviving members of HIRYU's crew had already begun to transfer to KAZAGUMO. Captain Abe, commander of the destroyer division, crossed over to the carrier in a vain effort to persuade Admiral Yamaguchi and Captain Kaku to leave the ship. As the last survivors were leaving the ship, these two officers climbed to the bridge, where they were last seen waving goodbye to the men who had served them so long.

The destroyers then pulled clear of the carrier, and Captain Abe gave the order to administer the *coup de grâce* in accordance with Admiral Yamaguchi's final instructions. As the torpedoes from KAZAGUMO and YUGUMO found their mark at 0510, there were deafening explosions, and the big carrier started to go down. The first streaks of dawn were just reaching into the eastern sky as Captain Abe witnessed the explosions, and, satisfied that his work had been accomplished, he ordered the destroyers to retire. His report that HIRYU had been scuttled in position 31° 38′ N, 178° 51′ W was received in YAMATO at 0540. An hour and twenty minutes later, however, a plane from light carrier HOSHO, which had been sent eastward to locate Nagumo's force, discovered HIRYU still afloat. The plane reported that men could be seen on board, and several pictures were taken of the smoldering derelict.

Upon receiving this information, Admiral Yamamoto relayed it to Nagumo, ordering him to verify the scuttling and make every effort to rescue any survivors. Admiral Nagumo immediately detached TANIKAZE for the mission and ordered a seaplane launched from flagship NAGARA to cooperate in the search. But HIRYU was never seen again.

In the light of American data obtained after the war, it is now known that HIRYU remained afloat until around 0820. The men seen on deck were survivors of the engine-room crew, who had miraculously escaped from their entrapment belowdecks when the torpedoes from Abe's destroyers blasted open a way of exit. When the carrier sank, they were set adrift and subsequently picked up by an American ship. HIRYU's last battle cost the lives of 416 crewmen, in addition to the two commanders who elected to perish with her.

With the death of Admiral Yamaguchi the Japanese Navy lost one of its most brilliant officers. He had generally been considered the most likely successor to Admiral Yamamoto for the post of Commander in Chief Combined Fleet. His great courage and ability had inspired the confidence of his superiors, as it did the trust and faith of his subordinates. Grief at his loss was shared by every man who knew him.

His classmate, Combined Fleet Chief of Staff Ugaki, recorded an appreciation of Yamaguchi in a diary entry of 6 June:

"He was indeed a farsighted man. He was considerate of everyone, kind of heart, prompt of decision. His constructive recommendations, forcefully presented to his superiors, contributed
greatly to the success of operations; in this matter particularly
he stood out from other commanding officers and earned a place
of greatness."

The commander of the Second Carrier Striking Force, Rear
Admiral Kakuji Kakuta, also paid a warm tribute to Yamaguchi
when news of his death reached the Aleutians Forces. He confided to Lieutenant Commander Okumiya of his staff, "How I
wish that Yamaguchi had commanded this Force. Gladly would
I have served under him." And Yamaguchi had been a full year
his junior.

10. RETREAT

Now let us return to flagship NAGARA where the transfer of
Admiral Nagumo's flag was completed at 1130. Two minutes
earlier a CHIKUMA search plane had radioed, "Enemy in position bearing 070°, 90 miles from our force. Time 1110." There
was a brief interval of shocked surprise at this information.
Then the senior staff officer, Captain Oishi, suggested to the Admiral: "The enemy is much closer than we thought. If we advance at full speed, we might be able to engage him in a
surface action."

The enemy was now believed to have seven cruisers and five
destroyers accompanying his carriers. If our two fast battleships,
two heavy cruisers, one light cruiser, and twelve destroyers
could engage them in a daytime surface action, we might be able
to destroy the enemy ships with gunfire and torpedoes. In
NAGARA's immediate company at this time were only five destroyers. The others were standing by the three damaged carriers or steaming northward with battleships HARUNA and

VICE ADMIRAL (THEN REAR ADMIRAL) TAMON YAMAGUCHI

Editors' Note: Commander Okumiya calls attention to the fact that Admiral Yamaguchi attended Princeton at one time.

Japanese War Art Painting in Custody of U. S. Army.
Title "Last Moments of Admiral Yamaguchi"

Kirishima, heavy cruisers Tone and Chikuma, and carrier Hiryu.

Admiral Nagumo considered Oishi's proposal until 1153 and then acted upon it. A terse radio order was flashed to all units of the Force: "We will go to the attack now. Assemble!" The order was repeated at 1156 and again at 1159, the last of these messages directing the formation of a battle line on course 170° in the order of Destroyer Squadron 10, Cruiser Division 8 and Battleship Division 3. Nagara meanwhile had set course to the northeast at a speed of 24 knots to make the rendezvous.

Just before issuing these orders, Admiral Nagumo had dispatched a message to Admiral Yamamoto and Midway Invasion Force Commander Vice Admiral Kondo to notify them of his present situation and plans. The message, sent at 1150, stated: "As a result of enemy bombing attack at about 1030, Akagi, Kaga and Soryu sustained considerable damage, outbreak of fires rendering them inoperational. I have transferred to Nagara and plan to withdraw to the north with my entire force after attacking the enemy. . . ."

At 1300, however, Tone's search plane reported the discouraging news that the enemy was withdrawing. Since he had air superiority, it was to be expected that he would maintain a safe distance from the Japanese force and make repeated air attacks. With his screening force limited to cruisers and destroyers, it would have been foolish for him to risk a duel of gunfire and torpedoes. Moreover, his ships were supported by Midway-based air forces, and he had plenty of planes for reconnaissance. It was clear that, however desperately we dashed ahead, there would be little chance of engaging in a successful battle. We would only be throwing ourselves into the enemy's trap.

Consequently, after Nagara had been speeding northeastward for a little more than an hour, Nagumo and his staff de cided to give up the idea of a daylight battle. But something had to be done, and the next best possibility was a night engagement. Accordingly Admiral Nagumo decided to retire westward temporarily while preparing to engage the enemy in a night battle.

By 1445 NAGARA had caught up with HIRYU and the other ships, and the Force reformed with the flagship taking the lead, the carrier in the center, and the battleships and cruisers on the flanks. At 1620 Nagumo received word from Rear Admiral Yamaguchi that HIRYU was preparing to launch her remaining planes for a dusk attack on the enemy carriers. The Striking Force Commander assented to this plan, but he nevertheless ordered the Force to head due west, away from the enemy, while the attack preparations were being made.

Yamaguchi planned to launch his planes at 1800. At 1703, however, as already related, enemy dive bombers struck again, disabling HIRYU and depriving the Nagumo Force of its last remaining air strength. Nagumo's staff realized that the battle was lost and that the only hope was to avoid further destruction. But each man felt a personal responsibility for the defeat, and none could bring himself to suggest withdrawal.

The grim situation was painfully clear. Our air strength was wiped out. The enemy still had at least one carrier intact, we had failed to render the Midway airfields ineffective, and some of our ships were still within striking range of planes based there. With command of the air firmly in enemy hands, the outcome of the battle was a foregone conclusion.

What slim hopes remained for carrying out a night engagement faded considerably when, at 1733, another plane reported that the enemy task force was still withdrawing eastward. Nagumo's irritation at this news was obvious. Nevertheless, Oishi continued his efforts to pave the way for a night battle. He requested NAGARA, which carried the only night-scouting plane in the Force, to ready it for a search to locate the enemy.

An engagement was, of course, impossible unless the enemy was located, and it was generally recognized that there was little chance that a single plane could find the enemy ships in the dark of night. This gave rise to a growing skepticism among the rest of Nagumo's staff officers, but Oishi pressed his plan persistently. He further recommended that all destroyers standing by the damaged carriers be summoned to augment the force for the night engagement. Admiral Nagumo gave his approval to this suggestion and the order was issued for all forces, including the stand-by destroyers, to assemble.

This action came as a complete surprise to the other staff officers. What would become of the crews if these ships should sink with no rescuers at hand? Furthermore, unless a withdrawal could be effected before dawn—after rescuing the crews and disposing of the damaged carriers—all would become daylight targets for rampaging enemy planes. These thoughts must have occurred to everyone, but they remained unspoken.

At 1830 a blinker message from CHIKUMA served further to deepen the gloom in NAGARA. It read: "At 1713 this ship's No. 2 plane sighted four enemy carriers, six cruisers, and fifteen destroyers at a point 30 miles east of the burning carrier. The enemy force is proceeding westward."[14]

This message forced a re-examination of our plans, since it showed the enemy to be far stronger than we had estimated. It would take more than good luck for our Force, with no radar and only one night-scouting plane, to find and successfully engage this enemy. And if we failed in a night engagement, there would be no chance of eluding dawn attacks. Our ships

[14] *Editors' Note:* This report was correct as to total ship count but sadly amiss in that two cruisers were mistaken for carriers. But for the "burning carrier" (YORKTOWN), the two U.S. task forces were still undamaged and at this time comprised two carriers, eight cruisers, and fifteen destroyers.

would be like sitting ducks. Realizing this, Admiral Nagumo finally decided to forego a night action attempt and chose the wiser course of retiring to live and fight another day. The rescue destroyers were ordered back to the disabled carriers.

The battle lost, Nagumo withdrew to the northwest. Burning HIRYU tagged along, but she was soon outdistanced and had to be left behind with destroyers KAZAGUMO and YUGUMO standing by.

CHAPTER 10 **Admiral Yamamoto's Operations**

1. ON THE BRIDGE OF YAMATO

The early morning of 4 June found Combined Fleet flagship YAMATO heading eastward at a point 800 miles northwest of Midway. Sunrise was at 0452, but the fog which had enshrouded the force for days still remained so dense that from YAMATO's deck the other ships in the formation could not be seen.

All was silent on the bridge of the flagship. The thoughts of every man were with the Nagumo Force, then proceeding in the van of the whole Fleet. Was it, too, surrounded by fog? It was impossible to dispel the grave apprehension that this might disrupt the whole operation.

Spirits brightened as the sun finally burned through and the fog thinned. An order was issued to carry out last-minute refueling, and battleship NAGATO took lines from fleet tanker TOEI MARU for that purpose.

At 0535 YAMATO received the message sent by TONE's seaplane when it sighted an enemy flying boat. Yamamoto and his staff waited expectantly, figuring that the American PBY would soon discover Nagumo's ships.

The succeeding message from TONE's plane at 0555, announcing the approach of 15 planes, made it appear that an attack on the Nagumo Force was imminent. This did not disturb Combined Fleet, however, for it was presumed that the Midway strike had already been safely launched and that Nagumo's combat air patrol could easily take care of so few American planes. The action was now opened, and everything was going as planned. Attention focussed on the loudspeaker from the radio room, which relayed incoming messages to the bridge. Scout-plane reports were coming in, but there was nothing from Nagumo's flagship, which apparently was still keeping radio silence. Presently Lieutenant Tomonaga, commander of the Midway strike, reported the completion of his mission and recommended a second strike. Yamamoto and his staff waited expectantly for word that the second attack wave had been launched, confident that enemy air strength on the island would soon be destroyed.

Admiral Yamamoto had been suffering from a stomach ailment since the day before, but he was now in high spirits as he listened to the reports of his jubilant staff officers. The entire staff felt that the operation was going smoothly.

The next report, therefore, came as a startling surprise. Received at 0740, it was the 0728 message from Tone's search plane announcing that it had sighted "ten ships, apparently enemy." This made it evident that, contrary to all our estimates, enemy surface forces were in the vicinity. On the bridge excitement ran high. An enemy force within distance to engage! The enemy's unusual radio activity of a week before suddenly came to mind and took on meaning.

The question now was, What was in the enemy force? There was a tense silence until, at about 0820, another message from the Tone plane gave the composition of the enemy fleet as five cruisers and five destroyers. This was followed about ten minutes later by a supplementary report that the enemy had one carrier bringing up the rear.

Here was big game, and the excitement on Yamato's bridge rose to fever pitch! Kuroshima, the senior staff officer, asked if Nagumo's plan had called for the second attack wave to be held ready for a possible attack on an enemy surface force.

Sasaki, the Air Officer, answered with perfect confidence, "Yes, Sir, and it will make short work of them, too."

Miwa, the Operations Officer, interrupted, "But hasn't the second attack wave already been launched for another strike at Midway?"

This remark jolted everyone to the sudden realization that only a moment before they had been expecting the Nagumo Force to launch the second wave against Midway to complete the destruction of the enemy's shore-based air forces. Sasaki was covered with confusion. He immediately phoned the radio room and asked if there had been any report that the second attack wave had taken off for Midway.

"No, Sir. There is no indication that it has."

The reply brought a deep sigh of relief. The enemy carriers, it was thought, would quickly be disposed of by planes of our second attack wave.

This optimism was amazing in view of the fact that not only in the planning of the operation, but even up to just a few moments before, no one had even dreamed that enemy carriers might be encountered on the approach to Midway. Now with this calculation suddenly proven wrong, there was momentary surprise, but nobody seemed greatly concerned about it or about the fact that Combined Fleet Headquarters had been guilty of a serious oversight. Everyone appeared fully convinced that the Japanese forces would be able to smash the enemy, however prepared he might be, as soon as his fleet was located. The situation reminds one of a Japanese wrestling champion who, confident in his own strength, stands majestically in the middle of the ring, allowing his opponent to act first.

At 0847 still another message from TONE's scout plane reported the sighting of two additional enemy cruisers 250 miles northeast of Midway. The pilot obviously was doing a good job of maintaining contact, but he radioed shortly afterward that he was running low on fuel and would have to return. This caused momentary concern on board YAMATO, as contact might be lost; but a message sent by Rear Admiral Abe, Commander Cruiser Division 8, was soon picked up, ordering the plane to continue its contact until relieved.

Abe's alert move drew praise from Chief of Staff Ugaki, who voiced the opinion that the Nagumo Force was fully equal to the task at hand. These pleasant speculations were abruptly halted, however, by a scout plane report at 0900 that 10 carrier-borne enemy planes were heading for the Nagumo Force. This was the last information received concerning that Force for almost two hours. Yet, despite the temporary blackout, Yamamoto and his staff did not feel the least bit uneasy about the impending action.

Then the blow fell. At 1050 the Chief Signal Officer, Commander Yushiro Wada, painfully and without words handed Admiral Yamamoto a radio message from Rear Admiral Abe in TONE. It said: "Fires raging aboard KAGA, SORYU, and AKAGI resulting from attacks by enemy carrier and land-based planes. We plan to have HIRYU engage enemy carriers. We are temporarily withdrawing to the north to assemble our forces."

Instead of the expected easy victory, the picture had suddenly become one of catastrophic defeat! Of Nagumo's four carriers, three, including the flagship, were obviously out of action, and only HIRYU was left to carry on the fight. The enormity of the disaster was such that Admiral Yamamoto and his staff could scarcely believe it. Too stunned to speak, the Commander in Chief just groaned as he read the tragic words of Abe's message. The jubilant optimism of the staff changed instantaneously to black despair.

There was only one course that offered any hope of staving off the immediate collapse of the entire operation. This was to concentrate all forces at the scene of battle and overwhelm the enemy by sheer weight of numbers. Admiral Yamamoto decided to rush immediately with his own battleships to the support of the crippled Carrier Striking Force, and personally to direct subsequent battle operations.

NAGATO and other ships engaged in refueling were again scarcely visible from the flagship, as the fog had once more begun to settle. Although speed was vital, it was fully an hour before the force was finally able to assemble and get under way. Course was set at 120°, and fuel was poured on until all ships were making 20 knots. This speed was maintained through the thickening fog, which soon rendered each ship invisible to every other.

Such hazardous maneuvers were quite beyond the imagination of peace-time navigators and, indeed, beyond all common sense. But this was battle—and battles, like the wars which occasion them, are often fought beyond the compass of common sense.

At 1220, Admiral Yamamoto dispatched the following order to his forces:

> All forces will operate as follows and attack the enemy in the Midway area:
>
> (1) 1200 position of Main Body 35° 08′ N, 171° 05′ W, course 120°, speed 20 knots.
>
> (2) The Midway Invasion Force (Kondo) will detach part of its strength to cover the Transport Group and will direct it to retire temporarily to the northwest.
>
> (3) The Second Carrier Striking Force (Kakuta) will join the First Carrier Striking Force (Nagumo) as soon as possible.
>
> (4) Submarine Squadrons 3 and 5 will redeploy on cordon line C.[1]

It was evident from this order that Yamamoto and his staff had not abandoned their hope of destroying the American surface force and capturing Midway. An additional directive sent

[1] *Editor's Note:* A line along 168° W longitude from 26° to 36° N latitude.

out shortly thereafter fixed a stand-by position for the Transport Group at a point 500 miles west of Midway, so that it would be sufficiently close if called upon to occupy the island.

2. VACILLATING COMMAND

Yamamoto and his staff were now vitally concerned with the question of how much air strength the enemy still had at Midway, as this was a key consideration in laying plans for the impending operations. Although three Japanese carriers had been put out of action, HIRYU was still intact and could be used for striking the enemy carriers. Also, a night surface action and other offensive measures could be resorted to. But against enemy shore-based air, our only weapon had been the Carrier Striking Force, and the results of its first Midway attack were not clear. Rear Admiral Ugaki therefore addressed a message to Admiral Nagumo on board his new flagship NAGARA, asking for a detailed report on the first raid results. When this inquiry brought no answer, Yamamoto concluded that Tomonaga's attack could not have been very successful. This conclusion, which was supported by the fact that Tomonaga himself had recommended a second attack, gave rise to the fear that unless the Midway air base was destroyed without delay, the Americans might move in more planes from Hawaii, making the island even more difficult to capture.

Captain Kuroshima therefore urged the dispatch of a surface force to bombard the island during the night. Admiral Yamamoto promptly accepted the proposal and decided to assign the mission to Vice Admiral Kondo, whose Invasion Force Main Body was nearest to the target and included high-speed warships. It was also decided to defer the scheduled landing operations on Midway and the Aleutians until after the enemy carrier force had been destroyed. In accordance with these decisions, Admiral Yamamoto issued the following order at 1310:

(1) Attack Method C will be employed against the enemy Fleet.

(2) Commander Midway Invasion Force will dispatch part of its strength to bombard and destroy air bases on Midway.

(3) Landing operations on Midway and the Aleutians are temporarily postponed.

Attack Method C called for the concentration of all combat forces from both the Midway and the Aleutians areas to engage the enemy fleet in decisive battle.

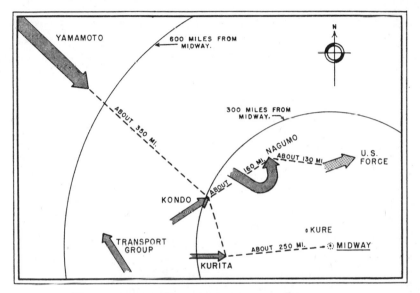

DISPOSITION OF FORCES, 1915 ON 4 JUNE 1942
(West Longitude Date, Zone plus 12 Time)

A little more than an hour before this order was issued, Admiral Yamamoto had received Admiral Nagumo's 1150 message, the first since Nagumo's transfer to NAGARA, reporting the extent of damage to his carriers and also announcing his intention to attack the enemy with his remaining strength and then retire to the north. Shortly after 1430, YAMATO picked up a further message sent out by Nagumo, this time addressed to Rear Admiral Kakuta's Second Carrier Striking Force cruising south of the Aleutians. It said:

(1) Position of First Carrier Striking Force at 1400 June 4 30° 48′ N, 178° 31′ W. We are planning to head north after destroying enemy task force to the east.

(2) Second Carrier Striking Force will rendezvous with us immediately.

Obviously, a great deal depended on how soon Admiral Kakuta, with his two carriers, RYUJO and JUNYO, could come south to bolster the Nagumo Force. Kakuta's reply, received at 1530, was not encouraging:

> The Second Carrier Striking Force will rapidly proceed south after recovering planes from the Dutch Harbor attack. It will refuel at Lat. 44° 40′ N, Long. 176° 20′ W during the morning of the 6th and thereafter will operate so as to join the First Task Force. Position as of 1500 June 4 is 120 miles southwest of Dutch Harbor.

This report made it clear that the Kakuta Force had been able to execute its planned strike on Dutch Harbor despite the dense fog. However, it was equally apparent that the Force could not be expected to join the battle in the Midway area before the afternoon of the 8th.

Meanwhile, reconnaissance reports were so contradictory that Combined Fleet had no accurate information on the strength of the enemy carrier force until 1615 when Admiral Yamaguchi radioed, "From our returning pilots' reports, the enemy force is apparently composed of 3 carriers, 5 large cruisers, and 15 destroyers. Our attacks succeeded in damaging 2 carriers." This was formidable opposition by any standard, but it was a bright note in the otherwise gloomy picture to learn that Yamaguchi's fliers had succeeded at least in damaging two of the enemy's carriers.

At 1736 a CHIKUMA search plane radioed that it had spotted the enemy force a mere 100 miles or so to the east of Nagumo's battleships and cruisers, and that the enemy ships were withdrawing eastward. As sunset this day would be at 1832, there was still hope that the Kondo Force might engage the enemy in a night action to turn the tide of battle in our favor. In its training program the Japanese Navy had always emphasized night battle, and these tactics were particularly favored by our commanders. It now seemed the only chance for our salvation.

But Japanese misfortunes were not yet at an end. A further stupefying message came from Admiral Nagumo at 1755: "HIRYU hit by bombs and set afire, 1730." With this crippling of Nagumo's last remaining carrier, our offensive spearhead was completely smashed.

In the light of the whole situation, an order sent by Admiral Yamamoto to his entire command at 1915, an hour and twenty minutes after the news of HIRYU's loss, was so strangely optimistic as to suggest that Commander in Chief Combined Fleet was deliberately trying to prevent the morale of our forces from collapsing. It said:

> (1) The enemy fleet has been practically destroyed and is retiring eastward.
> (2) Combined Fleet units in the vicinity are preparing to pursue the remnants of the enemy force and, at the same time, to occupy Midway.
> (3) The Main Body will reach 32° 08′ N, 175° 45′ E at 0300 on the 5th. Course, 090°; speed, 20 knots.
> (4) The Carrier Striking Force, Invasion Force (less Cruiser Division 7), and Submarine Force will immediately contact and attack the enemy.

Jangled nerves and bloodshot eyes on board YAMATO testified to the prevailing anxiety. Every man was eager for a night action in which our losses might be avenged. The futility of such hopes was manifest, however, when Nagumo reported at 2130: "Total enemy strength is 5 carriers, 6 heavy cruisers, and 15 destroyers. They are steaming westward. We are retiring to the northwest escorting HIRYU. Speed, 18 knots."

Ugaki voiced the dejection of the entire Combined Fleet staff when he remarked gloomily, "The Nagumo Force has no stomach for a night engagement!"

But Admiral Yamamoto was still determined to attempt the night attack. Realizing the need for unified command, he ordered Admiral Kondo to take charge of the attack force.

YAMATO soon picked up an order which Kondo dispatched at 2340 to his Night Action Force:

(1) The Invasion Force Main Body (Kondo Force) will reach position 30° 28′ N, 178° 35′ W, 0300 June 5. Thereafter, searches will be made to the east in an effort to engage the enemy at night.

(2) The First Carrier Striking Force (less HIRYU, AKAGI[2] and their escorts) will reverse course immediately and participate in the night engagement.

From this order itself, it was all too evident that there was little hope of contacting the enemy fleet before dawn. And this was our only chance! So the last flame of hope among the anxious men on board the flagship slowly flickered out.

3. ANXIETY IN NAVAL GENERAL STAFF

Back in Tokyo the Naval General Staff had been following the progress of the battle with steadily mounting apprehension. When the report came in that HIRYU had suffered the same fate as AKAGI, KAGA and SORYU, they felt that the operation was already doomed.

Our four finest fleet carriers were lost. Enemy air strength on Midway was not destroyed. The enemy still had at least one, and probably two, undamaged carriers. Under these circumstances the Tokyo strategists concluded that it was folly to pursue the operation further.

Admiral Nagano and his subordinates were concerned over more than the postponed invasions of Midway and the Aleu-

[2] *Editors' Note:* Both Yamamoto and Kondo already knew by this time that KAGA and SORYU had gone down, leaving only HIRYU and AKAGI still afloat.

tians, or even the loss of the four carriers. The Japanese Navy still had more warships of every category than the United States Navy had in the Pacific. What troubled these planners most was the fear that Admiral Yamamoto, in a desperate effort to recoup Nagumo's defeat, might take some long gamble and sacrifice his entire force to the overwhelming enemy air strength in the Midway area. Yet the Naval General Staff did not intervene. Captain Sadatoshi Tomioka, Chief of the Operations Section, later recalled that although the atmosphere was charged with anxious tension, the whole development of the battle was watched in silence. There were no instructions, no orders, no advice issued from Tokyo. Command of the operation was left completely to the discretion of Admiral Yamamoto.

4. ABANDONMENT OF THE OPERATION

Once the idea of a night engagement had been abandoned, the Combined Fleet staff in YAMATO turned to pondering the next move. Everyone inwardly recognized that we were defeated, yet not a single member of the staff proposed suspension of the operation. Instead, they desperately cast about for a way to salvage something from the defeat. They were like drowning men grabbing at straws.

Various temporizing measures were proposed. An air staff officer advocated a further air attack on the enemy fleet, employing a makeshift force consisting of the small number of planes available in light carriers HOSHO (Yamamoto Force) and ZUIHO (Kondo Force), supplemented by the float planes of the battleships and cruisers. Such an attack, he argued, might at least inflict some damage on the enemy carriers and reduce their offensive power, thus affording a better chance for the Japanese battleship and cruiser forces to swing the tide of battle.

The Gunnery Officer favored stronger action along the line of the already planned night bombardment of Midway air base by heavy cruisers of the Kondo Force. He expressed the opinion that if a sufficient number of heavily-gunned ships were employed, the bombardment might succeed in inflicting enough damage to keep the enemy's Midway-based air forces neutralized for at least a day. Another staff officer voiced the optimistic belief that the antiaircraft fire power of the battleships would be adequate to repulse any air attacks that might be launched against the Yamamoto Force by the enemy carriers.

The tentative plan drawn up by Captain Kuroshima as a result of these staff discussions was little short of fantastic. It called for all the battleships, including Yamato, to close Midway in broad daylight of the following day, 5 June, and shell the air base installations with their main batteries. When this proposal was laid before Rear Admiral Ugaki, he at least recognized it for what it was—a face-saving plan of suicidal recklessness and folly. He rejected it without mincing words:

"The stupidity of engaging such shore installations[3] with a surface force ought to be clear to you. The airfield on Midway is still usable, a large number of American planes is based there, and some of the enemy carriers are still intact. Our battleships, for all their fire power, would be destroyed by enemy air and submarine attacks before we could even get close enough to use our big guns.

"If circumstances permit, we will be able to launch another offensive after the Second Carrier Striking Force (Kakuta) has joined. But even if that proves impossible and we must accept defeat in this operation, we will not have lost the war. There will still be eight carriers in the Fleet, counting those which are to be completed soon. So we should not lose heart. In battle, as in chess, it is the fool who lets himself be led into a reckless move through desperation."

Ugaki's level-headed intervention thus scotched the plan, but not all members of the staff were satisfied. To some the

[3] *Editors' Note:* What shore installations on Midway caused such concern is not clear. Japanese ship firepower was still far superior to the power of American guns, ship *and* shore-based, at Midway.

thought of having to shoulder responsibility for defeat was unbearable, and they were ready to gamble everything for a chance to save face. Their attitude was plainly expressed by one of the officers who protested to Ugaki, "But how can we apologize to His Majesty for this defeat?"

Admiral Yamamoto, who had remained silent during the discussions, spoke up now. "Leave that to me," he said abruptly. "I am the only one who must apologize to His Majesty."

It was evident from this brief remark that Admiral Yamamoto himself had all but decided to abandon any further attempts to engage the enemy fleet or to capture Midway. At 0015 on 5 June, he took the first step toward such abandonment by ordering Vice Admiral Kondo and Vice Admiral Nagumo, whose forces were still maneuvering for a night attack on the enemy carriers and a bombardment of Midway, to suspend these operations and join the Main Body. The order read:

> (1) The Midway Invasion Force (less the Transport Group presently standing by, but including Cruiser Division 7) and First Carrier Striking Force (less AKAGI, HIRYU and their escorts) will join the Main Body.
> (2) At 0900 today the Main Body will be in position 32° 08' N, 179° 01' E. Course 090°, speed 20 knots.

Admiral Yamamoto now faced another painful decision regarding the scuttling of AKAGI. Earlier, when AKAGI's skipper had requested permission to sink her, Yamamoto had ordered that this action be delayed because his own and Kondo's forces were advancing to engage the enemy. Now, however, hope of an engagement was virtually gone, and Kondo and Nagumo had been ordered to pull back toward the Main Body. The decision could therefore be delayed no longer. Yet the fact that the Japanese Navy had never before scuttled one of its own warships made the decision an exceedingly hard one to take. Admiral Yamamoto finally accepted this grave responsibility and ordered the destruction of AKAGI at 0250.

Only five minutes after this order went out from YAMATO, Commander in Chief Combined Fleet, at 0255 June 5, issued a further order which set the seal on the defeat of the Japanese forces. It read:

(1) The Midway Operation is cancelled.

(2) The Main Body will assemble the Midway Invasion Force and the First Carrier Striking Force (less HIRYU and her escorts), and the combined forces will carry out refueling during the morning of 6 June at position 33° N, 170° E.

(3) The Screening Force, HIRYU and her escorts, and NISSHIN will proceed to the above position.

(4) The Transport Group will proceed westward out of range of Midway-based planes.

Thus, the Midway operation was finally abandoned. But there still remained the difficult and hazardous task of rounding up the scattered Japanese forces and effecting their retirement from the battle area under the ever present threat of enemy attack. The enemy had tasted blood and would thirst for more.

Meanwhile, in the Aleutians, Rear Admiral Kakuta's carriers had delivered another air attack on Dutch Harbor during 4 June, in spite of adverse weather. The attack was carried out by a picked force of nine fighters, eleven dive bombers, and six level bombers. Availing themselves of narrow cloud gaps, these planes destroyed fuel storage tanks, hangars, large merchant vessels, and other targets with notable success. On the return flight JUNYO's planes encountered some American P-40 fighters over Otter Point, at the northeast end of Umnak Island. A dogfight ensued, in which four enemy planes were reported shot down. During the action the Japanese pilots noticed an airfield directly below them, the only one discovered by our planes during the whole Aleutians operation.

Our attack force lost one fighter and two bombers in aerial combat, and two other bombers, badly damaged, failed to get back to the carriers. This ended the air offensive of the Second Carrier Striking Force against enemy territory in the Aleutians.

CHAPTER 11

Finale

1. KURITA'S BOMBARDMENT MISSION

Almost simultaneously with the issuance of Admiral Yamamoto's order calling off the Midway operation, misfortune overtook the Japanese forces again. But this time the enemy was only indirectly responsible. When Combined Fleet, at 1310 on 4 June, had ordered Vice Admiral Kondo to carry out a night bombardment of Midway with part of his force, he had assigned this mission to Rear Admiral Takeo Kurita's Support Force made up of Cruiser Division 7's four heavy cruisers —KUMANO, SUZUYA, MIKUMA, and MOGAMI—and two destroyers of Destroyer Division 8. The cruisers carried ten 8-inch guns and were the fastest ships in the Japanese Navy. Admiral Kondo had also considered including fast battleships KONGO and HIEI in the attack unit because their 14-inch guns would markedly heighten the effectiveness of the bombardment. However, the battleships were in his own Invasion Force Main Body, which was more distant from the target, and they consequently could not reach Midway before sunrise on the 5th.

Admiral Kurita received Kondo's order assigning his force the bombardment mission at about 1500 on the 4th. He immediately increased speed for the run-in, but as he was 400 miles west of Midway, his chances of reaching the target before dawn the next day were extremely slim even if his cruisers ran at their best speed of about 32 knots. Even if he did make it, his withdrawal would undoubtedly have to be made in daylight under the menace of enemy air attack. He therefore informed Admiral Kondo that he desired the cooperation of other forces to insure the success of the attack. Kondo, whose own force included light carrier ZUIHO with a small complement of fighter planes, forwarded this recommendation to Admiral

Yamamoto, but the latter decided that it could not be accepted. Kurita would have to go it alone.

With heroic determination, Kurita's ships raced eastward at top speed. Unable to keep pace with the cruisers, the destroyers soon fell behind and by 2300 were out of sight. On board the cruisers preparations were actually made to send a suicide demolition party ashore as a last resort if the bombardment failed.

Meanwhile, on board YAMATO, the Combined Fleet staff rechecked Kurita's position, as last reported, and found that he was farther away from Midway than they had figured. Their calculations showed that the projected bombardment could not possibly be made on schedule. Consequently, at 20 minutes past midnight, an order was sent to the Kurita Force cancelling its mission. By the time he received the order, Kurita had already closed to within 90 miles of Midway.

In compliance with the Combined Fleet directive, Kurita turned his speeding cruisers about and set a northwest course. Shortly thereafter, flagship KUMANO, leading the division, sighted a surfaced enemy submarine four degrees off the starboard bow. Kurita instantly ordered his ships to execute an emergency 45-degree turn to port. The signal, "Red! Red!" was flashed to SUZUYA, next astern of the flagship, by a low-powered directional signal lamp, and KUMANO then swung to port. SUZUYA, in turn, also relayed the signal and turned left, as did MIKUMA, the third ship.

It was about two hours before sunrise. Clouds hung low, veiling everything in darkness. Tension had relaxed in the cruisers when the force turned away from Midway, and perhaps the let-down gave rise to lack of vigilance. Whatever the reason, MOGAMI, the last ship in line, failed to get the emergency turn signal in time, with the result that she ploughed into MIKUMA's port quarter.

All of the cruisers had reduced their speed somewhat since the turnabout, but they were still making 28 knots. As a result of the collision MOGAMI lost her bow section forward of the first turret and was forced to halt. MIKUMA suffered only slight hull damage which did not affect her combat efficiency or maneuverability.

Notified of the accident, Admiral Kurita immediately turned back to stand by the cripple. MOGAMI's skipper, Captain Akira Soji, soon reported that he could make 12 knots, so the Admiral ordered Captain Sakiyama, in MIKUMA, and two ships of Destroyer Division 8, ARASHIO and ASASHIO, to escort her. Kurita, with KUMANO and SUZUYA, then headed for the designated rendezvous with Admiral Yamamoto's Main Body. By this time dawn was breaking, and MOGAMI and her escorts limped westward at 12 knots, every man in the four ships apprehensively expecting momentary attack by enemy planes, and perhaps pursuit by the enemy fleet.

2. EXPLOITS OF SUBMARINE I-168

Despite the important role which Combined Fleet's Midway plan had assigned to the submarine forces, only one submarine actually made any noteworthy contribution to the operation. This was I-168, commanded by Lieutenant Commander Yahachi Tanabe.

After reconnoitering Midway on 1 June, as mentioned in an earlier chapter, I-168 maintained a stealthy vigil around the island and was still there on the 4th when the battle began. Tanabe could not follow the development of the battle in detail, but radio messages picked up by the submarine told enough for him to know that it was going against the Japanese forces. Shortly after 2030 on 4 June he received an order from Commander in Chief Combined Fleet in YAMATO directing him "to shell and destroy the enemy air base on Eastern Island." The order instructed Tanabe to keep up his bombardment until 0200 on the 5th, after which time Rear Admiral

Kurita's heavy cruisers were scheduled to take over and complete the destruction of the air base.

Tanabe promptly moved his submarine into position, brought her to the surface and opened fire at 0130. The shelling did

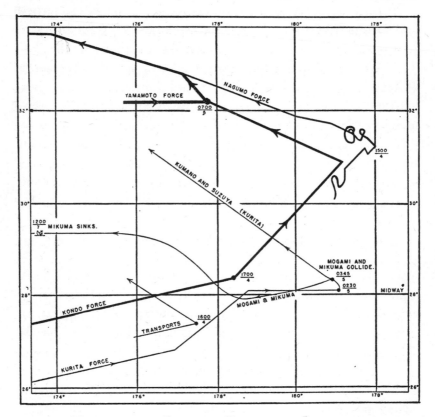

MOVEMENT OF JAPANESE FORCES, 4-5 JUNE 1942
(West Longitude Date, Zone plus 12 Time)

little if any physical damage, although it may have had some psychological effect in making the defenders think that there was still danger of an invasion. Searchlights from the island began probing the darkness in the direction of 1-168, and presently shore batteries opened fire. It was too unhealthy for the submarine to remain, so she promptly dove and withdrew. After dawn, enemy patrol planes spotted her and made a heavy depth-charge attack, but 1-168 escaped unscathed and went looking for bigger game.

Tanabe had received an early morning report that an enemy carrier was damaged and adrift in the waters north of Midway, not more than 150 miles from 1-168. Once freed of pursuers, he headed for this fetching target, making a careful approach through the heavy enemy patrol cordon around Midway. His caution was finally rewarded on the 6th when he looked through his periscope at 1331 to see seven U.S. destroyers swarming around crippled YORKTOWN in position 30° 35′ N, 177° 20′ W. He closed to within 1,900 yards before firing four torpedoes, which were certain to get hits at that distance.

As soon as the torpedoes were away, 1-168 dove for the safety of the depths. Shocks from the explosions were felt within five minutes, followed shortly by the first of many depth charges bursting close by, each one shaking the submarine like a leaf. Sixty near-misses were counted before the violent shocks finally caused damage which forced 1-168 to surface. The hunters closed in immediately, forcing the submarine to submerge again in spite of her injuries. It seemed that the destroyers would never give up the chase, and finally Tanabe was forced to surface once more. What could be more miserable than a submarine in this predicament? Fortunately, however, the enemy destroyers had at last abandoned pursuit just a short while before, and 1-168 thus escaped what would otherwise have been certain destruction.

As a result of Captain Tanabe's bold venture, the American carrier YORKTOWN was left staggering under the effects of two direct torpedo hits, and destroyer HAMMANN, which had been alongside the carrier, was blasted in two by a torpedo and sank almost instantly.

3. RE-ASSEMBLY OF FORCES

Although abandonment of the Midway operation had been finally ordered at 0255 on 5 June, Admiral Yamamoto kept his battleships headed eastward through the remaining hours of darkness in order to join with the Nagumo and Kondo Forces withdrawing from the battle area. Grim determination permeated the flagship as everyone realized that this maneuver would bring the Yamamoto Force, too, within range of enemy attack, thus creating the danger of further losses and casualties to the Japanese forces.

The sun rose at 0440 in a clear and cloudless sky, affording visibility in excess of 40 miles. It was the finest weather since the Fleet had left the homeland ten days earlier.

This day would see the battleships of Combined Fleet, excluding the four old ones in Vice Admiral Takasu's Guard Force, make their closest approach to the enemy since the war's start. Every ship maintained a strict alert against air raids.

Admiral Yamamoto's ships sighted and joined Kondo's Invasion Force Main Body shortly after sunrise. By 0700 they had closed and, from their position 320 miles northwest of Midway, set course to the northwest.

Meanwhile, Nagumo's scattered ships continued retreating northwesterly, as they had since early morning, to join the Main Body. According to calculations and plans, Nagumo should also have joined at this time and position. When he failed to appear, a search plane was launched from HOSHO to find him. It did, some 40 miles to the northeast, and by 1155 most of his ships had caught up with and joined the others. What was left bore little resemblance to the mighty force which had sailed from the homeland. Not one carrier remained, and only half the original number of destroyers was present, six having been assigned to stand by the stricken carriers. It was a sight that brought home to those on board the flagship the full tragedy of the defeat.

Courtesy Shizuo Fukui

SUBMARINE *I-168*

Official U. S. Navy Photo

SINKING OF THE USS *Yorktown* IN THE BATTLE OF MIDWAY

JAP HEAVY CRUISER OF THE *Mogami* CLASS ON FIRE AFTER ATTACK BY TASK
FORCE 16 IN THE BATTLE OF MIDWAY

About this time a HOSHO search plane reported sighting the smashed and drifting hulk of HIRYU, still afloat despite the *coup de grâce* administered by her destroyer escorts many hours earlier. Admiral Nagumo immediately dispatched destroyer TANIKAZE to rescue survivors reported on the derelict and ordered a seaplane launched from NAGARA to aid in the search. NAGARA's plane arrived at the reported spot but found no trace of HIRYU, and TANIKAZE also searched the area in vain. While the destroyer was conducting its search, enemy carrier planes subjected her to a fierce bombing attack. The first wave of 4 dive bombers struck at 1636, the second wave of 26 an hour and a half later, and a third wave of 6 more at 1845. But luck was with the destroyer and she suffered only slight damage from a near-miss, which did not affect her battle efficiency. She succeeded in shooting down one enemy plane.

Thanks to TANIKAZE's absorption of these attacks, the big concentration of Japanese ships close by escaped the notice of enemy planes, and the transfer of survivors of the four sunken carriers from the rescuing destroyers was carried out in the afternoon without interference. Immediately on joining, the loaded destroyers began shifting their passengers to battleships MUTSU, NAGATO, HARUNA and KIRISHIMA. Even without an enemy attack, the transfers were difficult enough. The sea was rough, and the long swells made it impossible to bring the destroyers alongside the battleships. The fleet finally hove to, and boats had to be lowered to shuttle the survivors. The most seriously wounded had to be carried by stretcher. Darkness came and the work continued into the pitch-dark night. Not a single star glimmered through the low-hanging clouds. All crews kept frantically at the arduous task until it was finally completed. The sickbays and living quarters of the battleships were jammed with wounded, mostly victims of burns.

Some distance to the south, limping MOGAMI and her three companions were the target of air attacks by 12 American B 17s and as many Marine Corps dive bombers during the day. The former had little success, scoring only a near-miss on MOGAMI, killing two men. The pilot[1] of the leading dive bomber, however, after being hit by antiaircraft fire, attempted a daring suicide crash into MIKUMA's bridge. He missed the bridge but crashed into the after turret, spreading fire over the air intake of the starboard engine room. This caused an explosion of gas fumes below, killing all hands working in the engine room. This was a damaging blow to the cruiser, hitherto unscathed except for the slight hull damage received in the collision with MOGAMI. Both cruisers were now hurt, and they continued their westward withdrawal with darkening prospects of escaping the enemy's fury.

At 1259 June 6, Vice Admiral Kakuta's Second Carrier Striking Force was ordered to rejoin Admiral Hosogaya's Northern Force to permit execution of the suspended Aleutians landing operations a day later than originally scheduled. To assist in this project, Admiral Yamamoto issued a further order at 2320 designating additional units to be released shortly to Hosogaya's command. These were battleships KONGO and HIEI, cruisers TONE and CHIKUMA, light carrier ZUIHO, seaplane tender KAMIKAWA MARU, and 14 submarines from Submarine Squadron 2 and Submarine Division 13. The dispatch of these reinforcements was aimed primarily at discouraging a possible enemy attempt to recapture the islands of Kiska and Attu, but hope was also entertained that the northern operations might give rise to an opportunity for destroying the enemy fleet.

After the transfer of survivors to the battleships of the Main Body was completed, the combined forces got underway again and headed for the scheduled refueling rendezvous at 33° 00' N, 170° 00' E. By dawn of the next day all ships except MOGAMI, MIKUMA, and their two destroyer escorts would

---

[1] *Editors' Note:* This brave sacrifice hit was made by Capt. R. E. Fleming, USMC. The Japanese account given here indicates that his action caused much greater damage to MIKUMA than hitherto believed.

be beyond the attack range of Midway-based planes, though not of planes from the enemy carriers if the latter chose to pursue.

A striking aspect of this great assemblage of warships was that it contained no fleet carriers. Light carriers ZUIHO and HOSHO had the distinction of being the only flattops present, and their decks were intermittently aflurry with the activity of launching and recovering planes for antisubmarine patrol.

What were the feelings of the men in the ships as their westward withdrawal continued? Were there any who found solace for the loss of our four great carriers in the fact that the battleship "main strength" remained intact? There could hardly have been many, now, who did not realize with bitter regret that big guns alone were powerless to win a battle. With our carriers had gone the backbone of our offensive power. Virtually every man in the Fleet was weighed down by the sad realization that the Imperial Navy had just suffered a crushing defeat.

4. RETIREMENT

By the morning of 6 June (Japan 7 June)—the day Midway was to have been invaded—flagship YAMATO was over 600 miles from Midway and headed for Japan. The weather had again turned foul, visibility was poor, and another siege of heavy fog was threatening. The main portion of the fleet was now out of range of American land-based planes, but still there was cause for anxiety because the whereabouts of the enemy task force was not known. Some consolation was taken from the thought that if American carriers were in pursuit, the foul weather would provide a welcome cloak of concealment from air attack.

On YAMATO's port quarter followed NAGARA, from whose truck Admiral Nagumo's flag seemed to flutter in shame. It must have been humiliating for this commander, who for six months had feared no enemy, to be retreating from such a bitter defeat.

On the bridge of YAMATO her Captain's nervous commands betrayed his concern over pursuit by enemy planes and submarines. Light carrier HOSHO, to the rear of the battleship group, intermittently launched and recovered antisubmarine planes. In the operations room below YAMATO's bridge, a growing uneasiness prevailed among the staff officers. Throughout the night they had been gathered around the large table awaiting developments and absorbed in troubled thoughts. There was an apprehensive feeling that the battle was not yet over.

Most immediate concern was for the safety of the damaged cruisers, MIKUMA and MOGAMI, and their stand-by destroyers, ARASHIO and ASASHIO. These fears materialized at 0630 when word came from Captain Shakao Sakiyama of MIKUMA, "Two enemy carrier planes sighted." Successive reports from the beleaguered ships told the story of events all too clearly:

"Attacked by six dive bombers which scored one hit. Enemy carriers seem to be pursuing."

"0645. Bombed by many carrier-based planes. One enemy seaplane sighted."

"Three enemy seaplanes are shadowing us. Enemy surface force appears to have joined in the pursuit."

"0745. MOGAMI received one hit causing minor damage. Three planes shot down."

"0800. We are being pursued by enemy carriers and other ships operating in this area. We are heading for Wake Island. We are in position bearing 030°, distant 710 miles from Wake Island."

The damaged cruisers had reached a point 500 miles west of Midway when the first wave of enemy carrier planes struck. MIKUMA was hit once and MOGAMI twice in this attack, but the bombs inflicted only minor damage. Successive attacks, however, brought more hits and increased damage. Five bomb hits on Mikuma at 1030 spread fires throughout the ship, forcing her to a stop. The fires rapidly increased in fury until 1058, when they set off a tremendous internal explosion which eliminated all hope of saving the ship. Efforts to transfer her crew to a destroyer were under way when another attack of 10 planes came at 1200, scoring more hits and sending the cruiser to the depths.

Captain Sakiyama was wounded in the third attack of the day, but he continued in command until Mikuma went down. He was thrown clear of the sinking ship and picked up by a destroyer. However, death overtook this valiant officer on 13 June in the sickbay of cruiser Suzuya.

In the course of the day's raids, Mogami suffered a total of six bomb hits. Nine officers and 81 men were killed, but quick and effective damage control saved the ship from sinking, and she succeeded in shooting down eight planes. Her skipper, Captain Soji, assumed command of the three remaining ships, and, after picking up Mikuma's survivors, resumed the westward withdrawal.

The accompanying destroyers had managed to shoot down two attacking planes during this action, but each was hit by a bomb. On board Arashio 37 men were killed and Commander Ogawa, Commander Destroyer Division 8, was seriously injured, while 22 men were killed in Asashio. Neither ship, however, was damaged enough to impair navigation, and both did their utmost to fulfill their screening duties.

Aside from the carriers lost in the preceding two days, Mikuma was the largest Japanese warship to be sunk since the start of the war. The constant companion of her sister ship Mogami, they had fought together in the battle off Batavia on 1 March, sinking USS Houston and the Australian cruiser Perth. They had seen action in the invasions of the Andamans and of Burma, as well as in the Bengal Bay operations. And they had been together to the last, when Mikuma, standing by her crippled sister, perished in her defense. Her gallant action commanded the respect and admiration of men throughout the Navy.

As Admiral Yamamoto received the increasingly dismal reports from MIKUMA, he decided on a course of action. At 1230 he detached Kondo's Invasion Force and Cruiser Division 8 to speed to the rescue of Captain Sakiyama's ill-fated ships. As a further precaution he also turned his own Main Body to follow them southward.

At this juncture it was believed that the enemy fleet consisted of at least one carrier, two converted carriers, and several cruisers and destroyers. If the enemy continued in pursuit, the Kondo Force might engage him during the night, or Yamamoto's entire force could meet the enemy in decisive battle the next morning. In the latter case it would be necessary to first knock out the opposing air power. To achieve this, Yamamoto could mobilize a total of about 100 planes, counting those of light carriers HOSHO and ZUIHO and the seaplanes of the battleships, cruisers, and tenders. To augment this limited air strength, it was considered desirable to lure the enemy within range of the 50 or so medium bombers based on Wake Island. These planes could reach to within a few miles of the position of MIKUMA's sinking.

On the basis of these considerations, Admiral Yamamoto issued the following order at 1500 to all the ships of his command:

(1) Combined Fleet units operating in this area will catch and destroy the enemy task force within attack range of air forces based on Wake Island.

(2) At 1530, from position 33° 24′ N, 169° 00′ E, the Main Body (Yamamoto), Striking Force (Nagumo), and the second section of Battleship Division 3 will proceed on course 180° at 18 knots.

(3) The Guard Force (Takasu) will support the Northern Force.

(4) The Land-based Air Force (Tsukahara) will take every opportunity to attack the enemy.

This grand scheme was actually followed until the next morning (7 June) when, with no enemy in sight and his ships in need of fuel, Yamamoto called off his vain pursuit and retired toward the homeland.

MOGAMI, in the meantime, had continued westward in her effort to lure the enemy. Through the untiring efforts of her crew, a speed of 20 knots was achieved by 1515 despite the heavy bomb damage she had sustained and the loss of her bow. She was fortunate that no enemy planes had appeared since MIKUMA's sinking, and she was able to creep out of the very jaws of death, the last Japanese warship to come clear of enemy attacks in the Midway battle. Kondo's force finally rendezvoused with crippled MOGAMI and provided escort to Truk.

Further American attempts to hit the retreating Japanese Fleet this day were made by 26 B-17s from Midway, but the foul weather thwarted these efforts and no contacts were made. Alert to the possibility of attack by planes based on Wake Island, the enemy carriers also gave up the chase, and the action was over.

Thus fell the curtain on a spectacular and historic battle. Japan's sole consolation for the defeat lay in the minuscule success of having captured two Aleutian bases. The northern operations, resumed after their earlier cancellation, had progressed smoothly and led to the occupation of the islands of Attu and Kiska on 7 June. But these unimportant acquisitions were small compensation for the devastating fleet losses suffered to the south, and in the end they were to bog us down still deeper in the quicksands of defeat.

The catastrophe of Midway definitely marked the turning of the tide in the Pacific War, and thenceforward that tide bore Japan inexorably on toward final capitulation

CHAPTER 12 Analysis of the Defeat

1. GENERAL SUMMARY

Such, then, is the Japanese story of the Battle of Midway—its place in the evolution of Japan's Pacific War strategy, how it was conceived and planned, and how it was actually fought. In conclusion, the author wishes to attempt a summation of the principal causes of the Japanese defeat, adding some reflections on aspects not already dwelt upon in detail in the preceding chapters.

The distinguished American naval historian, Professor Samuel E. Morison, characterizes the victory of United States forces at Midway as "a victory of intelligence." In this judgment the author fully concurs, for it is beyond the slightest possibility of doubt that the advance discovery of the Japanese plan to attack was the foremost single and immediate cause of Japan's defeat. Viewed from the Japanese side, this success of the enemy's intelligence translates itself into a failure on our own part—a failure to take adequate precautions for guarding the secrecy of our plans. Had the secret of our intent to invade Midway been concealed with the same thoroughness as the plan to attack Pearl Harbor, the outcome of this battle might well have been different.

But it was a victory of American intelligence in a much broader sense than just this. Equally as important as the positive achievements of the enemy's intelligence on this occasion was the negatively bad and ineffective functioning of Japanese intelligence. This was eloquently illustrated by the Naval General Staff's persistent misestimate, maintained until the very eve of battle and communicated to the advancing Japanese forces, that an American task force was operating in the Solomons

area, strongly implying that the enemy had no suspicion of
the impending Japanese attack on Midway. Nor was Combined
Fleet's intelligence a great deal better. For despite the unusual
enemy activity noted in the Hawaii area around 30 May-1
June, Combined Fleet did not consider it a serious enough sign
of enemy counter-preparations to warrant warning the Nagumo
Force.

Another fundamental cause of the Midway defeat was the
faulty basic planning of the operation. The most striking and
obvious error in this regard was the manner in which the various naval forces were disposed. Here the planners indulged in
one of their favorite, and in this case fatal, gambits—dispersion. Instead of massing what could easily have been the
most formidable single naval task force ever seen, Combined
Fleet chose to scatter its forces, reducing them thereby to
comparative feebleness. Strategically, the Aleutian arm of this
dispersion was unimportant since it aimed only at destroying
U.S. installations, occupying for a short time and then abandoning these northern islands. Tactically, the objective of the
Northern Forces was to effect a diversion to the main thrust at
Midway, but to sacrifice the sure advantage of concentrated
strength for the dubious advantage of a diversion that might
not—and actually did not—work was unjustifiable beyond
question.

But the dispersion was not limited merely to the main split of
forces between the Aleutians and Midway; there was a further
dispersion of forces within each of these two sectors. In the
north, Kakuta's Carrier Striking Force was to operate on its own,
300 miles in advance of Takasu's Screening Force of battleships.
The dispersion of the Midway forces was much more extreme—
Nagumo's carriers northwest of Midway, Yamamoto's battleship Main Body 300 miles back, Kondo's Invasion Force Main
Body to the south or southwest of Midway, and Kurita's Close
Support Group moving in with the invasion transports from

the southwest. Lack of concentration is one of the basic tactical weaknesses of war on land, sea, or in the air. At Midway it facilitated the enemy's destruction of the Nagumo Force, with the other Japanese forces too far away to strike even a blow. And once Nagumo's carriers had been destroyed, the Japanese weakness caused by dispersion became almost total impotence. In contrast, consider the effective compactness of the American forces. Concentrated at the outset, they remained that way throughout the battle, thus achieving a maximum of strength, offensive as well as defensive.

As just one concrete example of how a wiser disposition of forces might have led to a different outcome of the battle, think of the vastly increased strength that would have resulted if the Main Body and the Nagumo Force had operated together, with Admiral Yamamoto's big battleships serving as screen for the carriers. The tremendous firepower of the battleships and their escorts would have warded off many attacking enemy planes and doubtless would have drawn some of the attackers away from our ill-fated carriers. In addition, Admiral Yamamoto would have had a direct control over the prosecution of the battle which he did not have as a result of being too far away. Properly used, the battleships could have had real purpose and effectiveness in the action.

Another error in planning was the failure to keep the emphasis firmly fixed on the central goal of the operation—the destruction of the enemy fleet. The original concept behind the operation was to use the invasion of Midway as a means of luring out the enemy fleet for decisive battle. But this concept was violated the moment that Combined Fleet, in its tactical plan, strapped the carriers to a fixed schedule and to a supporting mission for the invasion of Midway. Thereby the carriers lost the flexibility of movement that was imperative for a successful fleet engagement. Perhaps Combined Fleet thought it was safe to do this because of its firm conviction that the enemy would not depart his base until after the island had been attacked. But it should certainly have provided for the contrary eventuality. Destruction of the enemy fleet should have been unequivocally fixed as the foremost aim of the operation, and all else subordinated to that goal. Upon this basis it would have been wiser to delay the entire operation until such time as carriers ZUIKAKU and SHOKAKU could have been readied to add their strength to the Striking Force. Combined Fleet refused to do this out of undue emphasis on securing the best possible meteorological conditions for the Midway landing operations.

Equally defective and inadequate were the plans for preinvasion scouting and reconnaissance. The fact that the submarines were delayed two days in sortieing from the homeland removed all possibility of their arriving on station in time to observe the enemy's approach to the battle area and give warning to our fleet. But even if they had conformed to the schedule, there is some question whether they could have succeeded in sighting the American forces because of the more or less static position to which each submarine had been assigned. Not only should it have been made absolute that the schedule be kept, but these submarines should have been ordered to sweep along the line of the Hawaiian Islands from the waters northeast of Midway. The Operation "K" plan for aerial reconnaissance of Pearl Harbor also, although vitally important to the success of the Midway attack, was narrowly and loosely worked out, allowing for no alternatives when the basic plan did not succeed.

As a result of these grave defects in the basic plans, the commanders of our forces in the battle had two strikes against them from the start. But, even so, had it not been for the blunders committed by them in the tactical conduct of the operations, the conclusion seems justified that the outcome would not have been so miserable as it was. Elsewhere, mention has been made of the saying that battles are a succession of errors on both sides and that victory goes to the side that makes the fewer. There is no question about which side committed the greater number of mistakes in the Battle of Midway. Indeed, from a study of the operations of the American as well as the Japanese forces, it is hard not to acknowledge that *all* the errors in this action were committed on our side.

That Admiral Nagumo was guilty of most of these does not warrant the conclusion that he was less competent than the other force commanders. It was his misfortune, because the Nagumo Force was the only Japanese force actually to come to grips with the enemy, to be placed in the position of having to make most of the decisions which influenced the outcome of the battle. The other commanders—even including Admiral Yamamoto, who supposedly was to direct the operations of all the Japanese forces—found themselves reduced to the position of helpless spectators. They could not commit errors if they were not called upon, as Nagumo was, to take critical decisions.

Having said that much to soften the criticism that must be made of our Force Commander, let us proceed to the criticism itself. It now appears, with the benefit of hindsight, that Admiral Nagumo committed three serious blunders.

The first of these was his failure to enforce adequate search dispositions on the morning of the Midway strike. Had he employed an earlier, two-phase search, the unsuspected enemy task force would probably have been discovered soon enough to permit Nagumo to strike the first blow instead of taking it. At the very least, as soon as it was learned that CHIKUMA's and TONE's float planes could not be launched promptly on schedule, Admiral Nagumo should immediately have ordered other planes out in their place to fill the gap in his search pattern. Of course, the failure of CHIKUMA's No. 5 plane to spot the enemy carriers, despite presumably flying right over them, cannot be blamed on Admiral Nagumo.

Nagumo's second mistake had to do with the method he

employed in dividing up his carrier planes between second attack waves. Each attack wave was made up portionate numbers of planes from all four carriers instead having just two carriers supply the first attack wave and the other two carriers supply the second. Though the use of planes from four carriers simultaneously meant less time consumed in launching and recovery, it necessarily increased vulnerability to enemy attack during and immediately after recovery operations, because all carriers were then engaged and unable to get their planes swiftly in the air to fend off an attack. It also meant that, during such periods, the Striking Force was incapable of launching an attack on the enemy carriers however urgently this might be required. Had Nagumo launched his Midway strike from just two carriers and held the other two in reserve, ready for any eventuality, he would not have found his hands tied at the critical moment of the battle.

The third and perhaps gravest error committed by Nagumo was his failure, as soon as it was discovered that the enemy task force included a carrier, to launch immediately all available planes for an attack, whether properly armed or not and even if fighter protection could not be provided. The risks were admittedly grave, but were they not far less grave than the risk of being caught by the enemy's carrier planes with all his own planes on board and with refueling and rearming operations in full swing? Had Nagumo the right to count upon the enemy's not attacking him at just this moment of his greatest vulnerability? What becomes of his refusal to take the risk of sending his unprotected and improperly armed bombers against the enemy when the course he elected resulted in their destruction without even having been able to strike a blow in compensation for their loss? Yamaguchi's judgment in this crucial situation was the only correct one. Nagumo chose what seemed to him the orthodox and safer course, and from that moment his carriers were doomed.

brought about the emascula-
Admiral Yamamoto could do
rds, the defeat of the Japanese
fore Commander in Chief Com-
judgment to bear one way or
this grave situation, did Admiral
course that was open to him? Was
e same vacillation and indecisiveness
mo's action? The plan conceived by his
stan   himself for an attempt to turn the tide
of battle by   the enemy in night surface battle was all
too plainly a plan of desperation, with the odds all against it
from the start. And when finally forced to the realization that
the plan had no chance of success, Admiral Yamamoto promptly
gave up the battle as lost beyond repair.

The question is, Was there really nothing that could have
been done? Was defeat irreparable? Nagumo's carriers were
gone, it is true, but Admiral Yamamoto had reason to believe
that two out of three enemy carriers had been disabled by
HIRYU's planes. This meant that the enemy would have had
but one carrier left intact, with no others available to throw
into the battle, whereas Yamamoto had two undamaged carriers
left in Kakuta's Second Carrier Striking Force to the north and
two more, ZUIHO and HOSHO, left in his own and Kondo's
force. Instead of ordering resumption of the once-suspended
Aleutians operation, then, why did Commander in Chief Combined Fleet not leave in force his order to Kakuta to come down
and join the Midway forces and, when Kakuta had arrived, add
ZUIHO and HOSHO to the latter's two carriers to form a new
and not inconsiderable Carrier Striking Force? Admiral Yamamoto's failure to do this is the more difficult to understand in
the light of his plan, formulated two days later, to engage the
pursuing enemy task force in decisive battle with only the
planes of ZUIHO and HOSHO, plus the float planes of his battle-

ships and cruisers, to provide air support—except for the dubious indirect support of shore-based planes from Wake.

The reasons for Admiral Yamamoto's decision against this course, if he considered it, are difficult to guess. He was not the type of commander to shirk or seek to minimize his responsibility for failure. If he had been, one might suspect that he was seeking in the Aleutians a success to soften the blow of his defeat at Midway.

There was also a serious fault in the command arrangements set up for the Midway operation, and this was a product of the Japanese Navy's tradition that in warfare a commander's place is at the front. Accordingly, Admiral Yamamoto kept his flag in YAMATO and put to sea to serve as inspiration for the actual fighting forces. It is clear that this outworn notion has no place in modern naval warfare. It is far more important than any morale factor involved that the commander be informed of what is going on and be able to inform and keep control over all the forces for which he is responsible. Evidence that the United States recognized and acknowledged this situation is seen in the fact that Admiral Nimitz's headquarters was maintained ashore throughout the war, first at Pearl Harbor and later at Guam. Afloat in YAMATO, as he was, Admiral Yamamoto was unable to communicate with the other units of his fleet because of the radio silence imposed until the last moment on all ships taking part in this operation. He was, therefore, unable to communicate to Nagumo the latest information received from Tokyo, and he was unable to exercise any control over the conduct of the operation until it was too late. If Combined Fleet Headquarters had been ashore, preferably at Tokyo, which was the intelligence and communications center, there would have been no limitation on his use of radio and Yamamoto could not only have kept his forces informed of late developments and information, but he could have maintained close control throughout the operation.

2. MYTH OF THE ALMIGHTY BATTLESHIP

Much has been said here and elsewhere about the anachronistic views of the "old school" Navy men and their notion of battleship supremacy. It was appalling to air-minded men to see the tremendous effort and expense put into the construction of super-battleships YAMATO, MUSASHI, and SHINANO. True, SHINANO was wisely altered to a carrier while under construction, but then suffered the indignity of being sunk by an enemy submarine in Tokyo Bay on 28 November 1944, just seventeen days after her launching and within 24 hours after weighing anchor for her first service cruise—perhaps the shortest-lived warship of all time.

Neither technological progress nor the changes wrought by it in warfare seemed to affect the thinking of the "Battleship Admirals" until long after it was too late. As early as the 1930s and the Sino-Japanese conflict, it was apparent that air power had to be reckoned as a real force in modern warfare. This view was verified and accentuated by the fabulous achievements of Japanese air power during the opening months of war in the Pacific. But the die-hards still deprecated the value of the airplane in combat and concluded that these early victories had been achieved purely by luck. They asserted that carriers were too vulnerable by their very nature, that shore-based air did not have enough range to be of importance in the far-flung reaches of the Pacific Ocean, and that, as before, the final decisions of naval war would still be rendered by the battleship. These advocates believed that the fire power of a modern battleship was adequate to provide its own defense against enemy air attack.

At the other end of the scale were the extremist air power advocates who interpreted the early aerial successes as evidence that planes and carriers alone were able to win battles and wars. This view was unfortunate too, because it blocked consideration of battleships for the roles they properly should have played in World War II. The result was that airmen generally dismissed the battleship force as completely useless and made it the butt of contemptuous jokes about the "Hashirajima Fleet."

Naval air power had indeed taken the place of the battleship as the decisive striking force at sea. This was convincingly shown in the first two days of war when Japanese naval aircraft, carrier and shore-based, smashed the battleship strength of both the U.S. Pacific Fleet at Pearl Harbor and the British Far Eastern Fleet off Malaya. It is interesting to observe that it was also carrier and land-based aerial operations which were employed in the American offensives which converged on the homeland and ultimately brought about the defeat of Japan. So it was throughout the war. While Japan enjoyed initial successes at the expense of the United States, the latter profited by the bitter experiences of the early months and marshaled its forces, adapting what it had and developing what it had not, to win the war in the Pacific.

A graphic example of resourcefulness is seen in the U.S. Navy's employment of battleships. Merely because air power and aircraft carriers came into a position of prominence did not mean that America's powerfully gunned battleships stood idle in the nebulous hope of being able to fight an engagement in the grand manner. Instead the U.S. battleships were skilfully employed for preinvasion bombardment of Japanese island outposts, and they did a terrific job of it, as any survivors of such garrisons will attest. The U.S. Navy also used its battleships to advantage in screening forces for aircraft carriers. Their tremendous antiaircraft barrages served effectively to keep our planes from making successful approaches to attack the carriers.

It was not that Japanese naval leaders were unaware of the changes taking place in ocean war, but they seemed reluctant to face realities. On 1 March 1942, for example, Rear Admiral Takijiro Onishi was transferred to Tokyo from his position as

Chief of Staff of the Eleventh Air Fleet in the Southern Area. On the way he reported to Combined Fleet on the combat situation in the Philippines and Dutch East Indies. He stressed the shift in emphasis taking place in engagements with the enemy, showing that surface gunnery actions were taking a back seat to air and air-surface actions. The slight impression made by his report was evidenced by the response it evoked from Combined Fleet Chief of Staff Admiral Ugaki, who said that on such a fundamental issue a decision based solely on the limited operations in the south was premature. An entry of this date in Ugaki's diary is illustrative of high-level thinking on the problem:

> In vast ocean areas land-based air forces can be employed only on a limited scale, and I doubt that carriers alone can provide adequate air power for aggressive action. Fukudome [Chief First Section, Naval General Staff] told me that he had postponed the decision advocated by [Navy Minister] Shimada to halt construction of MUSASHI. It is generally considered that the battleship is a worthy instrument of service, and until there are other means for nullifying the enemy's battleships, our own battleship strength must be maintained.

Such was the determined view of the men who believed in battleship supremacy.

3. MISTAKEN NAVAL AIR POLICY

Another important cause of Japan's defeat was what may be called the "crack-man policy" of the Navy Air Force. Under this policy all our best pilots were assigned to and kept on combat duty with the carrier air groups. Opponents of the policy contended that this was shortsighted and that some of the best and most experienced flyers should be sent to naval air stations as instructors to impart their wisdom and battle experience to fledgling students. But the crack-man policy had worked so successfully at Pearl Harbor and in the Indian

Ocean that few, if any, pilots from the carriers were transferred to duty as instructors.

As a result, there was no reserve of able pilots available to fill the ranks left vacant by losses in the battle of the Coral Sea— none, that is, who were combat ready. The best replacement pilots available after Coral Sea required weeks of practical training in carrier take-offs and landings alone, plus additional weeks of training in combat techniques, before they would be ready for combat operations. This shortage of combat-ready pilots was the sole reason for ZUIKAKU's inability to take part in the Battle of Midway. And if our repair facilities had been as efficient as those of the United States, we might have effected repairs to damaged SHOKAKU to permit her participation, but again, only *if* replacement pilots had been available.

Thus, the battle was fought with at least one valuable (or even vital) carrier fewer than there might have been but for the short-sightedness of our leaders, who failed to realize that aerial warfare is a battle of attrition and that a strictly limited number of even the most skillful pilots could not possibly win out over an unlimited number of able pilots.

4. TECHNOLOGICAL BACKWARDNESS

In technological achievement, too, Japan started out the Pacific War in an inferior position and remained there. The clearest and most serious example of this deficiency was our lack of radar. Two days before the sortie for Midway, radar installations were made in battleships ISE and HYUGA, the first Japanese warships to be so equipped. Months earlier, naval authorities had been urging that radar sets be provided for our carriers, but development in this field of electronics lagged so pitifully that the two sets available at the last minute were only experimental models, and even these were not to be had for the carriers. Had we been six months farther along in our radar development it would have been an invaluable asset in this decisive battle. Radar could have pierced the fog that hampered the Nagumo Force's outward passage and approach to the battle area. What is more important, it could have detected and located enemy scout planes in time for our fighters to destroy them before the enemy fleet could be informed of our position; it could have given earlier warning of planes which attacked our carriers, and—installed in our reconnaissance planes—it could have detected the enemy task forces far sooner than was done by visual sighting.

This speculation brings to mind an ironic circumstance concerning radar development in World War II. One vital component of radar is the directional antenna. Early success in perfecting such an antenna was achieved by a Japanese college professor, Dr. Hidetsugu Yagi, who made public his discovery in Japan in 1932 and soon thereafter visited the United States, where his findings were honored by publication in several scientific journals. It was a matter of but fleeting pride to Japanese forces invading Shanghai to find electronic installations there employing the "Yagi antenna." England and the United States had availed themselves of this invention and developed it to their use while Japan had neglected to do so.

It must be remembered that the people of Japan are not by nature suited to mass production work. The individual is much more inclined toward craftsmanship than toward the assembly line. As with training pilots, repairing or building warships, and all the many vital endeavors of war, so with technological developments: Japan found herself behind at the outset and became more and more outdistanced as time went on.[1] There were exceptions to this, to be sure, such as our oxygen-fueled torpedo, whose performance seems not to have

---

[1] *Editors' Note:* There was one field of wartime effort in which Japan remained not only supreme, but absolutely unique, and that was the suicide tactics which were resorted to beginning in late 1944. Articles on the subject are in *U.S. Naval Institute Proceedings* for September 1953 and May 1954.

been matched by American torpedoes. There was also the Japanese Zero fighter plane, which was easily superior to anything that the Allies had ready in the Pacific, but which was soon outclassed by new arrivals from the United States. Japanese optical instruments have always been highly regarded and there is no question that the quality of the night glasses used in our warships was an important contributing factor to our success in night naval actions. But night glasses were no match for radar.

5. ARROGANCE

From the Manchurian Incident until December 1941, Japan had experienced nothing but easy victories over weak enemies, and it was with some apprehension that she embarked on war in the Pacific. She was as surprised as every other country was at her rapid succession of great victories in the early months, and her initial apprehensions were soon dispelled. People at home as well as soldiers at the front went wild with joy as the advance continued, and it was not long before they were thinking very lightly of the enemy's ability to fight or resist. In this framework there developed an arrogant attitude on the part of the Japanese toward the enemy. By the time of the Midway battle this arrogance had reached a point where it had permeated the thinking and actions of officers and men in the fighting services. This malady of overconfidence has been aptly called "Victory Disease," and the spread of the virus was so great that its effects may be found on every level of the planning and execution of the Midway operation.

The war had gone so well for Japan up to the spring of 1942 that the Midway planners seemed to work entirely on the basis of what the enemy would *probably* do, rather than of what he might possibly do or what he was capable of doing. A fleet engagement was our goal, and the surest way to achieve it was by striking the enemy's most vital position. If he failed to come out in defense of Midway, well and good; we would secure that island as another outpost, as well as Aleutians bases in the north. Thereby our defensive perimeter would be extended and we could make the next move along the Hawaiian chain, each advance serving as support for the next move, until finally the enemy would have to come out and fight. In this reasoning, however, we were blind to the possibility that the enemy might act differently than we expected. Combined Fleet was not alone in this blindness. In a joint planning conference for the Midway operation, a spokesman of the Naval General Staff announced, "What we are most concerned with in this operation is that the enemy will be loath to meet our fleet and will refuse to come out from his base."

This arrogant underestimation of the enemy could not have been more wrong. Far from reluctant to meet our advance, the enemy was eager and ready to do so. Our blithe assumption that he would be taken by surprise was attributable to our own cocksureness that our plans had remained secure from the enemy. But they had not.

The dispersal of our forces was another evidence of arrogance. They were divided in complete reliance on the idea that the various groups could easily be assembled as occasion might demand, when and if the enemy should rise to our lure. The fallacy of this scheme was clearly shown by the inability of our widely scattered forces to assemble for effective combat when the battle was joined.

No less than our commanders, our junior officers and enlisted men were infected with the victory disease. Here the ramifications were not so sweeping nor the results so far-reaching, but the symptoms were unmistakable. When our aircraft carriers were fatally hit on 4 June, the majority of our casualties were caused not by explosions or shell fragments but by burns. Many of these burns could have been avoided if the crews had been properly clad for combat. Instead they wore only half-sleeved shirts and tropical shorts, and why not? Summer in the tropics is warm and there was nothing to fear from enemy attacks, so why be encumbered with the heavier clothing needed to protect against fire and flash? Joined with this same episode was the haphazard handling of bombs as they were removed from our planes to be replaced by torpedoes. Never mind the precaution of stowing the bombs in protected places. Just pile them on the deck. The enemy will never hit our ships. But he did.

No more vivid example of thoughtless and stupid arrogance can be conceived than the attitude which pervaded the war games in preparation for the Midway operation. When, following the established rules of the games, nine enemy hits were scored and two Japanese carriers sunk thereby, these results were arbitrarily reduced, first, to only three hits scored, sinking one carrier and damaging another, and finally to no carriers lost at all. The same flexible system of calculation was employed to establish plane losses, highly favorable of course to the Japanese.

In the final analysis, the root cause of Japan's defeat, not alone in the Battle of Midway but in the entire war, lies deep in the Japanese national character. There is an irrationality and impulsiveness about our people which results in actions that are haphazard and often contradictory. A tradition of provincialism makes us narrow-minded and dogmatic, reluctant to discard prejudices and slow to adopt even necessary improvements if they require a new concept. Indecisive and vacillating, we succumb readily to conceit, which in turn makes us disdainful of others. Opportunistic but lacking a spirit of daring and independence, we are wont to place reliance on others and to truckle to superiors. Our want of rationality often leads us to confuse desire and reality, and thus to do things without careful planning. Only when our hasty action has ended in failure do we begin to think rationally about it, usually for the purpose of finding excuses for the failure. In short, as a nation, we lack maturity of mind and the necessary conditioning to enable us to know when and what to sacrifice for the sake of our main goal.

Such are the weaknesses of the Japanese national character. These weaknesses were reflected in the defeat we suffered in the Battle of Midway, which rendered fruitless all the valiant deeds and precious sacrifices of the men who fought there. In these weaknesses lies the cause of Japan's misfortunes.

APPENDIX 1 # U.S. and Japanese Losses in the Battle of Midway

The results of the Midway Battle, as compiled on the Japanese side after the operation from ship and air unit reports, were as listed below. Since the losses claimed to have been inflicted on the American forces were inevitably exaggerated, the actual losses sustained by those forces have been compiled from American sources and are given at the right for purposes of comparison with the Japanese claims.

U.S. LOSSES

Claimed by Japanese	*Actual*

1. SHIPS

2 ENTERPRISE-class CVs sunk	CV YORKTOWN sunk
1 SAN FRANCISCO-class CA damaged	DD HAMMAN sunk
1 DD sunk	

2. AIRCRAFT

Shot down or destroyed in Midway air strike 45	U. S. carrier-borne aircraft lost .... 109[1]
Shot down in strikes against U. S. carriers 15	U. S. shore-based aircraft lost
	Marine—28
Shot down by combat air patrol 90	Navy — 6
Shot down by AA fire of Japanese ships 29	Army — 4
	Total shore-based 38
Total 179	Total ....147[2]

[1] *Editors' Note:* This figure includes operational as well as combat losses on 4, 5 and 6 June, plus 11 planes lost with YORKTOWN when she sank on the 7th.
[2] *Editors' Note:* U.S. aircraft losses are taken from S. E. Morison, *History of U.S. Naval Operations in World War II*, Vol. IV, pp. 90-93.

3. GROUND INSTALLATIONS

Eastern Island:

1 hangar set afire
3 buildings set afire
Airstrip damaged in two places

Marine command post and mess hall destroyed, powerhouse damaged
Airstrip damaged but still usable

Sand Island:

1 seaplane hangar set afire
Seaplane platform destroyed
2 fuel storage tanks set afire
2 AA emplacements destroyed

Seaplane hangar destroyed
Fuel storage tanks destroyed
Aviation fueling system damaged
Hospital and storehouses set afire

JAPANESE LOSSES

1. SHIPS

Sunk: 4 CVs (Akagi, Kaga, Hiryu, Soryu)
1 CA (Mikuma)
Severely damaged: 1 CA (Mogami)
Medium damage: 2 DDs (Arashio, Asashio)
Slight damage: 1 oiler (Akebono Maru, by aerial torpedo)
1 DD (Tanikaze, by bomb near-miss)
1 BB (Haruna, by bomb near-miss)

2. AIRCRAFT

Lost in Midway air strike 6
Fighters of combat air patrol lost 12
Lost in attacks on U.S. carriers 24
Lost with carriers when they sank . . . . 280 (approximate)

Total . . . . 322[3]

[3] *Editors' Note:* Total Japanese plane losses as given here considerably exceed the approximate 250-plane figure given in U.S. sources. Since they also are in excess of the actual operational complement of the four Nagumo Force carriers, aggregating 261 planes, it is presumed that the 280 planes listed as lost with the carriers when they sank includes reserve aircraft carried in addition to the actual operational strength.

APPENDIX 2 Combined Fleet Task Organization, 5 June 1942

COMBINED FLEET

Admiral Isoroku Yamamoto, in YAMATO
Chief of Staff, Rear Admiral Matome Ugaki

MAIN FORCE (First Fleet), Admiral Yamamoto

Main Body, Admiral Yamamoto

BATTLESHIP GROUP (BatDiv 1), Admiral Yamamoto

YAMATO, Captain Gihachi Takayanagi

NAGATO, Captain Hideo Yano

MUTSU, Captain Teijiro Yamazumi

CARRIER GROUP, Captain Kaoru Umetani

HOSHO (CVL), Captain Umetani

Air Unit (8 bombers), Lieutenant Yoshiaki Irikiin

YUKAZE (DD), Lieutenant Commander Shizuka Kajimoto

SPECIAL FORCE, Captain Kaku Harada

CHIYODA (seaplane carrier),[1] Captain Harada

NISSHIN (seaplane carrier), Captain Katsumi Komazawa

SCREEN (DesRon 3), Rear Admiral Shintaro Hashimoto

SENDAI (CL, flagship), Captain Nobue Morishita

DesDiv 11, Captain Kiichiro Shoji

FUBUKI, Commander Shizuo Yamashita

SHIRAYUKI, Commander Taro Sugahara

HATSUYUKI, Lieutenant Commander Junnari Kamiura

MURAKUMO, Commander Hideo Higashi

DesDiv 19, Captain Ranji Oe

ISONAMI, Commander Ryokichi Sugama

URANAMI, Commander Tsutomu Hagio

SHIKINAMI, Commander Akifumi Kawahashi

AYANAMI, Commander Eiji Sakuma

---

[1] *Editors' Nota:* Seaplane carriers CHIYODA and NISSHIN, serving as tenders, carried midget submarines in this operation.

1ST SUPPLY UNIT, Captain Shigeyasu Nishioka
  NARUTO (oiler), Captain Nishioka
  TOEI MARU (oiler)
Guard (Aleutians Screening) *Force,* Vice Admiral Shiro Takasu, in
  HYUGA
        Chief of Staff, Admiral Kengo Kobayashi

BATTLESHIP GROUP (BatDiv 2), Vice Admiral Takasu
  HYUGA, Captain Chiaki Matsuda
  ISE, Captain Isamu Takeda
  FUSO, Captain Mitsuo Kinoshita
  YAMASHIRO, Captain Gunji Kogure
SCREEN, Rear Admiral Fukuji Kishi
  CruDiv 9, Rear Admiral Kishi
    KITAKAMI (CL, flagship), Captain Saiji Norimitsu
    OI (CL), Captain Shigeru Narita
  DesDiv 20, Captain Yuji Yamada
    ASAGIRI, Commander Nisaburo Maekawa
    YUGIRI, Captain Masayoshi Motokura
    SHIRAKUMO, Commander Toyoji Hitomi
    AMAGIRI, Captain Buichi Ashida
  DesDiv 24, Captain Yasuji Hirai
    UMIKAZE, Commander Nagahide Sugitani
    YAMAKAZE, Commander Shuichi Hamanaka
    KAWAKAZE, Commander Kazuo Wakabayashi
    SUZUKAZE, Commander Kazuo Shibayama
  DesDiv 27, Captain Matake Yoshimura
    ARIAKE, Commander Shoichi Yoshida
    YUGURE, Commander Kiyoshi Kamo
    SHIGURE, Commander Noboru Seo
    SHIRATSUYU, Lieutenant Commander Kimmatsu Hashimoto
2ND SUPPLY UNIT, Captain Matsuo Eguchi
  SAN CLEMENTE MARU (oiler), Captain Eguchi
  TOA MARU (oiler)

FIRST CARRIER STRIKING FORCE
(First Air Fleet), Vice Admiral Chuichi Nagumo, in AKAGI
    Chief of Staff, Rear Admiral Ryunosuke Kusaka

Carrier Group, Vice Admiral Nagumo

CARDIV 1, Vice Admiral Nagumo
  AKAGI (CV), Captain Taijiro Aoki

Air Unit, Commander Mitsuo Fuchida
   21 Zero fighters, Lieutenant Commander Shigeru Itaya
   21 dive bombers, Lieutenant Takehiko Chihaya
   21 torpedo bombers, Lieutenant Commander Shigeharu
     Murata
KAGA (CV), Captain Jisaku Okada
  Air Unit, Lieutenant Commander Tadashi Kusumi
   21 Zero fighters, Lieutenant Masao Sato
   21 dive bombers, Lieutenant Shoichi Ogawa
   30 torpedo bombers, Lieutenant Ichiro Kitajima

CARDIV 2, Rear Admiral Tamon Yamaguchi, in HIRYU
  HIRYU (CV), Captain Tomeo Kaku
    Air Unit, Lieutenant Joichi Tomonaga
     21 Zero fighters, Lieutenant Shigeru Mori
     21 dive bombers, Lieutenant Michio Kobayashi
     21 torpedo bombers, Lieutenant Rokuro Kikuchi
  SORYU (CV), Captain Ryusaku Yanagimoto
    Air Unit, Lieutenant Commander Takashige Egusa
     21 Zero fighters, Lieutenant Masaharu Suganami
     21 dive bombers, Lieutenant Masahiro Ikeda
     21 torpedo bombers, Lieutenant Heijiro Abe

Support Group, Rear Admiral Hiroaki Abe, in TONE
  CRUDIV 8, Rear Admiral Abe
    TONE (CA), Captain Tametsugu Okada
    CHIKUMA (CA), Captain Keizo Komura
  2ND SECTION, BATDIV 3, Captain Tamotsu Koma
    HARUNA, Captain Koma
    KIRISHIMA, Captain Sanji Iwabuchi

Screen (DesRon 10), Rear Admiral Susumu Kimura
  NAGARA (CL, flagship), Captain Toshio Naoi
  DESDIV 4, Captain Kosaku Ariga
    NOWAKI, Commander Magotaro Koga
    ARASHI, Commander Yasumasa Watanabe
    HAGIKAZE, Commander Juichi Iwagami
    MAIKAZE, Commander Seiji Nakasugi
  DESDIV 10, Captain Toshio Abe
    KAZAGUMO, Commander Masayoshi Yoshida
    YUGUMO, Commander Shigeo Semba
    MAKIGUMO, Commander Isamu Fujita

DESDIV 17, Captain Masayuki Kitamura
  URAKAZE, Commander Nagayoshi Shiraishi
  ISOKAZE, Commander Shunichi Toshima
  TANIKAZE, Commander Motoi Katsumi
  HAMAKAZE, Commander Tsuneo Orita

Supply Group, Captain Masanao Oto
  KYOKUTO MARU (oiler), Captain Oto
  SHINKOKU MARU (oiler)
  TOHO MARU (oiler)
  NIPPON MARU (oiler)
  KOKUYO MARU (oiler)
  AKIGUMO (DD), Commander Shohei Soma

MIDWAY INVASION FORCE (Second Fleet)

Vice Admiral Nobutake Kondo, in ATAGO
Chief of Staff, Rear Admiral Kazutaka Shiraishi

Invasion Force Main Body, Vice Admiral Kondo
  CRUDIV 4 (less 2nd Section), Vice Admiral Kondo
    ATAGO (CA), Captain Matsuji Ijuin
    CHOKAI (CA), Captain Mikio Hayakawa
  CRUDIV 5, Vice Admiral Takeo Takagi
    MYOKO (CA), Captain Teruhiko Miyoshi
    HAGURO (CA), Captain Tomoichi Mori
  BATDIV 3 (less 2nd Section), Rear Admiral Gunichi Mikawa
    KONGO, Captain Tomiji Koyanagi
    HIEI, Captain Masao Nishida

Screen (DesRon 4), Rear Admiral Shoji Nishimura
  YURA (CL, flagship), Captain Shiro Sato
  DESDIV 2, Captain Masao Tachibana
    MURASAME, Commander Naoji Suenaga
    SAMIDARE, Commander Takisaburo Matsubara
    HARUSAME, Commander Masao Kamiyama
    YUDACHI, Commander Kiyoshi Kikkawa
  DESDIV 9, Captain Yasuo Sato
    ASAGUMO, Commander Toru Iwahashi
    MINEGUMO, Commander Yasuatsu Suzuki
    NATSUGUMO, Commander Moritaro Tsukamoto

Carrier Group, Captain Sueo Obayashi
  ZUIHO (CVL), Captain Obayashi

Air Unit
   12 Zero fighters, Lieutenant Moriyasu Hidaka
   12 torpedo bombers, Lieutenant Kaji Matsuo
Mikazuki (DD), Lieutenant Commander Saneho Maeda

Supply Group, Captain Jiro Murao
  Sata (oiler), Captain Murao
  Tsurumi (oiler), Captain Toshizo Fujita
  Genyo Maru (oiler)
  Kenyo Maru (oiler)
  Akashi (repair ship), Captain Tsunekichi Fukuzawa

Close Support Group, Vice Admiral Takeo Kurita
  crudiv 7, Vice Admiral Kurita
    Kumano (CA, flagship), Captain Kikumatsu Tanaka
    Suzuya (CA), Captain Masatomi Kimura
    Mikuma (CA), Captain Shakao Sakiyama
    Mogami (CA), Captain Akira Soji
  desdiv 8, Commander Nobuki Ogawa
    Asashio, Commander Goro Yoshii
    Arashio, Commander Hideo Kuboki
  Nichiei Maru (oiler)

Transport Group, Rear Admiral Raizo Tanaka
  transports[2]
    Kiyozumi Maru
    Zenyo Maru
    No. 2 Toa Maru
    Argentina Maru
    Brazil Maru
    Azuma Maru
    Keiyo Maru
    Goshu Maru
    Kano Maru
    Hokuriku Maru
    Kirishima Maru

[2] *Editors' Note:* Transports carried the Midway Landing Force of approximately 5,000 troops, with Captain Minoru Ota (Navy) in overall command. The Landing Force comprised the 2nd Combined Special Naval Landing Force, under Ota's direct command, and the Army's Ichiki Detachment, commanded by Colonel Kiyonao Ichiki.

Nankai Maru
Patrol Boats Nos. 1, 2, 34 (carrying troops)
Akebono Maru (oiler)
ESCORT (DesRon 2), Rear Admiral Tanaka, in Jintsu
  Jintsu (CL), Captain Torazo Kozai
  DesDiv 15, Captain Shiro Sato
    Kuroshio, Commander Tamaki Ugaki
    Oyashio, Commander Tokikichi Arima
  DesDiv 16, Captain Shiro Shibuya
    Yukikaze, Commander Kenjiro Tobita
    Amatsukaze, Commander Tameichi Hara
    Tokitsukaze, Commander Giichiro Nakahara
    Hatsukaze, Commander Kameshiro Takahashi
  DesDiv 18, Captain Yoshito Miyasaka
    Shiranuhi, Commander Jisuo Akasawa
    Kasumi, Commander Kiyoshi Tomura
    Arare, Commander Tomoe Ogata
    Kagero, Commander Minoru Yokoi

Seaplane Tender Group,[3] Rear Admiral Ruitaro Fujita
SEAPLANE TENDER DIVISION 11, Rear Admiral Fujita
  Chitose (CVS), Captain Tamotsu Furukawa
    16 fighter seaplanes
    4 scout seaplanes
  Kamikawa Maru (AV), Captain Tarohachi Shinoda
    8 fighter seaplanes
    4 scout planes
Hayashio (DD), Captain Kiyoshi Kaneda
Patrol Boat No. 35 (carrying troops)

Minesweeper Group, Captain Sadatomo Miyamoto
MINESWEEPERS
  Tama Maru No. 3
  Tama Maru No. 5
  Shonan Maru No. 7
  Shonan Maru No. 8
SUBCHASERS Nos. 16, 17, 18
Soya (supply ship), Commander Toshi Kubota

[3] *Editors' Note:* The Seaplane Tender Group moved in company with the Transport Group. Its mission was to occupy Kure Island and set up a seaplane base.

MEIYO MARU (cargo ship)
YAMAFUKU MARU (cargo ship)

NORTHERN (Aleutians) *FORCE* (Fifth Fleet)
Vice Admiral Moshiro Hosogaya, in NACHI
Chief of Staff, Captain Tasuku Nakazawa

Northern Force Main Body, Vice Admiral Hosogaya
NACHI (CA), Captain Takahiko Kiyota
SCREEN, Commander Hajime Takeuchi
INAZUMA (DD), Commander Takeuchi
IKAZUCHI (DD), Lieutenant Commander Shunsaku Kudo
SUPPLY GROUP
FUJISAN MARU (oiler)
NISSAN MARU (oiler)
3 cargo ships

Second Carrier Striking Force, Rear Admiral Kakuji Kakuta
CARRIER GROUP (CarDiv 4), Rear Admiral Kakuta
RYUJO (CVL), Captain Tadao Kato
Air Unit, Lieutenant Masayuki Yamagami
16 Zero fighters, Lieutenant Minoru Kobayashi
21 torpedo bombers, Lieutenant Yamagami
JUNYO (CV), Captain Shizue Ishii
Air Unit, Lieutenant Yoshio Shiga
24 Zero fighters, Lieutenant Shiga
21 dive bombers, Lieutenant Zenji Abe
SUPPORT GROUP (2nd Section, CruDiv 4), Captain Shunsaku
Nabeshima
MAYA (CA), Captain Nabeshima
TAKAO (CA), Captain Bunji Asakura
SCREEN (DesDiv 7), Captain Kaname Konishi
AKEBONO, Lieutenant Commander Minoru Nakagawa
USHIO, Commander Yoshitake Uesugi
SAZANAMI, Lieutenant Commander Jiroshi Uwai
TEIYO MARU (oiler)

Attu Invasion Force, Rear Admiral Sentaro Omori, in ABUKUMA
ABUKUMA (CL), Captain Seiroku Murayama
DESDIV 21, Captain Toshio Shimizu
WAKABA, Lieutenant Commander Masakichi Kuroki

NENOHI, Lieutenant Commander Saburo Terauchi
HATSUHARU, Commander Hiroshi Makino
HATSUSHIMO, Lieutenant Commander Satoru Migihama
MAGANE MARU (minelayer)
KINUGASA MARU (transport)[4]

Kiska Invasion Force, Captain Takeji Ono, in KISO
  CRUDIV 21, Captain Ono
    KISO (CL), Captain Ono
    TAMA (CL), Captain Masaharu Kawabata
  ASAKA MARU (auxiliary cruiser), Captain Jiro Ban
  SCREEN (DesDiv 6), Captain Yusuke Yamada
    HIBIKI, Lieutenant Commander Hagumu Ishii
    AKATSUKI, Commander Osamu Takasuka
    HOKAZE, Lieutenant Commander Tomoo Tanaka
  TRANSPORTS[5]
    HAKUSAN MARU
    KUMAGAWA MARU
  MINESWEEPER DIVISION 13, Captain Toshio Mitsuka
    KAIHO MARU
    SHUNKOTSU MARU
    HAKUHO MARU

Submarine Detachment,[6] Rear Admiral Shigeaki Yamazaki, in I-9
  SUBRON I, Rear Admiral Yamazaki
    I-9, Commander Akiyoshi Fujii
  SubDiv 2, Captain Hiroshi Imazato
    I-15, Commander Nobuo Ishikawa
    I-17, Commander Kozo Nishino
    I-19, Commander Seigo Narahara

[4] *Editors' Note:* KINUGASA MARU carried the Attu Landing Force (Army North Sea Detachment) of 1,200 troops, commanded by Major Matsutoshi Hozumi.

[5] *Editors' Note:* HAKUSAN MARU carried the Kiska Landing Force (Maizuru 3rd Special Naval Landing Force) of 550 troops, commanded by Lt. Cdr. Hifumi Mukai. KUMAGAWA MARU carried construction equipment and 700 labor troops.

[6] *Editors' Note:* At the end of May *I-9* scouted Kiska, *I-15* scouted Adak, *I-17* scouted Attu, and *I-19* scouted Dutch Harbor. Subsequently, *I-19* patrolled Unimak Pass off Dutch Harbor, while *I-9*, *I-15* and *I-17* deployed on Cordon line "C" between lat. 49° N, long. 166° W and lat. 51° N, long. 166° W. *I-25* and *I-26* patrolled off Seattle after scouting Chirikof Island, Sitkinak Island and Kodiak. Subsequently, *I-25* bombarded Astoria, and *I-26* bombarded Vancouver.

SubDiv 4, Captain Mitsuru Nagai
I-25, Commander Meiji Togami
I-26, Commander Minoru Yokota

ADVANCE (Submarine) *FORCE* (Sixth Fleet)
Vice Admiral Teruhisa Komatsu, in KATORI at Kwajalein
Chief of Staff, Rear Admiral Hisashi Mito

KATORI (CL), Captain Noboru Owada
SubRon 3,[7] Rear Admiral Chimaki Kono
RIO DE JANEIRO MARU (sub-tender, flagship, at Kwajalein)
SUBDIV 19, Captain Ryojiro Ono
I-156, Lieutenant Commander Katsuo Ohashi
I-157, Lieutenant Commander Sakae Nakajima
I-158, Lieutenant Commander Soshichi Kitamura
I-159, Lieutenant Commander Tamori Yoshimatsu
SUBDIV 30, Captain Masao Teraoka
I-162, Lieutenant Commander Takaichi Kinashi
I-165, Lieutenant Commander Takae Harada
I-166, Commander Makio Tanaka
SUBDIV 13,[8] Captain Takeharu Miyazaki
I-121, Lieutenant Commander Yasuo Fujimori
I-122, Lieutenant Commander Sadatoshi Norita
I-123, Lieutenant Commander Toshitake Ueno

SHORE BASED AIR FORCE (Eleventh Air Fleet)
Vice Admiral Nishizo Tsukahara (at Tinian)
Chief of Staff, Rear Admiral Munetaka Sakamaki

Midway Expeditionary Force, Captain Chisato Morita
36 Zero fighters,[9] Lieutenant Commander Mitsugu Kokufuda
10 land bombers (at Wake)
6 flying boats (at Jaluit)

---

[7] *Editors' Note:* I-168 patrolled around Midway. I-174, I-175, I-169 and I-171 deployed on Cordon Line "A" between lat. 19° 30′ N. long. 167° W and lat. 23° 30′ N, long. 167° W.

[8] *Editor's Note:* I-121 and I-123 were assigned the mission of carrying gas and oil to French Frigate Shoals, and I-122 to Laysan Island, in connection with Operation "K."

[9] *Editors' Note:* These fighters, with their pilots and ground crews, were transported by carriers of the First and Second Carrier Striking Forces.

24th Air Flotilla, Rear Admiral Minoru Maeda[10] (at Kwajalein)
  CHITOSE AIR GROUP, Captain Fujiro Ohashi (at Kwajalein)
    36 Zero fighters
    36 torpedo bombers
  1ST AIR GROUP, Captain Samaji Inouye (at Aur and Wotje)
    36 Zero fighters
    36 torpedo bombers
  14TH AIR GROUP, Captain Daizo Nakajima
    18 flying boats (at Jaluit and Wotje)

[10] *Editors' Note:* Rear Admiral Maeda assumed command following the abortive Operation "K." His predecessor was Vice Admiral Goto.

Index

261

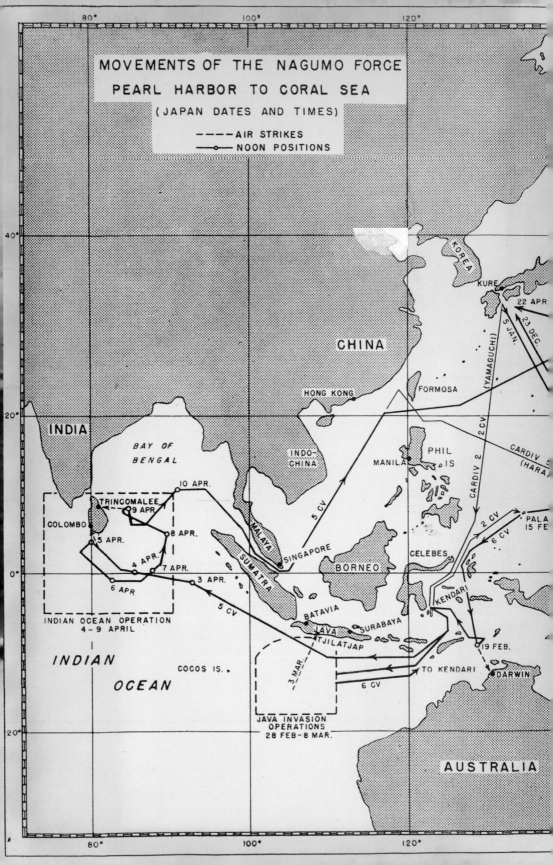